AF413129

Napoleon Bonaparte and the Napoleonic Wars

An Enthralling Overview of a Military Genius, His Rise to Power, and the Global Conflicts That Shaped an Empire

Free limited time bonus

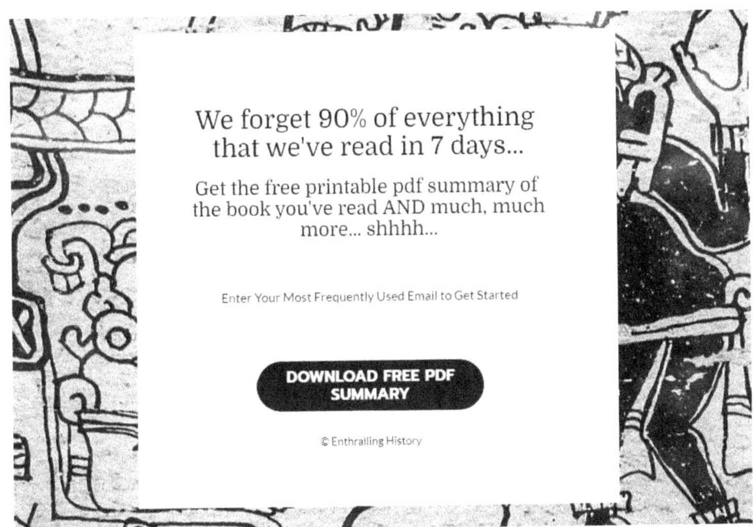

Stop for a moment. We have a free bonus set up for you. The problem is this: we forget 90% of everything that we read after 7 days. Crazy fact, right? Here's the solution: we've created a printable, 1-page pdf summary for this book that you're reading now. All you have to do to get your free pdf summary is to go to the following website:

https://livetolearn.lpages.co/enthrallinghistory/

Or, Scan the QR code!

Once you do, it will be intuitive. Enjoy, and thank you!

Table of Contents

PART 1: NAPOLEON BONAPARTE 1

  INTRODUCTION 3

  CHAPTER 1: NAPOLEON'S EARLY YEARS 4

  CHAPTER 2: FROM ARTILLERY OFFICER TO REVOLUTIONARY LEADER 11

  CHAPTER 3: THE EGYPTIAN CAMPAIGN 35

  CHAPTER 4: CONQUERING EUROPE: THE RISE OF NAPOLEON 47

  CHAPTER 5: NAPOLEON'S CORONATION AS EMPEROR 60

  CHAPTER 6: WARS OF THE THIRD AND FOURTH COALITION 65

  CHAPTER 7: THE PENINSULAR WAR: SPAIN AND PORTUGAL RESIST NAPOLEON 79

  CHAPTER 8: WAR OF THE FIFTH COALITION 89

  CHAPTER 9: THE RUSSIAN CAMPAIGN: NAPOLEON'S FATAL MISTAKE 96

  CHAPTER 10: WARS OF THE SIXTH AND SEVENTH COALITION AND NAPOLEON'S FINAL DEFEAT 106

  CHAPTER 11: NAPOLEON'S FINAL YEARS 116

  CONCLUSION 124

PART 2: THE NAPOLEONIC WARS 127

  INTRODUCTION 129

  CHAPTER 1: THE RISE OF NAPOLEON 131

  CHAPTER 2: THE REFORMATION OF FRANCE 141

  CHAPTER 3: REVOLUTIONARY BATTLEFIELD TACTICS AND WARFARE 149

  CHAPTER 4: NAPOLEON'S CONTINENTAL WARS BEGIN 158

CHAPTER 5: THE BATTLE OF TRAFALGAR: NAPOLEON'S DEFEAT AT SEA 168

CHAPTER 6: NAPOLEON'S ZENITH 177

CHAPTER 7: THE PENINSULAR WAR: NAPOLEON'S STRUGGLE IN SPAIN AND PORTUGAL 186

CHAPTER 8: THE CULTURE OF THE TIME 196

CHAPTER 9: THE INVASION OF RUSSIA: NAPOLEON'S CATASTROPHIC CAMPAIGN 205

CHAPTER 10: THE WAR OF THE SIXTH COALITION AND THE ABDICATION 216

CHAPTER 11: THE HUNDRED DAYS AND WATERLOO: NAPOLEON'S LAST STAND 226

CONCLUSION 236

HERE'S ANOTHER BOOK BY ENTHRALLING HISTORY THAT YOU MIGHT LIKE 238

FREE LIMITED TIME BONUS 239

BIBLIOGRAPHY 240

IMAGE SOURCES 249

Part 1: Napoleon Bonaparte

An Enthralling Guide to the Rise, Reign, and Legacy of a Military Genius and Emperor

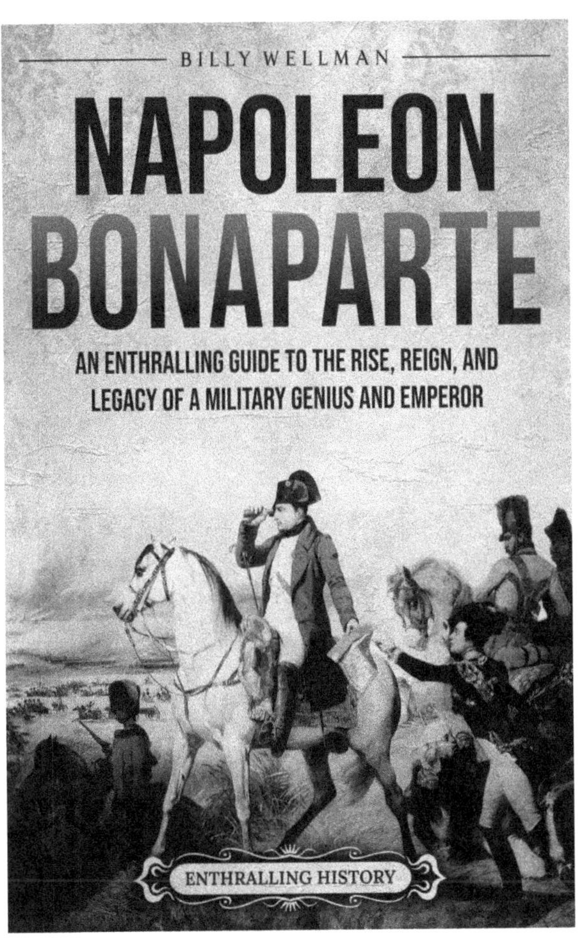

Introduction

Napoleon Bonaparte has been studied, analyzed, and written about by biographers, psychoanalysts, doctors, militarists, and novelists for centuries. Was he a hero, a liberator, a tyrant, a manipulator, an impatient genius, or all of these and more at different times to different people? He has been hated, despised, admired, adored, and hero-worshiped by contemporaries and generations to this day.

Napoleon loved order and discipline, and he felt compelled to eliminate chaos. He wanted to be in control at all times. He was a man of his time but also a visionary. Then again, there were times when he pushed the boundaries too far for his own capabilities and resources to meet his visionary ambitions. He learned the hard way that human nature can turn the tide in even the best laid-out plans.

At times, he was driven to achieve his objectives regardless of the cost to himself or others. His ego grew with his status until he came to believe his own propaganda. The same man whose belief in reason as the only viable motive for actions also believed that his ambitions were driven by a force beyond himself.

In this book, we aim to provide an overview of Napoleon's life, achievements, and legacy. We take a look at his rapid rise as an officer in the French Revolutionary army, his disappointments in Corsica, his remarkable ability to inspire death-defying courage and hope in his troops and followers, his sacrifices, and his amazing legacy.

Chapter 1: Napoleon's Early Years

When fourteen-year-old Maria-Letizia Ramolino married eighteen-year-old Carlo Maria Buonaparte in Ajaccio on the rugged island of Corsica in 1764, she had no idea that her family would be famous for centuries to come. Their son would become the first French emperor, Napoleon Bonaparte.

The newly married couple, both from minor nobility, were comfortable by Corsican standards. Carlo had been educated at the University of Pisa. He did not complete his legal studies, though. He went home to Ajaccio to tend to his family and his inheritance when his father passed away. Letizia, a descendant of the illustrious Lombard family, was a homemaker with no formal education. Letizia was a strong woman, as indicated by her insistence on accompanying her husband on a revolutionary campaign.

About two-thirds of Corsica is mountainous, and about one-fifth is thickly forested. Letizia braved this harsh terrain through all kinds of weather, carrying her toddler, Joseph, while pregnant with Napoleon. According to all accounts, she was a strict but loving mother to her eight children who survived infancy. The family's fortunes would wax and wane with the fortunes of the island.

Corsica is the fourth-largest island in the Mediterranean. It lies close to Italy, France, and Spain, and it is just north of Sardinia. Its geographical position made it strategically important as a launchpad or gateway into Europe. The island had been occupied by the Phoenicians, Carthaginians, Greeks, Etruscans, Romans, Visigoths, and numerous others over the millennia. Saracens and Moors from North Africa and Spain had raided it for years.

The native inhabitants of Corsica sought independence repeatedly over the centuries. A short-lived independent kingdom was established in 1736 by revolutionaries led by a German adventurer, Theodore von Neuhoff. The Italian Republic of Genoa soon squashed this independence.

In 1755, a well-educated revolutionary of noble descent, Pasquale Paoli, returned from exile in Naples, where he had lived since childhood after Genoa banished his father for leading an earlier revolt. Paoli established the Corsican Republic and became its elected leader. Inspired by Enlightenment ideals, he envisioned Corsica as a modern state governed by laws, representative institutions, and its own people rather than by foreign powers.

The Buonapartes' breadwinner, Carlo Buonaparte, was his personal assistant and a fervent supporter. Like many minor Corsican nobles, Carlo believed Paoli offered both political independence and social advancement. He saw this as a chance for educated local families to rise without Genoese interference.

Genoa, unable to suppress the rebellion or govern the island effectively, sold Corsica to France in 1768. French forces invaded soon after. Independence was lost after Paoli's defeat, most decisively at Ponte Novu, and he was forced into exile once again. With Paoli gone, the Buonaparte family lost their political patron, and their main income dried up.

They did retain a fairly substantial income from their olive oil business at Millelli. The olive grove had been in the family for generations on a long-term lease, and the olives were pressed in the house's basement.

As Corsica became French, so did the head of the Buonaparte family. Carlo Maria Buonaparte became Charles-Marie Bonapart, and Letizia became Laetitia. By 1777, Carlo had become Corsica's representative at the French court of Louis XVI through his friendship with the French governor of Corsica.

Napoleon was born during this turbulent period on August 15th, 1769, in the family home in Ajaccio. His birth came just over a year after Corsica officially became part of France. Had he been born earlier, Napoleon would have been Genoese. Instead, he was born a Frenchman, though one with deep Corsican roots and an Italian accent he would never lose.

Napoleon's Education

Napoleon's first taste of school was in a mixed class in Ajaccio, where nuns taught him some basic lessons. From here, he went to the local college where Letizia's brother Flesch taught him to read, and a family member of his father's taught him religion. He learned about Corsica's history and heroes and about the Buonaparte family during visits to his great-uncle's residence.

Even as a child, Napoleon was not like other boys. He was serious, observant, and intensely competitive. He was a quiet thinker, more drawn to books than rough play.

Through his French connections, Carlo was able to get his two oldest sons, Joseph and Napoleon, into a French school in Autun on the mainland. Napoleon was a small, thin boy of nine when the two mainly Italian-speaking Corsican boys were accepted at the school. He was bullied and teased for being a foreigner and of lesser nobility.

Napoleon was fiercely determined. He hated losing and being shown up. Teachers sometimes found him argumentative and sharp-tongued. Within three months, Napoleon had learned enough French to be admitted to the French military college in Brienne, although he never lost his heavy Italian accent. He spent five years at this college. He excelled at mathematics and also studied history, geography, and literature.

Despite awkward beginnings for the young Napoleon in France, he gained confidence and openly spoke about his patriotism and desire for an independent Corsica. At that time, he idolized Corsica and its valiant struggles for

Napoleon studying, a painting by François Flameng.[1]

independence and resented French control. Nevertheless, he remained in France and went on to study further at the École Militaire, a prestigious French military academy for nobility that also trained military officers to behave like gentlemen.

Napoleon completed his two-year training at École Militaire in just one year, graduating in 1785. He became a second lieutenant in the artillery division and was then stationed at Valence for further study and practical experience.

Return to Corsica

Napoleon's father passed away in 1785 of stomach cancer, leaving the family to face financial hardship. Napoleon returned to Corsica as soon as he could with his first leave from the military. It was September 1786, and he would remain in Corsica for nearly one year. He had assumed the role of head of the family, although he was not yet sixteen when his father died.

Return to France

Napoleon returned to his military duties in Valence in September 1787. By that time, France was a deeply unequal society on the brink of collapse. There were three classes of citizens: the clergy (the First Estate), the nobility (the Second Estate), and the commoners (the Third Estate). The Third Estate consisted of peasants, merchants, scholars, and laborers. They had almost no civil rights but did all the work and shouldered the tax burden.

The monarchy's finances were also in shambles. Decades of expensive wars had left the country drowning in debt. Attempts at tax reform failed because the nobility and clergy refused to give up their exemptions. Ministers warned the king that the state was on the edge of bankruptcy.

In June 1788, Napoleon's artillery regiment transferred from Valence to Auxonne, a small town in Burgundy. At the Royal Artillery School in Auxonne, Napoleon studied ballistics, military tactics, and strategy. He formed a strong connection with his mathematics professor, Jean-Louis Lombard, who later spoke highly of the young officer's abilities. Napoleon took part in artillery commissions studying how to fire bombs from siege guns.

The young officer continued his education through intensive reading, particularly of history, philosophy, and military strategy. He devoured works by Rousseau and Voltaire, along with classical histories and military treatises. His reading was wide-ranging, and his thinking was still taking shape. He hadn't yet developed a fully coherent political philosophy, but he believed that political change was necessary.

According to some accounts, Napoleon once nearly drowned in the Saône River when a swimming cramp seized him. He was saved only when the current pushed him onto a sandbank in shallow water. Another story suggests he narrowly avoided another accident when he declined to join fellow officers ice skating. The ice broke, and the men drowned.

Whether this second incident actually occurred remains uncertain, but it became part of the collection of near-misses that would follow Napoleon throughout his career.

The Revolution Erupts

In the spring of 1789, political tensions exploded across France. King Louis XVI called a meeting of the Estates General in May, the first such assembly since 1614. The Third Estate quickly grew frustrated. It was constantly overruled by the other estates, even though it had the most members. On June 17th, the Third Estate broke away and declared itself the National Assembly, claiming to speak for the people of France. It wanted to draft a constitution and limit the absolute power of the monarchy.

When representatives of the National Assembly were shut out of their meeting hall on June 20th, they gathered on the tennis courts of Versailles and took an oath to stick together and, if necessary, fight to change the country into a constitutional monarchy. This became known as the Tennis Court Oath.

The unrest wasn't confined to Paris. In early April, rioting broke out in Seurre, a town near Auxonne, sparked by famine following the poor harvests of 1788. Napoleon was sent with a detachment of about one hundred men to restore order. He arrived the next day, calmed the situation, and remained in Seurre until late May.

On July 14th, 1789, revolutionaries stormed the Bastille prison in Paris, a symbol of royal tyranny. Revolutionary fervor swept across France. News reached Auxonne within days. On July 19th, unrest broke out in the town amid high local tensions. This time, Napoleon commanded about 450 men in suppressing the riot. Napoleon and his fellow soldiers helped restore order.

Napoleon Returns to Corsica

In September 1789, Napoleon requested leave to return to Corsica. He left Auxonne on September 9th and arrived on the island on September 21st. This would be his longest stay in Corsica, lasting until late January 1791.

The young officer found Corsica in political turmoil. The island was deeply divided. Paoli's long-standing nationalist faction wanted independence. Moderate reformers saw an opportunity in aligning with the French revolutionaries. Traditional local elites were wary of any radical change. Napoleon threw himself into this complex political landscape, attending meetings and writing passionate letters and essays about Corsica's future. He was torn between his admiration for Corsican independence and his belief that the island needed French support.

In late October 1789, Napoleon helped draft a political address to the French National Assembly, signed by many in Ajaccio's Patriotic Club, including his brother Joseph. The appeal asked the Assembly to grant Corsica the right to self-rule while remaining united with France. Among other things, it requested an end to the island's military administration and permission for Corsicans to form a local national guard.

Napoleon traveled to Bastia, the administrative center of Corsica. He spoke with local leaders about the island's future and the possibility of organizing a Corsican national guard. His activism provoked alarm among authorities. The French governor, Viscount Charles Armand Barrin de la Galissonnière, ordered Napoleon to leave Bastia, an order he obeyed without any resistance.

Just weeks later, on November 30th, 1789, the Assembly passed a decree formally incorporating Corsica into the French constitutional order. Corsicans would now be governed by the same laws and enjoy the same civil rights as mainland citizens. It was not the full independence some still desired, but it was a major shift. Napoleon viewed it as a historic victory for Corsica.

Napoleon returned to Bastia shortly after the decree and attempted to press for enforcement of the Assembly's decisions, including the formation of a national guard. Local authorities, though, resisted carrying out these reforms, and Napoleon was ordered to depart from Bastia once again.

Paoli's Return

In 1790, the revolutionary government in Paris issued decrees allowing Corsican exiles to return to the island. Pasquale Paoli, the legendary Corsican patriot, came back to a warm reception after more than twenty years in exile.

For Napoleon, this was a momentous occasion. Paoli had been his childhood hero. Napoleon and his brother Joseph met with Paoli in the summer of 1790, but the encounter was disappointing. Paoli was wary of the Bonapartes. Years of political conflict had left their mark, including lingering resentment that Napoleon's father, Carlo, had made peace with the French after Corsica's defeat in 1769.

More fundamentally, Paoli and Napoleon held different visions for Corsica's future. Paoli favored an eventual separation from France. Napoleon believed that Corsica needed French backing and that revolutionary reforms offered the best path forward. These political differences would prove to be irreconcilable.

The rift between the Bonaparte family and Paoli deepened over the following months. By the time Napoleon left Corsica in early 1791, the relationship was clearly strained.

Return to France and New Commitments

Napoleon left Corsica in late January 1791 to rejoin his regiment at Auxonne. He traveled with his younger brother Louis, stopping briefly in Valence along the way before arriving at Auxonne in mid-February.

During this second stay at Auxonne, Napoleon joined the Jacobin Club. The Jacobins were one of several political clubs that had emerged in France to debate revolutionary policy and shape the new political order. By aligning with them, Napoleon had become an active participant in French revolutionary politics.

In March 1791, Napoleon arranged with a printer in the nearby town of Dole to publish one of his political letters. He sent copies back to Corsica, including one for Paoli, along with a note expressing his interest in writing a history of the island. According to surviving accounts, Paoli's response was dismissive; he suggested that history should not be written by young men.

On June 1st, 1791, Napoleon was promoted to first lieutenant and transferred to the 4th Artillery Regiment at Valence. He left Auxonne on June 14th and arrived at Valence two days later.

His time in the quiet garrison towns of provincial France was drawing to a close. The young Corsican artillery officer was becoming a French revolutionary.

A young Napoleon Bonaparte in 1792.'

Chapter 2: From Artillery Officer to Revolutionary Leader

After Napoleon arrived in Valence in June 1791, he did not settle into routine garrison life as one might expect. Although he was officially reassigned to the 4th Artillery Regiment, his thoughts and ambitions remained tied to Corsica. The island's political scene was still roiling. Old rivalries simmered, and reformers struggled to put the National Assembly's decrees into practice. One reform in particular, the creation of a Corsican National Guard, had been authorized, but local authorities, especially those allied with Paoli, dragged their feet.

Word of Napoleon's energy and his earlier appeals for reform had spread among Corsican deputies in Paris. In salons and committee rooms, names were floated for leadership, and Napoleon's name kept coming up. He wasn't just another lieutenant; he had shown intellectual curiosity, political nerve, and a willingness to step into the island's tangled politics.

By early 1792, the situation on Corsica had grown more urgent. Town councils were divided, tempers flared, and old loyalties were fraying. When the National Assembly finally ordered the implementation of the National Guard, it created an opening, and Napoleon was tapped for the job. He was appointed adjutant-major in Ajaccio, a post that put him directly in the middle of Corsica's internal struggles. That appointment, made over the objections of Paoli and his circle, widened the growing gap between the Bonapartes and the traditional leadership.

The Corsican National Guard was formed from volunteers loyal to the revolutionary reforms, but political tensions were high from the start. In 1792, factional violence spread through Ajaccio and other towns. National Guard companies faced their first real tests. Clashes broke out between reformist guards and opponents who resisted the new order. In one series of confrontations, Napoleon and his volunteers attempted to assert control over key positions in the town, only to meet stiff resistance from rival factions that held strategic points, such as the citadel.

Over the following months, Napoleon rose to the rank of lieutenant-colonel in the Corsican National Guard and continued to lead troops in efforts to stabilize the island. His actions against conservative and royalist elements showed his willingness to use force to uphold the revolutionary order. By doing this, he further alienated himself from Paoli.

The Road to War

When Napoleon left Auxonne in June 1791, France was still technically a monarchy. The National Assembly had spent two years dismantling the old regime and drafting a new constitution. In September 1791, Louis XVI accepted this constitution, which limited his powers and established a constitutional monarchy. France would be governed by an elected Legislative Assembly, with the king as a symbolic figurehead.

However, this compromise satisfied almost no one. Radical revolutionaries wanted to eliminate the monarchy entirely. Royalists wanted to restore the king's absolute power. Louis XVI secretly hoped foreign powers would intervene to restore his authority.

Europe's monarchies watched the French Revolution with growing alarm. If revolutionary ideas spread, their own thrones might be threatened. Emperor Leopold II of Austria and King Frederick William II of Prussia issued the Declaration of Pillnitz in August 1791, stating they would intervene in France if other European powers joined them. Though it had been carefully worded, French revolutionaries still saw it as a threat.

In France, different factions pushed for war for different reasons. The Girondins were moderate republicans who dominated the Legislative Assembly. They believed war would unite France and expose traitors. Radical Jacobins opposed war, fearing it would empower generals and lead to a military dictatorship.

On April 20th, 1792, France declared war on Austria. Prussia soon joined Austria, and the War of the First Coalition began. This would be the beginning of over two decades of near-constant warfare that would shape Napoleon's entire career.

The Fall of the Monarchy

The war went badly at first. French armies, weakened by the emigration of noble officers and poor organization, suffered defeats. Rumors spread that the king was secretly communicating with France's enemies; these rumors happened to be true.

On August 10th, 1792, Parisian crowds, convinced the king was betraying France, stormed the Tuileries Palace. The Swiss Guards defending the king were massacred. Louis XVI fled to the Legislative Assembly for protection, but his power was over. The National Assembly suspended the king and called for elections to a new National Convention, which would write yet another constitution.

But before the National Convention could meet, panic gripped Paris. With Prussian armies advancing toward the capital, rumors spread that imprisoned aristocrats and priests were plotting to break out and massacre patriots. In early September 1792, mobs stormed the prisons and killed over a thousand prisoners in what became known as the September Massacres. The violence shocked even committed revolutionaries.

The National Convention met for the first time on September 20th, 1792, the same day French forces turned back the Prussian invasion at the Battle of Valmy. Emboldened by this victory, the Convention's first act was to abolish the monarchy on September 21st, 1792. France was now a republic.

The Sardinia Expedition

In early 1793, revolutionary France mounted an expedition against Sardinia as part of its wider war against European monarchies. One effort targeted the southern port of Cagliari, and another focused on the tiny islands of the La Maddalena archipelago just off Sardinia's northern coast. Napoleon Bonaparte served with the artillery on the northern detachment.

This was a formal military assignment, not a casual volunteer action. Napoleon was responsible for positioning and directing the guns that his unit brought ashore. The attack, however, never gained traction. The landing force was poorly coordinated, and supplies were limited. Part of the command decided to pull back just as operations were beginning. In the confusion, Napoleon's artillery pieces were left on the beach, and the troops withdrew without securing any objective.

When it was over, Napoleon was deeply frustrated. He believed that elements of Corsican command, especially those close to Pasquale Paoli, had not fully supported the effort and that their lack of unity and political differences had weakened the campaign. Whether or not Paoli had intended to undermine the operation, many on the republican side saw his actions as unhelpful at best and obstructive at worst.

Breaking with Paoli

By the spring of 1793, whatever admiration Napoleon once felt for Pasquale Paoli had collapsed. What had begun as boyhood hero-worship turned into disappointment, frustration, and, eventually, outright hostility. Napoleon had watched the myth and reality of Paoli drift further and further apart. The man he had once pictured as a kind of Corsican liberator was different in practice. Napoleon found Paoli to be stubborn and increasingly committed to a form of Corsican autonomy that edged toward outright separation from

Pasquale Paoli.[8]

France. Napoleon was convinced that Corsica could not stand alone. He believed it needed the strength and protection of France to remain free of Genoese designs or other predatory powers.

Their differences were not just political but also personal. Years earlier, when Napoleon was still in the French artillery at Auxonne and dreaming of writing a history of his island, Paoli had dismissed the young man's efforts. That rejection wounded Napoleon's pride and dimmed his literary ambitions. Back home in Ajaccio, tensions simmered as well. Some of Paoli's supporters made life difficult for the Bonaparte family.

All of this lay beneath the surface when the expedition against Sardinia was mounted in early 1793. When that campaign collapsed, Napoleon saw confirmation of his growing suspicion that Paoli and his faction were not wholeheartedly committed to the French cause.

Napoleon wrote a letter to the French National Convention in which he denounced Paoli and asked for an inquiry. When investigators arrived in Corsica with warrants, Paoli's supporters drove them off and declared the island's independence from France. It was clear that Corsica was no longer on the same path as revolutionary France.

What went on between Napoleon and Paoli was deeper than a simple quarrel. Paoli was an older man shaped by decades of exile and defeat. He was wary of sweeping change and fearful of revolutionary excess. Napoleon, younger and fiercely committed to Jacobin republicanism, embraced the idea of a strong, centralized France as Corsica's best hope. One generation was clinging to cautious autonomy, while the other was swept up in the fervor of revolution.

Flight from Corsica

By May 1793, Corsica was in the early stages of open civil war. The fragile authority of the French National Convention had all but collapsed on the island. French commissioners sent to oversee affairs were intimidated or driven out. Revolutionary law had ceased to function. In its place rose factional violence and suspicion, where loyalty to one camp or the other could mean the difference between safety and danger. In this atmosphere, the Bonaparte family, which had openly identified with the French Republic, had become targets.

In May, Napoleon set out from Ajaccio with the intention of reaching Bastia, where representatives of the National Convention and their investigators were attempting to reassert French authority. The very real risk of arrest hung in the air. According to some accounts, Napoleon narrowly avoided capture by armed supporters of Paoli. With the danger too close, he turned back to Ajaccio.

Napoleon went into hiding. He was protected by political allies and, for a time, by the mayor himself. He managed to embark on a French ship and take part in an attempt to take back control of Ajaccio from Paoli's faction and other anti-Jacobin forces. The effort failed. Local resistance was too strong, and French power on the island was too weak to impose order.

The blow to the Bonapartes came swiftly. On the night of May 23rd, 1793, Paolist mobs ransacked the Bonaparte family home in Ajaccio. Letizia Bonaparte and her younger children fled. Her half-brother, Joseph Fesch, rode with them to the family's olive estate at Millelli outside town. However, they knew they were not safe. After a short rest, they continued their flight through marshland and rough scrub, aware that Paolist forces now held much of the surrounding countryside.

Their goal was the coast. At Capitello Beach, on land belonging to Letizia's Ramolino relatives, they found boats that could carry them north to Calvi. Some accounts suggest Napoleon stayed behind for a few days before rejoining them, but others say he was with his family immediately. What is certain is that when they reached Calvi, they stayed with Napoleon's godfather, Laurent Giubega, while they waited for passage to the French mainland. From Calvi, they sailed to Toulon, becoming exiles. Napoleon Bonaparte would never return to Corsica again.

France in Crisis

When the Bonaparte family arrived in France in 1793, they stepped into a country that was unraveling. Napoleon had been promoted to captain of artillery in July 1792, a rank he still technically held, but he had remained on leave in Corsica far longer than authorized. Under ordinary circumstances, that could have meant serious discipline or suspension. But these were not ordinary times. The French Army was stretched thin, and trained artillery officers were in short supply.

Napoleon's early ties with Augustin Robespierre, the younger brother of Maximilien, placed him within a network of rising Jacobins. Maximilien Robespierre was rapidly becoming one of the most powerful men in France; he would soon dominate the Committee of Public Safety. Augustin wasn't yet powerful enough to guarantee anyone's career, but his support likely helped place Napoleon in a more favorable light with the authorities in Paris. Combined with the army's desperate need for capable officers, this connection allowed Napoleon to resume active duty with his captain's rank intact.

Napoleon was also drawn into the political currents of the French Revolution. In July 1793, he wrote *Le Souper de Beaucaire* ("Supper at Beaucaire"), a short political pamphlet urging national unity and support for the Convention.

France in 1793 was no ordinary war zone. The French Revolution that had begun four years earlier had shredded the old social order and rewritten the rules of politics. The National Convention was deeply divided. The Girondins wanted a moderate republic. The Jacobins, led by Maximilien Robespierre, Georges Danton, and Jean-Paul Marat, pushed for more radical measures. A third group, the Plain, tried to navigate between the two extremes.

The fate of Louis XVI became the test case. Was he a traitor who deserved death, or should France show mercy? After a trial that was more political theater than legal proceeding, the National Convention voted narrowly to execute him. On January 21st, 1793, Louis XVI was guillotined in Paris. His death sent shockwaves across Europe, terrifying kings. The execution shocked Europe. Britain, Spain, Portugal, Naples, and the Dutch Republic would later join Austria and Prussia, which had been at war with France since 1792.

At home, France was ripped apart by civil conflict as much as by foreign war. Radical Jacobins in Paris were anxious to defend the republic from all perceived enemies. They created the Committee of Public Safety, a body with extraordinary powers to prosecute counter-revolutionaries and direct the war effort. Revolutionary tribunals soon sprang up. In the months that followed, the definition of "enemy" expanded from traitors and émigrés to include nobles, priests, moderates, and even rival revolutionaries who found themselves out of favor. The guillotine became the favored instrument of this new order.

At the same time that war and paranoia consumed France, revolutionary reforms were reshaping everyday life. Feudal dues were abolished, church lands were nationalized and sold, and a new revolutionary calendar replaced the familiar cycle of saints' days. The metric system appeared, hopes for universal education were proclaimed, and slavery was abolished in French colonies. But these gains came with tremendous cost. Food was scarce, inflation was rampant, the levée en masse required all able-bodied citizens to defend France, and civil war undercut national unity, particularly in the deeply Catholic Vendée, where peasants revolted against the French Revolution's attacks on the church and traditional life.

In Paris, the Jacobins' grip tightened. The National Convention suspended the constitution it had barely finished writing and unleashed a wave of conscription and repression that became known as the Reign of Terror. Maximilien Robespierre and his allies argued that only ruthless measures could save the republic from its enemies.

Across the provinces, resistance to the Parisian government flared. In Lyon, Marseille, Bordeaux, and especially Toulon, citizens rose up against Jacobin extremism. Some rebels even invited foreign armies to occupy French cities. Toulon fell to British and Spanish forces in 1793, a stunning loss that set the stage for Napoleon's first real opportunity to prove himself.

The Siege of Toulon

In the summer of 1793, the Mediterranean port of Toulon became the focal point of one of the French Revolution's most dramatic crises. Toulon was not just another town; it was France's main naval base on the Mediterranean. Its dry docks, arsenals, and fleet were linchpins of French sea power in the south. If the city fell into hostile hands, France's ability to control the Mediterranean and defend its southern coast would be gravely weakened.

Federalists, a faction of French revolutionaries who rejected the authority of the Jacobin government in Paris, believed that the revolution had gone too far in concentrating power. Many in Toulon had supported the French Revolution's earlier phases, but they now saw the government in Paris as tyrannical and dangerous. Desperate to keep control of their city, they took the extraordinary step of inviting British and Spanish warships into the harbor to protect them from Republican forces. Foreign armies were now in French territory.

The allied fleet that arrived was led by the British, although it had significant Spanish support. Other nations were involved more indirectly. They were not a tightly unified coalition under a single command; they were more like allied forces with a common interest in containing the French Revolution. The rebels raised the old royal standard over the forts that guarded the harbor and even proclaimed the young dauphin, eight-year-old Louis XVII, as king in a symbolic gesture.

The loss of Toulon was a staggering blow to the French Republic. Over thirty warships, countless cannons, and vast quantities of ammunition and naval stores sat in its docks. Recovering the port was a strategic necessity.

For months, Republican commanders struggled. The generals sent to retake the city were experienced soldiers, but too many were politically appointed and ill-suited to coordinate a siege against a fortified coastal position backed by enemy warships. The fighting dragged on. It was costly and frustrating, with neither side gaining a decisive advantage. Republican losses mounted.

Into this crucible stepped Napoleon Bonaparte, then twenty-four years old and a captain of artillery. The senior artillery commander had been badly wounded early in the siege, and the representatives of the National Convention who were overseeing the campaign needed someone with both technical skill and political reliability to step in. Napoleon's connections, particularly with the Corsican deputy Saliceti and with

Augustin Robespierre, helped bring him into view at just the right moment.

But it wasn't only networking that got him the job. Napoleon brought to the table an uncommon strength for his age: solid mathematical training and a deep grasp of artillery dynamics. Siege warfare in the late 18th century was not won by infantry charges alone, nor was it a simple matter of lining up cannons and trading shot. It was a matter of placing guns where they could dominate the field and of understanding how to shape the enemy's options before the first shot was fired. Many commanders at Toulon were experienced soldiers, but their focus tended toward traditional operations, like direct assaults, broad bombardments, or piecemeal cannon duels.

Napoleon at the Siege of Toulon.[4]

Napoleon saw that the key lay in controlling the harbor approaches. He urged that artillery be massed on the heights overlooking the harbor, where guns could fire into the heart of the enemy's defenses and break the support that the fleet provided. It was a bold departure from the conventional thinking of many of his seniors, but as the siege dragged on and frustration grew, his ideas gained traction.

Jacques François Dugommier replaced the previous commander of the siege in November 1793. He was more receptive to Napoleon's ideas. One battery after another opened fire from the ridges above the bay, and the allied guns began to fall silent.

When the British and Spanish commanders finally saw that their naval positions could no longer be held, they withdrew. During their retreat, they destroyed what they could of the French arsenal and scuttled ships, but they could not keep Toulon. It was a turning point in the war.

Napoleon was wounded in the fighting. A British soldier struck him with a bayonet in the thigh. The wound was painful, but it was not enough to remove him from the battlefield. Before the year was out, on December 22nd, 1793, he was promoted to brigadier general. His meteoric rise reflected both the chaos of the French Revolution and the French Republic's willingness to reward talent in a way the old army had rarely allowed.

The Reign of Terror

The Jacobin-led National Convention, backed by the Committee of Public Safety, passed the Law of Suspects in September 1793. The law defined "suspects" so broadly that almost anyone could be arrested based on rumors or past associations. This law became one of the legal foundations for the Reign of Terror.

For much of the following year, the guillotine at the Place de la Révolution (later renamed Place de la Concorde) was in constant use, executing people suspected of being royal sympathizers or brewing counter-revolutionary ideas. Many people used the opportunity to accuse personal enemies rather than enemies of the French Republic. Tens of thousands died during the Reign of Terror. About sixteen thousand to seventeen thousand were formally executed by revolutionary tribunals, while others died in prison, in massacres, or through extrajudicial killings.

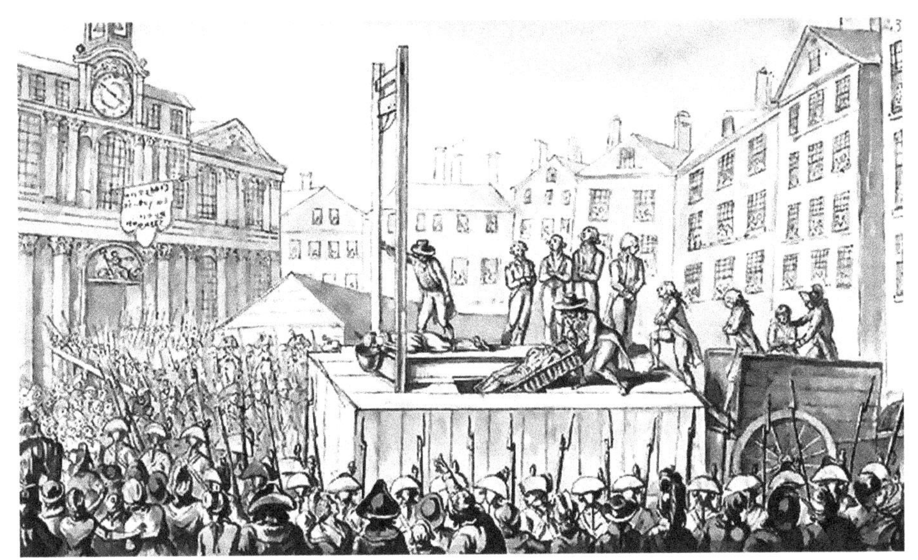

A depiction of the Reign of Terror.[5]

The Reign of Terror succeeded in its immediate goals. The Federalist revolts were crushed. French armies began winning victories against the First Coalition. In the Vendée region of western France, where staunch Catholics and royalists had risen against the French Revolution's attacks on the Catholic Church, the uprising was brutally suppressed, with tens of thousands killed.

But the violence spiraled beyond military necessity. Georges Danton, once a leading revolutionary, was executed in April 1794. He was accused of being too moderate. Maximilien Robespierre, who became one of the most influential figures associated with the Reign of Terror, began to take a more dominant role on the Committee of Public Safety. His influence was widely feared.

The Fall of Robespierre and the Thermidorian Reaction

As things escalated, deputies in the National Convention feared that no one, including themselves, was safe from accusation. On July 27th, 1794, members of the National Convention turned against Robespierre and his closest allies. Robespierre was arrested and executed by guillotine on July 28th, 1794. With his death, the Reign of Terror lost its central figure and much of its momentum.

The Thermidorian Reaction, named after the month of Thermidor in the revolutionary calendar, was a political backlash against the excesses of the Reign of Terror. In the weeks that followed Robespierre's fall, the National Convention moved to weaken the legal and political structures that had made mass repression possible. Committees lost power, laws were scaled back, and the Jacobin Club was closed.

Although the Reign of Terror officially ended, political violence did not; it merely shifted direction, now targeting former Jacobins. Anti-Jacobin groups called the Muscadins—well-dressed young men who were sometimes tolerated or even encouraged by local authorities—attacked those associated with Robespierre's regime. In southern France, particularly, royalists and moderates took revenge on former Jacobins and their supporters. This became known as the White Terror.

Because of Napoleon's vague associations with figures in Robespierre's circle, he was arrested on allegations of associating with that group. He was held briefly and released without formal charges, then returned to his duties, as the army still needed skilled officers.

The period from mid-1794 to late 1795 saw France searching for stability. However, France remained deeply divided. Royalists plotted restoration. Former Jacobins wanted to revive the radical republic. Food shortages and economic problems continued. The assignat, France's revolutionary paper currency, collapsed in value, causing widespread hardship.

The army, however, was transforming. The levée en masse had created the largest military force Europe had ever seen. Young officers like Napoleon could rise based on talent rather than birth. French armies were winning victories on multiple fronts, conquering the Austrian Netherlands, the Rhineland, and parts of Italy. These political and social upheavals created opportunities for military officers like Napoleon, as instability made military success increasingly valuable to whoever held power.

Unrest in Paris

Parisians were restless in 1795. After one of the harshest winters in memory, food was scarce, and bread prices were crushing. In May, riots broke out across the city. People were angry, hungry, and desperate. These uprisings weren't led by royalists; most of those who protested were working-class revolutionaries.

The government responded with force. Soldiers fired on the crowds, and the unrest was crushed.

Later that year, on October 5th, 1795 (which in the revolutionary calendar was 13 Vendémiaire), another threat hit Paris. This time, the crowd wasn't from the working class. Instead, a mix of royalists, frustrated National Guardsmen, and others opposed to the Thermidorian

Convention rose up. They marched on Paris. The National Convention feared it might be overthrown.

Paul Barras, a powerful revolutionary politician who helped overthrow Robespierre and was responsible for defending the government, turned to Napoleon Bonaparte, a young brigadier general who had already shown promise. Napoleon went to work. He placed his troops at key positions and put artillery where it could control the approach to the Tuileries Palace.

When the insurgents advanced, Napoleon ordered his guns to fire grapeshot, short-range iron balls packed into a cannon shot. The fire tore through the attackers, and the revolt collapsed within hours. What might have been another long, chaotic uprising was over before nightfall. The National Convention was saved.

A depiction of 13 Vendémiaire.[6]

Barras saw what Napoleon had done. Five months later, when the new government needed a commander for the Army of Italy, Barras's support helped Napoleon get the post.

The New Constitution

Even before Vendémiaire, France was working on a new constitution. The National Convention had appointed a committee earlier in 1795 to write it. This one was very different from the Constitution of 1793. The goal was to avoid a return to monarchy or to a Jacobin dictatorship.

The result was the Constitution of Year III. It was put to a vote in August 1795. Not many people turned out, and in some regions, the results were disputed, but the new constitution was approved. It limited political participation to property owners and set up two legislative chambers. The Council of Five Hundred proposed laws, and the Council of Ancients, which consisted of two hundred men over the age of forty, reviewed and approved them.

Executive power was given to a five-man Directory, which took office on October 27th, 1795. The idea was stability. After years of revolution, terror, and rebellion, the Directory promised a calmer, more orderly government. But it was still fragile. It depended heavily on the army to keep order and defend the republic.

Joséphine Bonaparte

Barras didn't just admire Napoleon's abilities on the battlefield; he also took it upon himself to help the young general's social fortunes. Among Barras's introductions was Joséphine de Beauharnais, a well-connected widow whose comfort in the political and social circles of Paris made her almost the opposite of Napoleon, who still felt slightly out of place in the capital's salons. Joséphine was six years his senior and had lived through more of Paris's twists and turns, but Napoleon appears to have been smitten almost from the start. She, for her part, was more cautious at first, taking her time before fully returning his affection.

A portrait of Joséphine.[7]

They were married on March 9th, 1796, just two days before Napoleon set out from Paris to take command of the Army of Italy. By marrying Joséphine, Napoleon tied himself to a network of influential people in Paris at a moment when alliances and connections could make or break a career. It was a step into a world that was not naturally his, and he would navigate it with as much energy and ambition as he brought to his campaigns.

The Italian Campaign

Several European monarchies had been at war with France since 1792. They didn't act as one neat alliance but as a series of shifting partnerships.

These loose, uneasy coalitions came together and fell apart as fortunes changed.

Despite the crisis at home, French armies began gaining the upper hand in the field around 1794 and 1795. They pushed into the Austrian Netherlands and overran the old Dutch Republic in the north, turning it into the Batavian Republic, a state friendly to Paris and dependent on French support.

In 1795, France pulled two major enemies out of the war. Prussia and Spain both concluded separate peace treaties at Basel, freeing up French forces to be used elsewhere. Austria remained defiant and continued the fight. In northern Italy, French troops were still locked in difficult, indecisive fighting against the Habsburg armies when the National Convention gave way to the Directory later that year.

With the situation in Italy unresolved, the new government needed a commander willing to take risks in what many still saw as a secondary front. In early 1796, with the political support of Paul Barras, the Directory appointed Napoleon Bonaparte to take command of the Army of Italy. Napoleon was only twenty-six and hardly a household name outside the army. To many in Paris, it looked like a gamble for a young general to be put in charge of a neglected army on a tough front.

Taking Command

Before Napoleon arrived, the Army of Italy was, by French standards, the service's black sheep. It was badly supplied, short on equipment, and chronically undermanned. Its officers and troops were scattered along the Ligurian coast around Nice and through the Alpine passes, watching experienced Austrian and allied units across rugged terrain. Pay was irregular and often poor, food was hard to come by, and desertion and unrest were serious problems. Some regiments were on the verge of open mutiny by the time Napoleon reached Nice.

The officer corps itself was a mixed bag. Many of the old aristocratic officers had fled or been purged after 1789, but a number of seasoned veterans remained. These men had served before the French Revolution or learned their mettle in the long wars that followed. These men were not impressed by Napoleon's sudden elevation. He seemed a risky choice to many of them.

Napoleon began where he always seemed to: by looking closely at the problem. He rode out to inspect the troops, met with his officers, and took stock of the army's supplies and equipment. The picture was grim, but Napoleon saw things clearly. To stop the army from falling apart, he moved fast to secure emergency funds and supplies. Suddenly, there was food where there hadn't been any before. Soldiers who hadn't been paid in months began to receive at least partial wages again. The discontent eased.

Units that were unruly or close to breakdown were broken up or reassigned. He brought cavalry back from winter quarters so the army could move. Slowly, order and direction returned.

Once the basics were under control, Napoleon turned to reorganization. He tightened discipline and clarified the chain of command. Rather than waiting in static positions, he began planning for rapid movement and bold action. He talked to men at every rank, rallying them with a mix of confidence and bluntness. To the officers, he showed off his technical skill and tireless energy. To the soldiers, he promised glory, honor, and rewards taken from the enemy.

Morale, which had been low, began to lift. Officers who had doubted him started to trust his judgment. The ordinary soldiers responded to his swagger and conviction. The neglected Army of Italy was transforming into a force that believed it could take the fight to the Austrians and their allies.

The Battles Begin

The war in northern Italy opened in April 1796 under odd conditions. Austria and Sardinia-Piedmont were supposed to be allies. However, they didn't trust one another. They had plenty of soldiers between them, but those troops were stretched thin along long mountain ridges. They expected the French to come through the well-known Alpine passes. So, they stacked up defenses there and left other routes lightly held.

Napoleon saw something most officers missed. Instead of attacking where the Allies were strongest, he sent his army through the gaps.

On April 11th, near a ridge called Montenotte (today Monte Legino), French troops ran into an Austrian advance guard under Count Eugène-Guillaume Argenteau. The weather was foul. The hills were steep. Yet the French pressed on. They pushed the Austrians back. Just as important, they cut them off from support. It wasn't a huge battle, but it changed things. Suddenly, the allied lines were in pieces, and coordination fell apart.

A painting of the Battle of Montenotte.[8]

Millesimo and Dego

After Montenotte, Napoleon didn't pause to admire his work. He shifted his attention south. The next targets were the Sardinian-Piedmontese positions around Millesimo.

On April 13th, French troops caught up with the enemy near the village. A stubborn pocket of resistance had gathered around Cosseria Castle, a stone fortress. The fighting was tough. The terrain was difficult. French attacks were not always in perfect sync. Soldiers waded through brush and shell-pocked fields. For a while, it looked as if this part of the campaign would be a grind.

The Piedmontese fought hard. They held their ground longer than many on the French side expected. When the castle finally fell, it wasn't because of a brilliant flanking maneuver. It was because the Piedmontese ran out of energy and supplies.

The next day, attention turned back to Dego, a crossroads town that linked the Austrian and Piedmontese lines. Napoleon knew that if the two enemy forces stayed connected, they could reinforce one another and blunt his thrust. So, he ordered André Masséna to take the town.

French soldiers captured Dego on April 14th, but victory came with a problem. After the fighting, discipline broke down. Troops began looting and celebrating. They wandered away from their posts, which left the town exposed.

The Austrians noticed. They sent a force back in and, for a short time, took Dego back from the French.

Napoleon was furious when he heard the news. A victory undone by careless soldiers was something he could not afford. He did not sulk, though. He gathered fresh troops and struck again on April 15th. The French retook Dego and drove the Austrians off.

That brief loss and quick recovery reinforced something Napoleon had already begun to make a hallmark of his command: soldiers could win battles, but only disciplined soldiers could hold positions.

Ceva, Mondovì, and the Collapse of Piedmont

After the hard fighting at Dego, the Sardinian-Piedmontese army pulled back toward prepared positions near Ceva. Their line of earthworks and redoubts looked strong on a map, and in many ways, it should have been tough for the French to break.

But Napoleon wasn't interested in a long siege. He kept his troops moving and his opponents guessing. The defenses at Ceva slowed him down, but they didn't stop him. On April 17th, the Sardinians began to realize they were in danger of being cut off from both sides. Rather than risk being surrounded, they chose to fall back again.

The road lay open toward Mondovì, a key town that stood between the French and the heart of Piedmont. Napoleon knew that a sharp blow here could decide whether Sardinia-Piedmont stayed in the war or not.

On April 21st, his army struck. The French outmaneuvered the main Sardinian force and engaged them where they were vulnerable. The Piedmontese fought, but they were running out of steam. When the French pressure came, their line gave way, and they began to retire in disorder.

With the road to the interior open and no sign of Austrian help coming in time, King Victor Amadeus III asked for terms. Within days, Sardinia-Piedmont agreed to an armistice, effectively pulling itself out of the war. In less than two weeks, the southern flank of the coalition in Italy had disappeared.

Austria now stood alone against France in Italy. And the French Army of Italy was suddenly a force that had tasted success.

Napoleon made a point of praising his troops. He shared their hardships and spoke to them plainly. He didn't sugarcoat their fear, the mud, or their weariness, but he gave them a sense of purpose. The men began to move with confidence, not just because they were ordered to but because they believed they could win.

From the Po to Milan: Fombio, Codogno, and Lodi

By early May, the Austrians under Johann Peter Beaulieu were trying to recover. Their plan was to fall back behind the Po and Adda Rivers, using the waterways as natural barriers to stop the French advance.

From May 7th to May 10th, French and Austrian troops skirmished around Fombio and Codogno as Napoleon looked for a weak point. The fighting wasn't dramatic at first; it was just probing and testing defenses. Napoleon wanted a way to get his army over the rivers and deeper into Lombardy.

On May 10th, he found it near Lodi. The French forced the crossing of the Adda River under fire. The Austrians had left a rearguard on the far bank to hold the bridge. It was a narrow piece of ground, making it easy for defenders to fire at anyone trying to cross.

Napoleon ordered repeated infantry assaults. French troops went forward in waves under artillery fire. The fighting was brutal and costly, with hundreds dying. The day was fading when the French finally forced their way across. Once over, they drove the Austrians back.

Lodi wasn't a massive battle by numbers, but it boosted their confidence, and it bolstered Napoleon's reputation. A short time later, the French entered Milan. Its capture gave Napoleon control of Lombardy's capital, as well as access to money, supplies, and political leverage. It was clear that Austrian authority in northern Italy had effectively collapsed.

Political Consequences in Italy

As Napoleon's army marched forward, the map of northern Italy began to change. Old governments disappeared. In their place, French-backed republics sprang up. These small states were organized on new, revolutionary lines. Some adopted French legal codes or republican symbols. Others were little more than shells, dependent on French troops and French money.

The French expected these new republics to help pay for the war. They asked for money, supplies, guns, and food. That was part of how Napoleon kept his army moving without collapsing.

But not everyone welcomed this. For some Italians, French rule looked like another foreign occupation rather than liberation. Resentment grew in towns and the countryside. In places where taxes or requisitions were heavy, hostility flared. The same army that brought defeat to Austria and Sardinia also brought new burdens to the ordinary people. In the months and years ahead, that resentment would simmer and occasionally boil over.

Borghetto and the Binasco Reprisals

By late May, Beaulieu's army was retreating east, and the French were pressing their advantage. On May 30th, Napoleon forced a crossing at Borghetto, slipping past Austrian defenses and keeping the enemy off balance.

Not long after, trouble flared in Pavia. Some locals rose up against French authority. In nearby Binasco, French troops responded with harsh reprisals. Civilians were executed, and homes and property were destroyed.

Later storytellers would exaggerate and mythologize what happened in Binasco, saying that Napoleon ordered all the males in the town to be killed. The truth is harder to pin down, but it is clear that the retaliation was brutal.

Expansion and Siege Warfare

In June 1796, Napoleon didn't waste time after Borghetto. French forces began extending control over the smaller states of Parma, Modena, Tuscany, and even the Papal States. Some local leaders agreed to terms without a fight. Others only came to the table under the clear threat of force. French artillery and cavalry were enough to convince most rulers that resistance was pointless.

At the center of the campaign was Mantua, one of Italy's strongest fortresses. The French reached it in July 1796 and began a siege that would last for months. Napoleon couldn't simply batter Mantua into submission. He would need to starve it out, blockade it, and prevent any Austrian effort to break through.

While the siege dragged on, Napoleon kept maneuvering elsewhere. He crossed rivers, cut supply lines, and kept pressure on Habsburg relief forces. Inside Mantua, conditions worsened. Food grew scarce, and disease spread. The civilians and soldiers trapped inside suffered more each passing week.

Rovereto, Bassano, Arcole, and Rivoli

Napoleon's enemies didn't give up after Mondovì. The Austrians pulled themselves together under Dagobert Sigmund von Wurmser, a professional soldier who knew the terrain and French tactics well. He wanted to break through the French lines and relieve Mantua before starvation and disease finished the garrison there.

What followed was a series of back-and-forth moves across the rugged ground of northern Italy. At Rovereto in late July and again at Bassano later in the summer, Wurmser tried to push toward Mantua. Napoleon kept shifting his lines, keeping pressure on multiple points so that the Austrian columns never found a clear path. These were not huge battles, but they kept Wurmser reacting instead of acting.

When the two armies met at Arcole in mid-November, the fighting was intense. For three days, French and Austrian soldiers struggled over marshy fields and narrow causeways. The terrain made it hard to see what was happening and harder still to form orderly lines. Men fought in the smoke and mud. In some accounts, it was a dramatic, almost mythic confrontation. Napoleon was said to have rushed forward, waving a flag to rally his men. The truth is that it was a brutal, grinding clash of infantry and artillery. On the third day, the Austrians simply pulled back. Wurmser's attempt to break the siege had failed again.

A depiction of Napoleon at Arcole.'

The last serious Austrian effort came in January 1797 at Rivoli. Wurmser tried to thread his forces through narrow mountain passes to reach Mantua from the northeast. Napoleon moved guns and men onto the steep ground that overlooked the passes. When the Austrian columns poured out into the open, they were met with concentrated cannon and musket fire. Parts of the enemy line collapsed under pressure. Pockets of Austrians were surrounded, and what had been a relief attempt dissolved into retreat and surrender.

With the Austrian advance stopped, Mantua's fall was only a matter of time. On February 2nd, 1797, after months of hopeless waiting, the garrison finally gave up. Tens of thousands of soldiers had passed through that fortress during the siege, but by the end, only about sixteen thousand were still fit for duty. Wurmser and his staff marched out with the honors of war, but the rest were sent home under parole. They pledged not to fight France again.

The fall of Mantua didn't bring the war to a close, but it did change its shape completely. With Austria's last effective army trapped and its forces in Italy broken, there was no longer a real field army south of the Alps capable of coordinated resistance. Napoleon did not pause to rest. Instead, he reorganized his army and pushed it across the mountains into Austrian territory.

This last chapter of the campaign didn't feature the big, pitched battles of northern Italy, but it put unrelenting pressure on the Habsburg government. French divisions moved steadily through Styria and Carinthia, keeping Austrian commanders off balance and approaching closer and closer to the heart of Habsburg lands. Vienna suddenly seemed vulnerable. Under that kind of pressure and with no army ready to stop Napoleon, the Austrian government chose negotiation over further destruction.

Peace Settlements

Napoleon's advance forced Austria to come to the table. On April 18th, 1797, he and representatives of Holy Roman Emperor Francis II signed what came to be called the Preliminaries of Leoben. Officially, Napoleon negotiated in the name of the French Directory, but in practice, he steered the talks, offering terms shaped by what his victories had made possible on the ground.

Under the agreement at Leoben, Austria agreed to withdraw from the war against France and acknowledged French control of the Austrian Netherlands (roughly today's Belgium). Austria also accepted the loss of Lombardy, which was folded into the French-aligned Cisalpine Republic. In return, Austria would receive territory taken from the Republic of

Venice, a state that had not yet been conquered.

Although the Republic of Venice had tried to stay neutral for most of the Italian campaign, Napoleon never really trusted it. To him, Venice was a problem waiting to be dealt with and a useful bargaining chip.

In the spring of 1797, unrest flared in Venetian territory. There were scattered attacks on French troops. French commanders accused Venetian officials of looking the other way, and Napoleon was quick to treat these incidents as proof that Venice could no longer be tolerated as an independent power. Whether the threat was real or exaggerated mattered less than the opportunity it provided.

French forces moved into Venetian lands in April and May. There was no dramatic showdown. The republic was old, diplomatically isolated, and militarily unprepared. On May 12th, 1797, the Venetian government simply dissolved itself rather than resist. A state that had survived for more than a thousand years vanished fairly quietly.

The preliminary terms agreed at Leoben were formalized later that year. On October 17th, 1797, Napoleon met Austria's negotiator, Count von Cobenzl, at Campo Formio and signed a peace treaty that effectively ended Austria's participation in the war. The First Coalition had collapsed, although Britain remained at war with France.

The results were dramatic:

- France's control of the former Austrian Netherlands was officially recognized.

- Northern Italy remained under French influence through allied client republics.

- Austria was compensated with territory from Venice.

- The centuries-old Republic of Venice effectively disappeared.

- French power expanded indirectly into nearby regions, including Switzerland, which would soon be reshaped under French pressure.

Campo Formio showed that Napoleon was no longer just a battlefield commander. By negotiating and signing the treaty himself, he demonstrated political authority. He had moved beyond commanding armies to shaping peace. That shift—from soldier to statesman—was unmistakable.

The Rise of a Legend

Napoleon's Italian campaign transformed a neglected, under-funded army into one of the most feared and effective fighting forces in Europe. When he arrived in Italy in 1796, the Army of Italy was poorly supplied, short of morale, and spread thin. By 1797, it had captured tens of thousands of prisoners, beaten multiple allied armies in the field, and forced major powers to negotiate on France's terms.

What made Napoleon's victories distinctive wasn't just that he won but how he won. He moved his forces quickly, often bypassing strongpoints and striking where the enemy was weakest. He didn't rely on long, secure supply lines; instead, his troops lived off the countryside and requisitioned what they needed along the way. He separated enemy forces rather than confronting them all at once. And he struck with concentrated force at the moments his opponents were least ready.

These approaches weren't brand-new in military theory, but Napoleon applied them with uncommon consistency. They became the backbone of his later campaigns and helped him turn battlefield successes into political power.

He also made a point of knowing his men personally. He rode with them, shared their hardships, and spoke to them directly. He praised their courage and framed each victory as their achievement, not just his. That fostered loyalty and pride. Young officers found in him a leader who recognized initiative. Ordinary soldiers felt seen instead of just commanded.

News of his accomplishments spread quickly. By 1797, Napoleon was more than just a successful general. He was a public figure, someone whose name echoed beyond Italy into the salons of Paris and the courts of Europe. People were beginning to speak of him not just as a man who won battles but as a man who was making history.

Chapter 3: The Egyptian Campaign

France and Austria had signed a peace treaty, but neither side trusted it would last. Britain posed the real threat in 1798. Napoleon knew a direct invasion wouldn't work. Britain's navy controlled the seas, and any attempt to land French troops on British soil would end in disaster.

A different strategy emerged. Egypt technically belonged to the Ottoman Empire, but it held enormous strategic importance. French control of Egypt would mean domination of the eastern Mediterranean. It would threaten Britain's trade routes to India, the centerpiece of the British Empire. Britain's economy could be crippled, all without landing a single French soldier on British soil. The French Directory approved the plan.

Military conquest alone didn't satisfy Napoleon's ambitions. He had read about Alexander the Great's explorations of Egypt and dreamed of following in those footsteps. The ancient Egyptian civilization beckoned. He wanted to study it, map the land, and gather knowledge. In March 1798, he convinced the Directory to establish the Commission of Sciences and Arts. One hundred sixty-seven scholars would accompany the military expedition.

An impressive group was assembled. Twenty-one mathematicians joined the commission, along with three astronomers, seventeen civil engineers, and thirteen naturalists. Dozens of artists and writers signed on. Interpreters who spoke Arabic and other Eastern languages completed the roster. Napoleon organized them into a military corps so they could travel with the army. Years later, between 1809 and 1829, these scholars published thirty-seven volumes simply titled *Description de l'Égypte*. It became a comprehensive study of Egypt's geography, history, and culture.

Malta: The First Stop

In May 1798, the French fleet set sail. Malta was their first target. The Knights Hospitaller controlled the island, a religious and military order dating back to the Crusades. Though they governed Malta as an independent state, European monarchies provided their support. Most of those monarchies opposed revolutionary France.

The French fleet requested permission to enter the harbor and collect fresh water and supplies. The Knights refused. French intentions made them wary, and they had aligned themselves with monarchies that viewed France as a threat.

Napoleon moved quickly. Valletta, Malta's fortified capital, surrendered on June 12th, 1798. Internal divisions weakened the Knights. Many French-born knights refused to fight against their homeland. The order's leadership was too old and unprepared for a determined assault.

Napoleon stayed on Malta for several days. He reorganized the government along French revolutionary lines and promised reforms and protections for the Maltese people. Reality quickly contradicted his words. The Maltese practiced Catholicism devoutly, while French revolutionary policies were aggressively secular. Church property was seized. Monasteries dissolved. Religious orders that had shaped Maltese life for centuries were dismantled. New taxes appeared, and pensions went unpaid. The promised reforms never materialized.

A small French garrison stayed behind when Napoleon's fleet sailed for Egypt. Anger over looted churches and attacks on their faith sparked a widespread rebellion. Initially, the Maltese people had welcomed liberation from the Knights' rigid rule, but now they fought fiercely to expel the French. The siege lasted until 1800, when Malta became a British protectorate.

Landing in Egypt

From Malta, the French fleet sailed to Egypt. Luck and careful navigation helped them avoid the British Mediterranean fleet. On July 1st, 1798, they landed near Alexandria.

A problem immediately presented itself. Egypt belonged to the Ottoman Empire, and France was not at war with the Ottomans. Napoleon's invasion was legally questionable and diplomatically provocative. He believed that the Ottomans were too weak and distracted to respond effectively. That gamble would have serious consequences later.

Proclamations went out to the troops before landing. They were entering a land with a radically different culture and religion. Napoleon wanted to emphasize that the enemy was not the Egyptian people but the Mamluks, a military caste originally from outside Egypt who had seized power and ruled harshly. Technically, the Mamluks were subjects of the Ottoman Empire. In practice, they governed Egypt as they pleased, extracting brutal taxes from the population while living in luxury.

Napoleon wanted his men to respect local customs and religion. Ancient monuments were to be protected. No unnecessary destruction would be tolerated. However, proclamations and reality would prove very different. French troops frequently disregarded these orders when plunder called to them.

Messages also went to Egyptian religious leaders and intellectuals. Napoleon claimed the French had destroyed the power of the pope and defeated the Knights Hospitaller of Malta. He was portraying France as an ally of Islam rather than an enemy of it. The French, he wrote, came as liberators to free Egypt from Mamluk oppression. Egyptian religion and customs would be respected.

Many Egyptians were skeptical about these promises. Foreign invaders were still foreign invaders, regardless of their intentions.

Taking Alexandria

Alexandria's defenses were weak and in disrepair when Napoleon arrived there. He moved quickly to take advantage, ordering an immediate attack rather than waiting for his full forces to assemble.

On the morning of July 2nd, Napoleon attempted to negotiate a peaceful surrender. Gunfire answered him. The French had to fight their way in. By afternoon, Alexandria was under French control, though two of Napoleon's generals had been wounded.

The city fell relatively easily, but this initial success would prove misleading. Other Egyptian cities and the countryside would offer far stiffer resistance.

The March to Cairo

No time was wasted. One battalion received orders to take the port city of Rosetta and secure provisions. Another seized a flotilla of riverboats on the eastern Nile Delta for transporting supplies. The main army would march directly toward Cairo.

The French faced harsh conditions as they marched across the desert. Water was scarce, and the heat was brutal. Bedouin raiders harassed the columns. Napoleon pushed his troops hard, determined to reach Cairo before the Mamluks could organize a coordinated defense.

On July 10th, they reached the Nile at the village of Ramaniyah. Several skirmishes with Mamluk forces had occurred along the way. The major engagement would come later at the Battle of Shubra Khit. For now, the troops could rest. They drank deeply and feasted on watermelons growing along the banks.

Two days of rest followed. Then scouts brought word that a substantial Mamluk force was approaching.

The Battle of Shubra Khit

To prepare for the conflict, Napoleon arranged his troops six ranks deep instead of the usual three, forming defensive squares. The French had faced Mamluk raiders during their march, yet they were still dealing with a style of warfare very different from European battles. Elite cavalry formed the foundation of the Mamluk army. They had little infantry and almost no modern artillery. They believed speed and personal skill would decide the battle.

On July 13th, the two armies faced each other. One of Napoleon's cavalry officers, Desvernois, later described what they saw. The Mamluks rode magnificent Arab horses with elaborate harnesses. Their riders wore dazzling armor inlaid with gold and jewels, dressed in brilliant colors with turbans adorned with egret feathers or golden helmets. They carried sabers, lances, maces, spears, rifles, axes, daggers, and three pairs of double-barreled pistols.

For more than three hours, the Mamluk cavalry rode back and forth. They were inspecting the French formations for weak points. The tension was unbearable, but Napoleon's disciplined men held.

Groups of impatient Mamluk warriors finally charged at different points in the French line. Muskets and cannons bristled on all sides of each French square, making it nearly impossible for cavalry to attack without being cut down by concentrated fire. Grapeshot from French field guns fired into the charging horsemen. The tightly packed formations were devastated.

Some Mamluks managed to penetrate between the French squares. They discovered the rear was as strongly defended as the front and were beaten back with heavy losses.

The Mamluks eventually retreated toward Cairo to regroup. For Napoleon, the battle proved the effectiveness of his tactics against Mamluk cavalry.

The Battle of the Pyramids

The village of Embabeh near the Giza Plateau became the Mamluks' fallback position. The ancient pyramids stood there. The Mamluk forces split into two. One division under Murad Bey took up a position on the west bank of the Nile. Another under Ibrahim Bey positioned itself on the east bank.

Several days of marching toward Cairo left Napoleon's troops exhausted. He gave them barely an hour to rest before ordering them into battle formation. This engagement, known as the Battle of the Pyramids, would take place on July 21st, 1798.

Napoleon created defensive squares again. These hollow squares were each made up of several units. Soldiers with muskets and bayonets faced outward on all four sides. Cannons were positioned at each corner. Inside each square, cavalry units and ammunition wagons waited for the right moment. The front row would kneel and fire. The second row would fire standing. The rear row would rotate forward as the front ranks reloaded. The system worked like a well-oiled machine.

French artillery opened fire first. Cannon shot tore through the charging Mamluk masses before they could close the distance. Those who survived the barrage met coordinated musket volleys from the infantry. The disciplined French firepower shattered charge after charge.

Napoleon reportedly told his troops that forty centuries of history looked down upon them from the pyramids. The message would become legendary, though whether he actually spoke these exact words remains uncertain. What is certain is that the battle was decided quickly. After the Mamluk charges were repelled, French infantry and artillery moved against the fortified Mamluk positions at Embabeh.

The Battle of the Pyramids by Louis-François, Baron Lejeune.[10]

French losses were minimal. Thousands of Mamluks were killed or captured. The Mamluk forces began to collapse. Ibrahim Bey, seeing the battle turn against Murad Bey's division, began withdrawing eastward before the French reached Cairo.

The remaining Mamluk positions were overrun by French troops. And then discipline broke down. The dead were looted by French soldiers. The Mamluks wore their wealth. Their bodies were adorned with jewelry and gold coins sewn into their elaborate clothing. Violence against Egyptian civilians also occurred, though the full extent remains disputed among historians. The promised respect for Egyptian people and culture gave way to the soldiers' desire for the riches they had been promised. Napoleon, for his part, looked the other way.

The victory broke the Mamluks' main resistance. French military power had shattered Egypt's ruling caste in a single afternoon. This was the turning point of the campaign. Within days, Napoleon would occupy the city and effectively control Lower Egypt.

Entering Cairo

News of the battle sent Ibrahim Bey's forces and the remaining Mamluk reserves fleeing to Syria. Napoleon marched into Cairo on July 24th, 1798.

His triumph would be short-lived, though. Just days after he entered Cairo, the British fleet under Admiral Horatio Nelson destroyed the French Navy at the Battle of the Nile on August 1st, 1798. This catastrophic defeat cut off Napoleon's army from France and left them stranded in Egypt with no hope of reinforcement or escape.

The scholarly corps that had traveled with the army finally had its moment. Tours were organized to the pyramids and the Sphinx. Napoleon, always aware of public relations, had himself painted visiting these monuments. He didn't actually explore inside the pyramids. His soldiers were less restrained. Several left graffiti inside, even in the topmost chambers of the Great Pyramid.

Napoleon immediately began reorganizing Cairo's government. To build relationships with Egyptian religious leaders, he attended meetings and carried a Quran. In August, he participated in an Islamic festival. Some French soldiers even converted to Islam to marry Egyptian women.

The Egyptians continued to observe how the French acted. The French claimed to be friends of Muslims and liberators. However, their actions were telling a different story.

Napoleon in Egypt by Jean-Léon Gérôme.[11]

Disaster at Sea: The Battle of the Nile

While Napoleon was securing Cairo, his fleet remained anchored in Aboukir Bay, east of Alexandria. The ships had served their purpose by transporting the army to Egypt. Now they waited at anchor.

British Admiral Horatio Nelson had been hunting the French fleet across the Mediterranean since the expedition began. Several times, the two fleets had barely missed each other in the darkness. On August 1st, 1798, Nelson finally found them.

Nightfall typically ended naval battles, but Nelson engaged despite the fading light. He executed a bold plan to attack inside the French line. Ships in two lines were sent directly into the gaps between the anchored French vessels, firing broadsides as they went. A few British ships even slipped between the French line and the shore, maximizing crossfire on the trapped French ships.

As darkness fell, the fighting intensified. The French flagship *L'Orient* was hit repeatedly. Small fires broke out and began spreading.

British captains, seeing the flames, concentrated their fire on *L'Orient*. If fire reached the gunpowder magazine, the ship would explode. The nearest British and French ships, fearful of the impact, cut their anchor cables and fled. They soaked their sails and decks with seawater to prevent flying sparks from igniting them.

For one terrible moment, *L'Orient* lit up the night sky. Then she exploded in spectacular fashion. More than a thousand men died, including French Vice Admiral François-Paul Brueys d'Aigalliers.

The Battle of the Nile: Destruction of L'Orient, 1 August 1798 by Mather Brown.[12]

The destruction of the French fleet left Napoleon's army stranded in Egypt, cut off at sea with limited hope of resupply or reinforcement. Britain now commanded the eastern Mediterranean.

The Cairo Revolt

Three months after the Battle of the Pyramids, Egyptian patience ran out. Resentment had been building among Egyptians. The French imposed heavy taxation, and property was seized. Despite their proclamations of respect, many Egyptians saw the French as disrespecting Islam and local traditions. Muslim sheikhs and imams had watched the French closely. Their promises of liberation rang hollow.

Local religious leaders and community figures played roles in fomenting resistance. Weapons were distributed, and people were urged to rise against the French occupation. On October 21st, 1798, the revolt began after a French brigadier general and Napoleon's personal assistant were killed. Street fighting erupted across the city.

Napoleon was engaged in negotiations elsewhere in Cairo when the violence started. The French garrison was already on edge, though, so the French response was swift and brutal.

Heavy weaponry and house-to-house fighting were used by French troops to suppress the uprising. Cannons positioned on the citadel fired into rebel positions. Napoleon led a street-by-street assault. The rebels were driven back to their stronghold at the Al-Azhar Mosque, a center of Islamic learning. The fighting there was fierce and led to significant casualties among the rebels.

The revolt was crushed. The pretense of French-Egyptian friendship was over.

The Syrian Campaign

Napoleon had miscalculated badly. The Ottoman government condemned the French invasion as an attack on imperial territory. Egypt was an Ottoman province, which meant Napoleon's invasion violated Ottoman sovereignty. Rather than welcoming French intervention against the semi-independent Mamluks, the Ottomans prepared for war with British support.

An Ottoman invasion of Egypt seemed likely, so Napoleon decided to strike first. In February 1799, he marched his army into Ottoman Syria. His forces captured several coastal towns with relatively little resistance from the mixed Mamluk, Arab, and Turkish garrisons. Gaza, Jaffa, and Haifa fell.

At Jaffa, French troops executed many prisoners, including Ottoman soldiers found wounded in hospitals. The exact number is debated; estimates range from several hundred to a few thousand. It was a significant massacre either way, and it tarnished Napoleon's reputation. Whether Napoleon ordered the killings or simply failed to prevent them, the slaughter would haunt him.

The campaign ground to a halt at Acre. Ahmed al-Jazzar, the experienced Ottoman governor, organized a fierce defense. The French would come to call him "the Butcher" for his ruthless resistance. The British navy blockaded the coast, preventing French reinforcements and supplies from arriving. For two months, Napoleon besieged Acre. Disease and food shortages ravaged his army. Eventually, he ordered a retreat to Egypt.

This was the first time Napoleon faced prolonged resistance. It drained French manpower and morale. It also led to Napoleon's eventual decision to leave Egypt and return to France.

The army that limped back to Egypt in May 1799 was a shadow of the force that had conquered Cairo. The men were tired, sick, and demoralized. However, Napoleon's instinct for public relations never failed. He staged a triumphal march through Cairo's streets with his healthiest, best-equipped soldiers. The sick and wounded were hidden in surrounding villages. The crowds cheered what appeared to be a victorious army.

The Battle of Aboukir

Napoleon knew his situation was desperate. His army was stranded in Egypt with no naval support. Disease and supply shortages were severe. Desertion occurred, as it commonly did in extended campaigns far from home. French forces were stretched across Egypt. One battalion watched Murad Bey in the south. Another kept Ibrahim Bey in check in Sinai. A third guarded the Libyan frontier.

In July 1799, reports arrived that Ottoman forces with allied support were preparing to challenge French control along the Egyptian coast. Napoleon gathered his available troops and marched toward Aboukir Bay. An Ottoman force under Mustafa Pasha had established defensive positions there.

Napoleon attacked on July 25th, 1799. French artillery tore gaps in the dense Ottoman formations, and as the enemy line began to buckle, the French cavalry surged forward. Leading the charge was Joachim Murat, whose aggressive use of cavalry proved decisive. Murat drove straight into the Ottoman center, fighting at close quarters and personally capturing the Ottoman commander, Mustafa Pasha, after a violent struggle in which Murat himself was wounded.

The Battle of Abukir, 25 July 1799 by Antoine-Jean Gros.[18]

The loss of their commander shattered Ottoman unity. Thousands of Ottoman troops fled or were driven back toward the shore, many drowning as they attempted to escape.

France celebrates the Battle of Aboukir as a great victory. It is even commemorated on the Arc de Triomphe in Paris. However, even this tactical success could not change the strategic reality. The French could not secure the region. The army remained isolated, stretched thin, and cut off from France. Egypt was beyond French control.

Learning the Truth

Disturbing news reached Napoleon from prisoner exchange negotiations and British newspapers. France was in trouble. A Second Coalition had formed. Austria, Russia, Britain, and others were closing in on the French borders. The Austrians had recaptured the Italian territories Napoleon had won in 1796 and 1797. In Paris, the Directory looked incapable of stopping anything. It was unpopular, divided, and unable to reverse defeats abroad or stabilize the situation at home.

Napoleon made his decision. He would return to France immediately. On August 22nd, 1799, he boarded a ship with a handful of officers and key members of his scientific corps. General Jean-Baptiste Kléber was left in command of the army.

Seventeen thousand French soldiers in Egypt were abandoned by Napoleon. Some contemporaries and later historians saw his departure as an abandonment of his army. Others view it as a calculated decision to pursue a broader political objective. Napoleon saw the situation clearly. The army was trapped with no hope of reinforcement or evacuation. His presence in Egypt changed nothing. But his presence in France could change everything.

Strong leadership was needed in France. The Directory was weak and divided. The country faced invasion from all sides. This was Napoleon's opportunity, not just to save France but to seize power for himself.

Remarkable work had been accomplished by the scholars who had traveled with him. Over the coming years, they would publish their monumental *Description de l'Égypte*, preserving knowledge of the ancient Egyptian civilization. One of them, an engineer named Pierre-François Bouchard, had discovered a stone tablet near Rosetta with text in three languages. This would eventually allow scholars to decipher Egyptian hieroglyphics.

The Egyptian campaign, on the other hand, was a military failure. The army was stranded. The fleet was destroyed. Thousands had been lost to battle, disease, and hardship. Yet through carefully managed news and propaganda, the expedition enhanced Napoleon's reputation at home as a daring commander willing to attempt the impossible. It also brought him home at exactly the moment when France needed, or at least would accept, a strong man to take control.

On October 9th, 1799, Napoleon landed in France. Within a month, he would overthrow the Directory and make himself ruler of France.

Chapter 4: Conquering Europe: The Rise of Napoleon

Less than a month after the French victory at Aboukir, Napoleon left Egypt. On the night of August 22nd, 1799, he boarded a ship with only a few trusted officers. His plans were kept secret. Even General Kléber, whom Napoleon left in command, only learned of his new position through a letter delivered that night. The troops had been told Napoleon was going north to inspect the Nile Delta. Then he was gone. The discovery of what had happened left the army feeling betrayed.

Napoleon arrived in France on October 9th, 1799, aboard the *Muiron*, one of only two frigates that escaped Lord Nelson's destruction at the Battle of the Nile. He set out for Paris immediately. Cheers and praise for his Egyptian campaign greeted him upon his arrival there on October 16th, 1799. His popularity was at a peak due to his propaganda. The French public remained ignorant of the losses he had suffered.

France had lost territories gained in previous battles while Napoleon was in Egypt. Several European countries were forming a Second Coalition. Internal strife between supporters of a constitutional monarchy and a democratic republican government added to the chaos. The five-member Directory was incompetent and ineffective. For an ambitious young general to seize power, the time was ripe.

Coup d'État of 18/19 Brumaire

Napoleon probably spent the voyage home planning and finalizing strategies to establish a new government and regain the territories France had lost while in Egypt. His arrival in Paris coincided with the plotting of a coup by Abbé Sieyès and Talleyrand. According to historical accounts, Sieyès, who was part of the Directory, was planning a constitutional coup but lacked a charismatic figure to execute it effectively. Napoleon's return gave the plan momentum, and he quickly overtook the process, sidelining Sieyès.

On November 9th, 1799, the two chambers of government were convinced by Sieyès to meet the next day at the Château de Saint-Cloud. Members were told it was for their safety amid a plot discovered among the Jacobins.

Napoleon's troops filled the Château de Saint-Cloud, lining corridors and surrounding the chambers. The members realized they had been duped, but it was too late to stop what was happening. The representative chamber of the Five Hundred was forced to dissolve, though not without resistance. Physical altercations broke out, and armed troops forcibly dispersed the council.

Lucien Bonaparte, Napoleon's brother and president of the Council of Five Hundred, played a crucial role in legitimizing Napoleon's actions. By presenting military intervention as a defense of the legislature rather than a coup, Lucien gave Napoleon the cover he needed to prevail. Without Lucien's aid, the coup might have failed or become violent on a larger scale.

Napoleon Bonaparte in the coup d'état of 18 Brumaire in Saint-Cloud by François Bouchot.[14]

After the coup, a new consular government, the French Consulate, was established. Napoleon took power as First Consul, alongside Sieyès and Roger Ducos, in a temporary leadership.

Within four days, Napoleon was settled in the Palace of Luxembourg. His power in France would become absolute over the next few years. One could almost say he was installed as a dictator through this largely bloodless coup of 18 Brumaire.

A New Constitution

Napoleon appointed a commission to draft a new constitution. The document was promulgated in mid-December 1799.

The new constitution drew symbolic inspiration from the Roman Republic, though it was not a direct legal or structural blueprint. This was to be a constitutional republic in name only. Napoleon and the drafters even used Roman terms when naming government assemblies, deliberately manipulating perceptions. Executive power was supposed to be vested in three consuls. An advisory body of senators was created. They were appointed for life to interpret the new constitution. The Tribunate was established as a body that could debate laws but had no voting power. The Corps législatif (the legislative body) could vote on laws but was not permitted to debate them. The Council of State, a key executive body, was created to draft legislation and advise the First Consul.

In effect, Napoleon, as First Consul, had all the power. The other two consuls were just figureheads. France was becoming a dictatorship. And like all dictators, Napoleon surrounded himself with family, loyal supporters, and bootlickers.

First Consul Napoleon in his office.[15]

Early in 1800, a referendum approved the constitution. Ninety-nine percent of France voted to accept it. Many scholars doubt the validity of that overwhelming percentage. The vote was not secret, and state pressure likely influenced the results.

A Bill of Rights was notably absent from the new constitution. The revolution had fought hard for equality and democracy, and many freedoms and public powers won by the common people during the revolution were left out. The constitution retained suffrage, but only indirectly. Citizens chose "communal notables," from which higher officials were selected, limiting any real democratic influence.

Napoleon convinced people they'd had enough chaos and bloodshed. Order, safety, stability, and peace were what they needed now. For the most part, the people trusted him. His military victories ensured he was admired throughout France and beyond.

Twice over the next few years, the constitution was amended. In 1802, Napoleon was made First Consul for life. In 1804, constitutional reform changed the consulate to an empire, with Napoleon installed as Napoleon I, Emperor of France. Napoleon's popularity allowed him to legitimize major changes through plebiscites, which were public yes-or-no votes. It was a win-win situation for Napoleon. The citizens felt they had a direct say in government. They didn't realize, or didn't mind, that they were increasing Napoleon's absolute control with every "vote."

Domestic Reforms

Napoleon was barely thirty years old when he took over the French government in 1799. The groundwork for transitioning France from a republic to an empire was laid during the Consulate period. His policies were aimed at stability, nationalism, and economic growth.

France's administration was centralized in the hands of the Consulate. As First Consul, Napoleon would soon have total control. The power of local authorities was reduced as a result.

The Bank of France was launched in 1800. A better tax collection system was implemented and regulated to balance the budget. The quality of tax collectors was improved through various means, focusing on their integrity and efficiency. Industrial development and exports were encouraged. A more stable currency system was established, restoring confidence after the collapse of revolutionary paper money.

The education system was reformed. The first secondary schools, known as lycées, were created based on the French military training system. These were intended to train civil and military servants for the state.

From 1801 to 1804, Napoleon developed France's first unified civil code. This was the Napoleonic Code, also known as the Civil Code. This will be discussed in more depth at the end of this chapter, but it covered individual rights, family, property, and colonial matters. The Napoleonic Code included progressive elements, such as legal equality before the law. However, it also restricted women's rights and reinforced patriarchal authority within families.

The Concordat with the Catholic Church

Before the French Revolution, the Catholic clergy held the highest status in the land. They were part of the First Estate. The nobility formed the Second Estate. Everyone else was the Third Estate. The church numbered around 0.5 percent of the total population but owned around 10 percent of the land in France. Less than 3 percent of the state's income came from their contributions.

Vast estates belonged to the church. Higher clergy, who came from the nobility, accumulated great personal wealth, both legitimately and through fraud and corruption.

Their privileges were extensive. They were granted an exemption from taxes on their assets and income. They were also exempted from military duties, and they could collect a tithe from peasants at will. Grants from the state came to them regularly. They were largely exempt from the state's legal system and could be prosecuted only through internal Catholic Church processes.

The Civil Constitution of the Clergy in 1790 attempted to subordinate the church to the state and reorganize dioceses. These reforms made the clergy state employees and contributed to significant conflict during the French Revolution. Revolutionary authorities confiscated and sold church lands. When Napoleon came to power, the relationship between church and state remained deeply fractured.

One powerful group around Napoleon suggested he officially break with the papacy and establish France's own religion as the Gallican Church. Napoleon thought about it, but he told his secretary, Bourrienne, that he'd rather endorse the old Catholic religion and allow the citizens of France to enjoy personal religious choices.

He didn't want religious quarrels within families and society to create too much tension. He was also convinced the majority of people were still

Catholics at heart. Acknowledging the Catholic Church's standing while allowing freedom of choice in religious matters would allow him to gain most French people's support.

At the beginning of 1801, Napoleon worked on an agreement to offer the pope. The document went back and forth between the pope and Napoleon for changes until June 1801. A delegation from the pope arrived in Paris to finalize the terms.

The final Concordat was signed in Paris and Rome on July 15th, 1801. The declaration acknowledged that the majority of French citizens were Catholic, though Catholicism was not the official state religion. French citizens would enjoy religious freedom, especially Protestants.

The French government was responsible for nominating bishops, but the papacy could depose bishops. France would pay clerical salaries out of state funds. The clergy had to swear an oath of allegiance to the state before serving.

The Catholic Church would not contest ownership of church properties that had been confiscated and sold after 1790. The Concordat also included a redistribution of dioceses, reducing their number and bringing them into line with France's civil divisions.

The Organic Articles

When the Concordat became law in April 1802, Napoleon promulgated the Organic Articles without papal approval. These state laws regulated how religious bodies, both Catholic and Protestant, operated in France and placed them under state oversight. The Organic Articles gave legal recognition to Protestant churches and extended state control over all religious activities.

They generated lasting tensions with the papacy. Napoleon's arrangement tilted church-state relations firmly in favor of the French state. He gained significant control over church finances and appointments while restoring Catholic worship. The Catholic Church regained some standing, but it remained subordinate to state authority.

Battle of Marengo

After dealing with France's most pressing domestic affairs and setting the country on a path of recovery, Napoleon set out against the armies of the Second Coalition in May 1800. Austria remained the primary opponent, backed by several lesser allies. Napoleon followed his usual strategy of preventing the loosely knit coalition from combining effectively. He was using Julius Caesar's playbook of divide and conquer.

The campaign in Italy began with Napoleon's crossing of the Alps via the Great St. Bernard Pass, a move that brought French forces into the heart of Austrian-held northern Italy. Before the decisive engagement at Marengo, French forces had already won at Montebello on June 9th, 1800.

Napoleon Crossing the Alps by Jacques-Louis David.[16]

On June 14th, 1800, the Austrian army under General Michael Melas launched an attack itat Marengo. The fighting moved across several battlegrounds during the day as both armies advanced, retreated, regrouped, and attacked again. Napoleon's rapid adaptation to changing circumstances kept the enemy off balance. His troops knew how to move fast. At one point, the Austrians were ambushed by Napoleon, who feigned a retreat.

By late afternoon, French reinforcements arrived under one of Napoleon's generals. They attacked with renewed energy. Their morale was boosted by Napoleon on the front lines, leading the attack. By nightfall, the Austrians were in retreat.

The Battle of Marengo by Louis-François, Baron Lejeune.[17]

General Melas agreed to a ceasefire that same night. The Convention of Alessandria was signed the next day, June 15th, 1800. The convention stipulated that Austria would pull its forces back beyond the Po and Mincio Rivers and cede several cities. It was a negotiated retreat rather than an unconditional surrender.

For Napoleon personally, the most important part of this victory was that it solidified his position as First Consul of France. He squeezed every drop of propaganda from it to boost his image as the savior of France. A bulletin published in France downplayed everyone else's contribution to the Italian campaign's success, except for those directly under Napoleon's control.

The Treaty of Lunéville followed in February 1801, solidifying French gains in Italy and along the Rhine. Austria was now out of the war.

The Treaty of Amiens

After the Treaty of Lunéville, Britain remained as the primary adversary. Russia and other coalition members had already withdrawn or become neutral. Spain was allied with France. Although Britain retained naval supremacy, it lacked the means to defeat France alone.

Napoleon, for his part, sought stability after years of conflict. He reasoned that peace with Britain far outweighed any sacrifices required of France. By proposing favorable and fair terms from the beginning, he was convinced he'd gain British trust. Britain was eager to sign because the hostilities were costing it a fortune through the loss of trade.

On March 25th, 1802, the two parties signed the Treaty of Amiens. The immediate end of hostilities was decreed, and all prisoners of war and hostages were to be returned.

France would evacuate Naples and return control of the Papal States. Egypt would be returned to the Ottomans. Britain would give up most of the conquests gained during the recent war. The Cape of Good Hope and its colony would be returned to the Dutch, and the Dutch colony of Ceylon was given to Britain. Spain gave Trinidad to Britain. Malta would be returned to the Knights of St. John and remain neutral. Gibraltar would remain under British rule.

However, the peace lasted only about fourteen months. It just gave both countries time to regroup and prepare for the future conflict. Under new leadership, Britain concluded that only total military victory would stop Napoleon's ambitious expansion plans.

Diplomatic tensions, especially over Malta and France's actions in Europe, led Britain to declare war again in May 1803. By this time, Napoleon had already been made First Consul for life.

Sale of Louisiana

Napoleon had ambitions for colonial expansion. He acquired Louisiana from Spain in 1800, intending it to serve as a breadbasket and base to support profitable Caribbean colonies, especially Saint-Domingue (now Haiti). France had claimed Louisiana in 1682, though effective control shifted over time. France retained claims and sporadic administration until the Treaty of Fontainebleau in 1762, which secretly transferred Louisiana to Spain.

By 1803, Napoleon's plans had collapsed. The Haitian Revolution in Saint-Domingue was a major factor. Saint-Domingue was France's most profitable colony, but its economy depended on plantation slavery enforced through extreme violence. Mortality rates among enslaved workers were high, but the population was constantly replenished through the slave trade.

The enslaved population on the island vastly outnumbered whites and free people of color. However, a small white planter class controlled all of the political power. Free people of color, many of whom were wealthy and educated, were denied equal rights. These tensions existed long before the French Revolution, but they intensified after 1789.

In 1794, the government in Paris abolished slavery, which transformed the conflict in Saint-Domingue. Formerly enslaved people became legally free and, in many cases, allied with France against foreign enemies. By the late 1790s, slavery had effectively ended on the island.

Napoleon reversed that policy. Seeking to rebuild a Caribbean empire, he moved to restore slavery in French colonies and sent a large expedition to Saint-Domingue in 1802. The possibility of being re-enslaved eliminated any remaining loyalty to France. People of color fought against the French forces, which were destroyed by disease and the conflict. The expedition collapsed. France permanently lost Saint-Domingue, which became the independent state of Haiti in 1804.

Without a productive Caribbean base, Louisiana was no longer valuable to Napoleon's colonial strategy. Financial pressure from the revolution and ongoing wars also weighed heavily on France's treasury. The imminent resumption of war with Britain presented another problem. Napoleon realized he could not defend Louisiana against the powerful British navy. Selling it to the United States was preferable to risking its capture by Britain.

French Treasury Minister François Barbé-Marbois, acting on Napoleon's instructions, offered Louisiana to American delegates Robert R. Livingston and James Monroe. The price was $15 million. They accepted the deal. The treaty was signed in Paris on April 30th, 1803. At the time of the sale, Spain still officially administered the territory despite the treaty returning it to France, so technically, France sold rights it had yet to exercise.

President Thomas Jefferson initially worried the purchase might not be constitutional because the United States Constitution did not explicitly authorize the acquisition of territory. In the end, though, the US Senate ratified the treaty, doing so on October 20th, 1803.

The funds gave Napoleon's war chest a welcome boost and freed France from unnecessary distractions and expenses across the Atlantic.

The Napoleonic Code: Progress and Regression

Before the French Revolution, France's legal system had severe problems. It served as a tool of oppression to maintain the status quo of the class structure. Common people were often harshly punished on charges that might receive leniency if brought against the privileged. The legal system was fragmented and complex, making it difficult for ordinary people to understand their rights and obligations.

Intellectuals like Montesquieu and Voltaire openly criticized France's legal systems and those of most of Europe. The judicial system drained state coffers. An inordinate number of courts existed. Court cases were expensive, drawn-out procedures. Suspects suffered extreme hardship even before a verdict was pronounced. Judges, prosecutors, and prison guards were often corrupt. They were also passionately hated by common citizens.

The French Revolution significantly reformed justice before Napoleon. The Penal Code of 1791 abolished many abuses of the ancien régime (the legal system in place before the revolution), eliminated many old crimes, and required that laws be published before conviction. Feudalism was abolished in 1789.

Napoleon Bonaparte believed in reason as the only acceptable basis for action and law since he was a young man. The disorder of the revolution and its aftermath showed that a revised legal system had become an absolute necessity. Though revolutionary reforms had begun modernizing justice, the interim system remained inadequate for the new nation.

A new commission was appointed by Napoleon in 1801 to consolidate revolutionary gains into a clear civil law system. The Napoleonic Code was designed to preserve concepts like equality before the law and the abolition of special privileges while creating a unified legal framework. Under his guidance and input, this civil code was drafted by 1801, although it was not officially promulgated until 1804.

Main Positive Changes

Distinction between Church and State: The Napoleonic Code made a definitive split between the power and authority of the state and the church in civil matters. Ecclesiastical control and influence over civil affairs, such as marriage and property, were removed, though religious freedom was protected.

Innocence: The revolutionary Penal Code of 1791 had already established protections regarding a person's innocence. The Napoleonic Code did not reverse these changes. It kept the principle that a person could not be punished unless a court first proved guilt.

Equality: All male citizens were equal before the law, regardless of social rank. Legal privilege based on birth was abolished.

Standardization: Crimes and punishments were written down. Judges were expected to follow the law as written instead of relying on custom or personal influence.

Personal Rights: People could own property and make contracts under the law. These protections mainly applied to men, though.

Privileges Abolished: Being born noble or into the clergy no longer brought special legal treatment. The law applied equally to everyone.

One Legal System: Local customs and regional laws were replaced by one national law code, the Napoleonic Code.

Publication of Laws: Laws had to be published and made public before they could be enforced. People could not be punished for rules they had never been told about.

Religious Tolerance: The law stopped treating people differently based on religion. Protestants and Jews gained the same civil standing as Catholics.

Tax Laws: Taxes were no longer tied to legal privilege. Nobles and clergy were not exempt simply because of their status.

Glaring Shortcomings

Despite these positive changes, the Napoleonic Code had several glaring injustices.

Gender Inequality: Men held legal authority over their households. Wives were subject to their husbands' control and had limited legal rights. Women could not act independently in many legal matters and faced restrictions on property and inheritance. The Napoleonic Code reinforced male authority over women and children, a feature common at the time but later heavily criticized.

Illegitimate Children: Children born outside marriage faced legal disadvantages. They had fewer inheritance rights and lower legal standing than children born within marriage.

Slavery: Slavery had been abolished in French colonies in 1794 during the French Revolution. In 1802, Napoleon restored slavery in the colonies, reversing that decision. This wasn't a part of the Napoleonic Code, but it greatly affected colonial law.

Criminal Law: The Napoleonic Code did not govern criminal punishment. Criminal law remained separate and was later codified in 1810. Harsh penalties, including execution and forced labor, continued.

Legacy

It is said that Napoleon once mentioned, while in exile on St. Helena Island, that he would not be remembered for his many glorious victories but for the Napoleonic Code. This code spread across many countries. Napoleon enforced it in conquered territories during the Napoleonic Wars.

The Napoleonic Code did not remain limited to France. As French influence spread, other countries adopted versions of the code, often adapting it to local customs and conditions rather than copying it exactly. One clear example is the Civil Code of Quebec, enacted in 1866. It drew heavily on the Napoleonic Code and remained in force, with revisions, until 1994.

In other regions, especially former Dutch territories, existing legal systems were not replaced. Dutch colonies in Africa, for example, retained Roman-Dutch law. Over time, however, elements of the Napoleonic Code were incorporated into these systems.

So, Napoleon was partially right. Even those who have no interest in his military skills or glorious victories may remember him through his influence on the basic structure of modern legal systems worldwide.

Chapter 5: Napoleon's Coronation as Emperor

After his successes as First Consul of France, the transition to an empire seemed inevitable. Napoleon Bonaparte had consolidated power, reformed the legal system, and achieved military victories that made him a hero to the French people. Moving toward an empire would solidify succession laws and create a dynasty, preventing the republic's return to an unstable government. It would also place Napoleon on equal footing with hereditary European monarchs.

In May 1804, the Senate approved a new constitution that ended the French Consulate and created the First French Empire. Napoleon was given the title "Emperor of the French," a deliberate choice meant to tie his authority to the nation rather than to a royal bloodline or territory. The rule would now be hereditary.

A public vote followed to approve the change. Official results claimed overwhelming support, with millions voting in favor and only a few thousand opposing. In reality, turnout was low, and the figures were almost certainly adjusted to make the results seem more impressive. The vote served more to confirm a decision already made than to test public opinion.

Preparation for the Coronation

Napoleon understood propaganda better than most of his contemporaries. He planned to use the pomp and circumstance of his coronation to maximize publicity for his new title. He was not above using strategic maneuvers to enhance the spectacle of the occasion and claim historical legitimacy.

The crown made for the occasion was called the "Crown of Napoleon." Napoleon claimed it was related to Charlemagne's crown and funded a publication in 1804 asserting its authenticity. The publication was presented as if it had been published in 1794. The crown was actually made for the coronation; it was not an ancient artifact passed down from Charlemagne.

The Crown of Napoleon.[18]

Napoleon also masterfully planned the ceremony to please multiple audiences. It had to satisfy the commoners and the aristocracy. It had to pacify the Catholic Church and the deeply religious in France. After the papal party arrived in Paris, Napoleon delicately maneuvered Pope Pius VII to accept his suggestions for incorporating elements from earlier French coronations with new imperial imagery, creating a ceremony that appeared traditional while placing authority firmly in his own hands.

Pope Pius VII agreed to anoint Napoleon's head, hands, and arms as part of the sacred rite. Napoleon would remain seated rather than kneeling while accepting the insignia of his office as emperor.

The most striking change was planned in advance and accepted by the pope. Napoleon would take the crown from the altar and place it on his own head, symbolizing that his authority came from himself and not from the pope. Joséphine would be crowned by Napoleon while she knelt before him. The pope's presence gave the ceremony religious weight, but when Napoleon crowned himself, it was clear that his power did not come from the church.

Coronation Day: December 2nd, 1804

Enormous crowds gathered in an excited and joyful atmosphere to watch the procession. Many had been gathering since the previous evening despite the winter cold. Snow had fallen overnight but was cleared by morning. Watchers and participants alike saw the ceremonially robed papal procession from the Tuileries Palace to Notre Dame in bright sunshine by 9 a.m.

According to Napoleon's valet, Louis Wairy, Napoleon left the Tuileries Palace at 11 a.m. He was attired in a gold-embroidered white velvet vest with diamond buttons. A short, satin-lined crimson coat covered his crimson velvet tunic. Like Julius Caesar and later Roman emperors, he wore a laurel wreath, a traditional symbol of victory and honor.

Six bay horses drew the imperial coach that transported Napoleon and Joséphine. Joséphine was dressed in a white empire-style dress with gold embroidery. Napoleon was cloaked in a long white satin tunic with gold embroidery at the entrance of Notre Dame. Both Napoleon and Joséphine wore ermine-lined crimson velvet mantels embroidered with golden bees during the coronation.

Napoleon drew inspiration from the distant past with the bee symbols instead of using the more recent fleur-de-lys used just before the French Revolution. The bee was the official symbol of the early medieval period's Merovingian dynasty.

The coronation of Napoleon I and Joséphine by Jacques-Louis David and Georges Rouget.[19]

The coronation lasted more than three hours, with prayers and music. The pope anointed Napoleon's and Joséphine's heads, hands, and arms as part of the religious consecration. The pope's blessings on the regalia followed. Each item was passed to Napoleon and then to Joséphine. Napoleon took the crown from the altar and placed it on his own head, then crowned Joséphine as she knelt before him, just as planned. The pope blessed them on their thrones.

Napoleon then swore an oath with his hand on the Bible. The oath was presented by the presidents of the Senate, the Corps législatif, and the Council of State. He pledged to govern in the interest of the French people and to protect their happiness and glory.

The herald proclaimed his crowning and enthroning. The people echoed his "Long live the Emperor!" They left the cathedral to the singing by the choir of four hundred voices. "God save our Emperor Napoleon!"

In yet another reflection of imperial Roman traditions, Napoleon handed the regalia from the ceremony to each of his regiments. The cost of the illustrious ceremony exceeded 8.5 million francs, according to historians. The coronation was both a state spectacle and a public event. A fortnight of celebrations followed, including fireworks and balls throughout Paris.

Why the French Accepted an Empire

The reported popular support for Napoleon raises questions. The French people had fought a bloody revolution for years to eliminate the monarchy and class distinctions. Why would they accept a virtual dictatorship so readily?

Well, Napoleon's war victories had raised him to hero status. He had brought fame and respect to their country. He brought order after the chaos and insecurity that followed the Reign of Terror.

The French Revolution had destroyed the old political culture. Many people desired a stable and predictable regime. The Directorate and early revolutionary governments had proven unstable, adding to the political turmoil. Napoleon promised to maintain revolutionary gains, such as equality before the law and property rights, while providing order. In the early years, he largely delivered on these promises.

Napoleon's reforms as First Consul benefited the people. The Bank of France provided financial stability. The Napoleonic Code modernized the legal system. Infrastructure improvements were visible across the country.

Napoleon gradually curtailed certain freedoms, including freedom of the press, and centralized power. French law did not grant women the right to vote in 1804. Political participation was limited to male citizens meeting certain criteria. Still, public tolerance for these restrictions remained high, given France's overall stability and prosperity.

Napoleon presented himself as the man who would protect what the French Revolution had achieved while restoring order. After a decade of upheaval, many people accepted the trade-off. Stability mattered more than abstract concerns about how much power he held.

Abroad, reactions were mixed. Some monarchs initially refused to recognize Napoleon's new imperial title. Others adjusted to it. Holy Roman Emperor Francis II, for example, adopted the title Emperor of Austria (making him Francis I of Austria) to place himself on equal footing. Napoleon's elevation forced Europe's rulers to reconsider how authority and rank would be defined after the French Revolution.

Chapter 6: Wars of the Third and Fourth Coalition

After the Peace of Amiens in March 1802, there was a brief pause in the war. However, it did not last. Britain watched Napoleon continue to expand French influence in northern Italy, Piedmont, and Switzerland. These moves did not formally break the treaty, but they made it clear that peace would not restrain him. In May 1803, Britain returned to war.

Napoleon's power had already grown since his victory at the Battle of Marengo. He focused on rebuilding France at home and reshaping its institutions. When he crowned himself emperor in December 1804, the war had already resumed. The coronation hardened opposition abroad, but it did not cause the fighting to restart.

Other European powers viewed Napoleon's rule with suspicion. Great Britain sought to contain France. Austria wanted to recover territory lost in earlier defeats. Russia aimed to preserve its influence in central and eastern Europe. They all knew Napoleon's expansion had to be checked before French power became overwhelming. This led to the formation of the Third Coalition.

The Third Coalition

Britain, Austria, Russia, Naples, and Sicily formed the Third Coalition in 1805. Sweden joined but played a limited role and did not participate in any major battles. Britain had no large land forces in central Europe. Instead, it was the financial backbone of the coalition and the naval enforcer. Naples and Sicily were peripheral and diplomatically unstable participants, not central actors. France had its client states and its ally, Spain. Prussia decided to remain neutral.

These conflicts were a continuation of the French Revolutionary Wars rather than a brand-new phase, though historians often group the warfare after 1803 as the Napoleonic Wars.

The Battle of Trafalgar

In 1804, the British and French fleets engaged in several skirmishes. Napoleon's plan was to force open a route to invade Britain, but the mighty British navy had to be defeated first. By March 1805, French and Spanish allied naval forces and the British navy were repeatedly engaging each other in the English Channel and beyond, in the North Atlantic and the West Indies.

Napoleon tried to manage the operation of drawing the bulk of the British navy out of the English Channel so he could land his already gathered troops on British soil. He understood naval strategy in theory, but he struggled to make it work in practice. His plans relied on poorly trained crews, fragile supply lines, and complicated maneuvers that rarely succeeded. He reportedly drew up four sets of complicated plans for crossing the Channel, each of which failed.

On October 21st, 1805, the British fleet under Vice Admiral Horatio Nelson dealt the combined French and Spanish fleets a destructive blow at Trafalgar. It was a crowning glory for the British fleet, despite the loss of Lord Nelson, who was killed by a sharpshooter from one of the Spanish ships. The French and Spanish fleets could no longer challenge British naval dominance.

The few ships that escaped were chased down in different parts of the ocean. The last ships surrendered after a few days of battle off the coast of Cape Ortegal during the first week of November 1805. Napoleon's immediate plans to invade and conquer Britain were over, though he continued to consider invasion scenarios intermittently in the following years.

Napoleon gradually lost confidence in his naval commanders. He believed they failed to act decisively and could not carry out his plans. His frustration was obvious, and the navy felt it. Without clear direction or trust from the emperor, French naval forces became sidelined.

Napoleon turned away from naval solutions. He focused instead on fighting Britain on land and through economic pressure, relying on continental warfare and blockade rather than fleets he no longer believed in.

The Campaign of Ulm

While the naval disaster unfolded at Trafalgar, Napoleon marched his massive army, originally gathered to cross the English Channel, to Bavaria to fight the Austrian-Russian part of the Third Coalition. He intended to separate the Austrians and Russians before they could join forces.

The Austrians assumed the main conflicts would be in northern Italy, so they focused on preventing Napoleon from crossing the Alps. However, Napoleon's intentions were to meet the Austrian army in Bavaria, so there was no need to cross the Alps.

When the first Austrian battalions met French forces in Bavaria, the Russians were still crossing Poland. The Austrian army advanced before the Russian forces were ready. Poor coordination and slow movement left the Austrians to fight the French on their own.

Napoleon's Grande Armée, his primary field army, moved with remarkable speed, executing a strategic encirclement of the Austrian army under General Karl Freiherr Mack von Leiberich. The Austrians found themselves surrounded and cut off from their supply lines. Skirmishes and battles began around October 8th across a wide area. The main Austrian army was forced to surrender at Ulm on October 19th, 1805.

The Austrian surrender at Ulm by René Théodore Berthon.[30]

Because of the protracted fighting and the large area, some historians prefer to call it the Campaign of Ulm rather than the Battle of Ulm.

Regardless of the name, Napoleon succeeded in capturing an entire Austrian army with minimum French losses. This enormous success was the precursor to what he himself would later call his greatest victory.

The Battle of Austerlitz

Before Austerlitz, Napoleonic forces were spread across the territories of various nation-states, with the goal of meeting in Vienna. The allied forces of Austria and Russia were positioning themselves for a decisive engagement. The Austrians were determined to clear the countryside of all available food that French troops would need. Napoleon had to force a confrontation as soon as possible.

Napoleon planned meticulously for the looming battle at Austerlitz. He deliberately weakened his right flank near the Pratzen Heights. He deployed his troops with a seemingly weak and thinly spread center line. The allied commanders would naturally attack what appeared to be the weak spot. Meanwhile, Napoleon strengthened his left flank into a force that could move quickly. When the allies committed to attacking his weakened right, Marshal Jean-de-Dieu Soult would launch a timed assault to seize the Pratzen Heights at the critical moment, cutting the allied army in two and encircling their forces.

Napoleon's total confidence inspired his commanders and spread down through the ranks. They trusted Napoleon fully, and every soldier fought with energy and determination to achieve a great victory.

One of Napoleon's aides-de-camp, Jean Rapp, gave his personal account to Napoleon's private secretary, Bourrienne, after the battle. Bourrienne recorded Rapp's words in his *Memoirs of Napoleon Bonaparte*.

Rapp described the dangerous situation that developed near the French center. A force from the Russian Imperial Guard, including elite cavalry, advanced through broken terrain that concealed their movement. This allowed them to strike suddenly, breaking into French infantry formations and threatening Napoleon's position.

Napoleon initially did not see the attack unfold. Once reports reached him, he reacted quickly. He ordered Rapp to investigate and counter the threat. Rapp led a mixed force drawn from the Imperial Guard, including cavalry and elite infantry.

Rapp discovered that the Russian Guard cavalry had already penetrated French lines and that additional Russian reserve forces were moving forward to support them. Acting immediately, he launched a direct attack against the Russian artillery and cavalry. The sudden charge overran the guns and drove back the enemy cavalry, disrupting the Russian advance.

Russian reserves attempted to restore the situation, but French Guard reinforcements arrived in time. Fighting became chaotic, with cavalry and infantry mixed together at point-blank range. Casualties were heavy on both sides; even senior officers fell. Eventually, the French Guard prevailed. The Russian Guard was forced to withdraw in disorder, ending the threat to the French center.

The Battle of Austerlitz, 2nd December 1805 by François Gérard.[21]

Rapp's account provides insight into aspects of the battle. The army was still using square formations. The cavalry included Mamluks. Perhaps more importantly, Rapp's words reflect the attitude and loyalty Napoleon inspired in his men. His promotion of Rapp right there on the battlefield to brigadier general demonstrates Napoleon's quick acknowledgment and reward of his officers.

The Battle of Austerlitz was a decisive victory. French losses were approximately nine thousand killed or wounded. The allies suffered losses of approximately twenty-seven thousand killed, wounded, or captured, including many who drowned in the frozen Satschan ponds while attempting to flee across the ice.

The Treaty of Pressburg

The Austrians had signed treaties with France twice before Austerlitz. This time, Napoleon forced them to accept much harsher terms in the Treaty of Pressburg, which was signed on December 26th, 1805.

Austria had to pay France a penalty of forty million gold francs. Austria gave up Venetia, Istria, and Dalmatia to Napoleon's Kingdom of Italy, which had been established earlier in 1805. The Tyrol, Vorarlberg, and

Augsburg regions were given to Bavaria. The Habsburg lands in western Austria were given to Württemberg and Baden. Austria received Salzburg as compensation for some of these losses.

Bavaria and Württemberg assumed royal titles, which Austria was forced to recognize under the Treaty of Pressburg. Napoleon encouraged and benefited from this elevation of his German allies, though he did not legally appoint their kings. Austria also had to confirm the withdrawal of all feudal ties to the Holy Roman Empire in the states it lost.

Napoleon's victory at Austerlitz increased his power and influence substantially. The Third Coalition effectively collapsed. Russia withdrew its forces, and Austria was forced out of the war. Only Britain remained at war with France.

The Reorganization of Germany

German princes of the old Holy Roman Empire established the Confederation of the Rhine in July 1806, almost certainly at Napoleon's prompting. It was made up of sixteen client states of France, which unified Napoleon's German interests. The league eventually grew to thirty-six member states with over fifteen million people. This was yet another strategic move by Napoleon as it provided his empire with a strengthened, loyal buffer zone against future aggression from either Austria or Prussia.

The creation of this confederation led to the dissolution of the Holy Roman Empire. Francis II, faced with the defection of so many German princes to Napoleon's confederation, realized that the empire could no longer function. In August 1806, he renounced the imperial crown.

The Holy Roman Empire, conventionally dated to 962 when Otto I was crowned, had existed for over eight centuries. By Napoleon's time, the Holy Roman Empire was no longer a strong, unified state. It was a patchwork of many semi-independent territories, most of them German-speaking. The Habsburgs still controlled major lands such as Bohemia and Moravia, but their authority over the wider empire was weak.

Napoleon's wars finished what centuries of decline had begun. In 1806, the Holy Roman Empire was dissolved and disappeared altogether.

The Continental System

Throughout Napoleon's reign, Britain remained a persistent adversary. The British refused to make peace with France and financed almost every coalition formed against Napoleon. After the annihilation of his fleet at Trafalgar, Napoleon shifted his strategy. He decided to hurt Britain through economic warfare.

Britain had been blockading French ports for years when Napoleon issued a decree from Berlin in November 1806. This decree prohibited the import of British goods into any countries allied to or dependent on France. This even included sending or receiving mail from Britain or its colonies. It became known as the Continental System.

This strategy had serious flaws. British naval superiority meant it could recoup losses suffered in the European market by increasing its trade across the rest of the world. France and its allies stood to lose as much economically as Britain did. Also, Napoleon could not effectively enforce his decree against countries that ignored it.

The system created severe economic problems for Napoleon's empire. Shortages of goods from the colonies, such as sugar, coffee, and cotton, drove prices to unprecedented levels. These shortages led to resentment among allies and subject populations. To enforce the blockade effectively, Napoleon found himself compelled to annex territories that were not complying. Holland was annexed in 1810, when his brother, Louis, proved too lenient in enforcing the law. Parts of northwest Germany along the coast were also annexed to close smuggling routes. Each annexation strained French resources further and created new administrative burdens.

Britain responded with Orders in Council, and Napoleon escalated with the Milan Decree in 1807. This embargo war would help drive future conflicts, including the Peninsular War. It would also eventually contribute to France's break with Russia.

Napoleon remained committed to the Continental System throughout his rule. He tightened customs laws and expanded inspection staffs, but enforcement was uneven. Smuggling was widespread, and British goods continued to circulate. In some places, they were openly available.

Napoleon's secretary Louis Antoine Fauvelet de Bourrienne later recalled one example from Hamburg. According to his account, sugar, coffee, and vanilla were smuggled into the city inside hearses. The scheme was only uncovered when officials noticed an unusual rise in funerals and opened a coffin packed with contraband. Whether the story is exaggerated or not, it reflects how difficult it was to enforce the embargo and how easily it could be evaded.

The Fourth Coalition Begins

By mid-1806, new tensions were emerging. Britain remained at war with France, providing financial aid to any power willing to oppose Napoleon and using its naval superiority to blockade French ports and support continental allies. Russia had withdrawn after Austerlitz but had not made a formal peace. Austria was bound by the Treaty of Pressburg to stay out of the conflict.

Prussia, which had remained neutral during the Third Coalition, grew increasingly alarmed by Napoleon's reorganization of Germany. The dissolution of the Holy Roman Empire and the creation of the Confederation of the Rhine threatened Prussian influence. Rumors circulated that Napoleon might offer Hanover to Britain in exchange for peace. Prussia wanted Hanover for itself.

Fear drove Prussia's decision. Napoleon's ever-increasing power threatened Prussian autonomy, domestic policies, and territorial integrity. At the Prussian court, the war party included influential voices like Queen Louise, the much-loved consort of King Frederick William III, though the ultimate responsibility for declaring war lay with the king and his military leadership.

On October 9th, 1806, Prussia declared war on France. Prussia would initially fight alone in central Europe. Russia would only enter operations after Prussia's defeat at Jena–Auerstedt. Sweden and Britain would contribute from the sidelines. Britain provided financial aid and maintained naval pressure on French forces, but it did not deploy significant land forces during this phase of the war.

The Battle of Jena–Auerstedt

Napoleon acted quickly. His main goal was to prevent enemy forces from joining up. His main forces had not returned to France after their battles against the Third Coalition in 1805. They instead spent the winter along the River Main in Germany. They were rested, fit, and well trained. These were seasoned, battle-hardened warriors led by exceptionally skilled officers who had earned their ranks based on merit.

The Prussians were an old-style battle force that trained in old-fashioned shoulder-to-shoulder infantry marches. Officers were appointed from the aristocracy and sometimes had no military training at all. Those who had previous battle experience were rather old.

Prussia had been neutral for eleven years. Its weaponry and methods were old-fashioned. But they had well-disciplined, valiant soldiers who were unafraid to die for king and country. Saxony fought reluctantly alongside Prussia but was similarly unprepared to face the superior French Army.

In addition to these obstacles, King Frederick William III only informed his Russian ally that he had declared war and was marching out to meet the French after he had already done so. There was no hope that the Russians would be able to join them in time.

The first contact was made at Saalfeld, where the brave young Prince Louis Ferdinand rallied his troops to stand their ground against a much larger French corps. He did this so the main Prussian-Saxon army could reach its destination in time. The small Prussian force held the French back until midday, when the prince was killed in hand-to-hand combat. Prussian losses totaled approximately 1,200 to 1,500, including prisoners.

The loss of the prince was a huge psychological blow to the Prussian commanders. They decided to hold off on an immediate attack, instead agreeing to retreat and regroup in Leipzig. Part of the Prussian Army had already fallen back to Jena by the evening of October 13th, 1806. Napoleon assumed it was part of the main force and sent an advance guard to attack them at dawn on October 14th, 1806, while he brought the rest of the army to Jena.

The Prussians fought valiantly, and Napoleon's army had to fight hard to gain the upper hand. By that afternoon, confusion, fog, and command paralysis had taken their toll on Prussian formations. The Prussian force began to slowly collapse. Napoleon's cavalry under Murat gave chase well into the late afternoon, killing and capturing soldiers as the retreat descended into disarray.

Napoleon inspecting his troops before the Battle of Jena by Horace Vernet.[22]

At neighboring Auerstedt, another fierce battle was fought when Marshal Louis-Nicolas Davout's III Corps unexpectedly encountered the Prussian main force falling back to Leipzig. The French corps was soon joined by several groups of reinforcements. The battle was over by mid-morning, when the Prussian commander gave the order to retreat. Napoleon only learned afterward that the main Prussian force was not in Jena but in Auerstedt. Davout's achievement in defeating the main Prussian force with his smaller corps was remarkable.

The Prussian Army had been totally defeated, and the Prussian command collapsed. Over the following weeks, major fortresses, including Spandau, Magdeburg, and Küstrin, capitulated quickly. On October 27th, 1806, the triumphant French Army marched into Berlin. True to his habit of rewarding those under him, Napoleon gave Marshal Davout the honor of leading the army into Berlin due to his outstanding victory against the main Prussian force at Auerstedt.

The Russian Campaign

After defeating Prussia, Napoleon pushed into Poland to confront the Russian Army. The Russians retreated slowly, fighting a series of minor engagements rather than risking a decisive battle. Heavy fighting took place in late December at Pułtusk and Gołymin, but neither side gained a clear advantage. Poor roads, bad weather, and growing supply problems slowed operations. With no clear end in sight, Napoleon halted the campaign and placed his army into winter quarters. Fighting still continued intermittently throughout the winter of 1806-07, though.

Poland no longer existed as a sovereign state when Napoleon entered Warsaw. It had been partitioned decades earlier by Prussia, Austria, and Russia, and its institutions had been dismantled. Napoleon occupied the former Polish territory that had been taken from Prussia after its defeat. Acting as a military occupier, he organized a provisional Polish administration to secure support and maintain order, while leaving Poland's ultimate status deliberately unresolved.

The idle French troops were bored and miserable in the cold winter. They were running low on food supplies by January 1807. One of Napoleon's commanders, Michel Ney, acted recklessly and, without orders, left the temporary quarters with his troops.

At the same time, the Russian armed forces were moving through dense forest to attack the French encampments. On January 17th, 1807, Ney encountered them by chance and hastily sent a message to warn

Napoleon. Napoleon immediately mustered his troops and prepared a trap for the Russians.

The Russians learned about it and avoided the trap by crossing over the River Alle. However, Napoleon was not to be stopped. The French Army crossed the river and chased after them. The two armies met in the town of Preussisch-Eylau on February 7th, 1807.

It was a bloody battle with heavy losses on both sides. A vicious snowstorm started overnight and continued into the next day. Combined casualties totaled approximately forty thousand to forty-five thousand. Napoleon himself reportedly narrowly escaped danger. The Russians only retreated after more divisions of Napoleon's troops arrived.

Neither army had gained an inch. The outcome of the battle was a draw. Napoleon's army was tired and hungry. Their clothes and shoes were worn out. Not even the sight or words of their beloved leader could lift their spirits. The Grande Armée was showing signs of exhaustion.

Over the next several months, both armies rebuilt and resupplied while minor fighting continued. By early June, Napoleon had regained his strength, and patience had run out. He decided to attack in full force on June 10th, 1807.

The Russians surprised him with an attack on Marshal Ney's corps on June 5th, 1807. Ney, with the help of reinforcements, managed to withstand the attack. Several skirmishes and battles followed, including Napoleon's attack at Heilsberg on June 10th.

The Battle of Friedland

On June 13th, 1807, Marshal Jean Lannes's advance scouts spotted large numbers of Russians crossing the Alle River at the small town of Friedland. Napoleon was informed and immediately commanded his forces to make for Friedland at top speed. At around 3:30 a.m. on June 14th, 1807, the Russians had started to cross the river on pontoons. Lannes, with approximately fifteen to seventeen thousand men, held the Russian force of about forty-five thousand to fifty thousand in place until Napoleon's other divisions began to arrive.

The Russian commander, like many before him, underestimated how quickly Napoleon could concentrate his forces. Expecting only a limited engagement, he allowed much of his army to cross the river near Friedland. As French forces arrived in strength, the situation worsened rapidly. Heavy fighting developed during the afternoon. French artillery fire and congestion at the crossings disrupted the Russian retreat, leaving much of the army trapped between the river and advancing French troops.

The battle collapsed by late afternoon. Many fleeing Russians drowned in the deep and fast-flowing river in their desperate efforts to get away. The French troops were not interested in chasing them down. They were tired and frantically rummaging through every nook and cranny of Friedland and the surrounding villages for food.

It was a decisive victory for Napoleon. Tsar Alexander I of Russia asked for a truce a few days later, and Napoleon agreed.

The Treaty with Russia

In early July 1807, after the defeat of Russia at Friedland, Napoleon Bonaparte and Alexander I agreed to meet face to face. The meeting took place on July 7th at the town of Tilsit on a raft anchored in the middle of the Neman River that had been deliberately positioned between their two armies. A pavilion had been built on the raft for the occasion. It was decorated with imperial symbols from both empires.

The isolation mattered. Away from advisers and generals, the two emperors spoke directly, man to man. They discussed not only peace terms but also their ambitions, grievances, and views of Europe. Contemporary accounts describe long conversations that continued for several days. Napoleon came away convinced he had found a partner who understood him. He believed they had met as enemies and parted as allies.

Napoleon meeting Tsar Alexander I of Russia on a raft in the Neman River at Tilsit by Adolphe Roehn.[28]

Not everyone shared that impression. Some later accounts claim that as Alexander departed, he quietly told the Prussian king that the friendship had been an act and that Napoleon was destined to fall. Whether true or not, the moment captured the uncertainty beneath the outward display of harmony.

The agreement that followed, known as the Treaty of Tilsit, reshaped Europe. Russia agreed to join Napoleon's Continental System, closing its ports to British trade and turning the struggle with Britain into a shared economic war. Napoleon, in return, offered support for Russian ambitions against the Ottoman Empire and accepted Russian expansion in northern Europe. This understanding soon led Russia into war with Sweden and the seizure of Finland, a long-standing Russian objective.

Napoleon also secured Russian acceptance of the creation of the Duchy of Warsaw, a new Polish state carved from former Prussian territory. This satisfied Polish hopes without fully restoring an independent Poland, while also keeping pressure on Prussia and Russia. At the same time, Napoleon promised to respect the independence of several small German states ruled by Alexander's relatives, including Oldenburg. He would later violate this promise, badly damaging relations between the two empires.

On paper, the Treaty of Tilsit created a powerful alliance. France stood at the height of its continental dominance, and Russia appeared to have joined Napoleon's new order. Together, the two empires eclipsed the remaining European powers. Yet beneath the formal friendship lay conflicting interests and mutual suspicion.

The Treaty with Prussia

Three days before the formal signing of peace between France and Prussia, Queen Louise of Prussia arrived at Tilsit. She was famous throughout Europe for her intelligence, grace, and beauty, and she was deeply admired by her people. Her journey was both personal and political. Louise hoped to soften Napoleon's terms and to save Magdeburg, the Prussian fortress city on the Elbe that she cherished.

She met Napoleon Bonaparte for roughly two hours. Accounts describe her appealing directly to his sense of honor and restraint. She pleaded for moderation and, at times, was visibly emotional. It made no difference. Napoleon listened politely but remained unmoved. His decision had already been made.

The peace imposed on Prussia was severe. Prussia was stripped of all territory west of the Elbe. It lost Danzig and had to surrender its Polish lands. Magdeburg, the city Louise had tried to save, was transferred into the newly created Kingdom of Westphalia, a French client state carved largely from Prussian territory. In total, Prussia lost more than half of its land and population.

Napoleon forced Prussia to recognize the Confederation of the Rhine and accept French dominance in Germany. The Prussian state was reduced to enforced neutrality; it was not treated as a true ally. Its army was cut down to forty-two thousand men, and it was forced to join the Continental System, cutting off trade with Britain. On top of this, a crushing indemnity of 140 million francs was imposed.

Napoleon became deeply hated in Prussia, not only by the public but by many within the elite. Even figures in Napoleon's own circle, including Charles Maurice de Talleyrand, warned that such harsh treatment of a defeated state was dangerous. Napoleon ignored them.

The shock of the treaty forced Prussia to confront its weaknesses. Reformers such as Heinrich Friedrich Karl vom Stein, Karl August von Hardenberg, and military reformer Gerhard von Scharnhorst began a far-reaching transformation of the Prussian state and army. These reforms would reshape Prussia and, in time, alter the balance of power in Europe.

The settlement at Tilsit was unstable from the beginning. Conflicts over the Continental System and Napoleon's later violations of its guarantees strained relations with Russia. The humiliation of Prussia ensured that resentment would endure. The peace ended the war on paper, but it planted the seeds for future conflict.

Chapter 7: The Peninsular War: Spain and Portugal Resist Napoleon

Portugal consistently resisted Napoleon's implementation of the Continental System. It was Britain's oldest European ally and maintained historically strong trade relations with Britain, as did Brazil, its colony in South America. Lisbon served as an important commercial and diplomatic hub where British ships had access to Portuguese ports, facilitating trade and communication that undermined Napoleon's economic blockade.

Napoleon was extremely irritated that this relatively small country persisted in refusing his demands. He was, after all, now master of most of Europe. He was an emperor and a conqueror whose family and closest associates ruled the reconstructed European landscape under his control.

In July 1807, bolstered by the terms of the Treaties of Tilsit and his new alliance with Russia, Napoleon dispatched orders to the Portuguese government demanding that they close its ports to Britain, confiscate British goods and property, and arrest British subjects in Portugal. When Portugal refused, Napoleon prepared for war.

What began as the enforcement of the Continental System would evolve into the Peninsular War, one of Napoleon's greatest strategic disasters.

The Invasion of Portugal

French troops gathered on the Spanish border to cross through Spain and invade Portugal. Napoleon and the king of Spain signed the Treaty of Fontainebleau in October 1807, dividing Portugal between them as though they had already conquered the country. In this treaty, Spain agreed to supply substantial forces to support a French invasion of Portugal, though many Spanish troops never cooperated.

The invasion relied on Spanish cooperation, though. French forces would enter Portugal through Spain, a move that would soon become a major problem. The presence of large French armies inside Spain destabilized Spanish politics almost immediately.

General Jean-Andoche Junot, who was personally close to Napoleon and chosen purposefully for this command, led French forces into Portugal in late October 1807. His corps advanced rapidly toward Lisbon. The French occupied the capital on November 30th, 1807.

The regent of Portugal, Prince John, and his family and courtiers escaped barely one day before the French arrived. They took with them the state's papers and treasures and fled aboard Portuguese ships protected by the British fleet. According to some accounts, they left treasure behind on the docks in their haste. Their destination was Brazil. Many Portuguese nobles and merchants joined their flight.

This flight to Brazil was momentous. It was the only time a European royal court relocated to a colony. This decision would reshape Brazil's political development and the Portuguese imperial structure.

Portuguese royals escape from Lisbon to Brazil by Henri L'Evêque.[34]

Britain provided a naval escort and would soon do far more. Within months, Britain would land troops in Portugal because it offered a secure base on the European mainland. It could be supplied by sea and was beyond Napoleon's reach. This move turned Iberia into a major theater of war rather than just an economic battleground.

The French occupation of Portugal was fragile from the start. Junot's forces were overextended, poorly supplied, and dependent on Spanish goodwill. This fragility explains why resistance erupted quickly. Napoleon, not for the first time, misjudged the mood of the people. Instead of feeling liberated from their old regime, most Portuguese resented the foreigners on their territory. They hated the new French laws imposed on them, and they were furious when new taxes were levied. The situation grew dangerous. Through early 1808, Junot imposed martial law, arrests, executions, and repression to quell the smoldering unrest.

Ruthless Ambition: The Takeover of Spain

Napoleon was still driven by his ambition to build an empire that controlled all of Europe. What began as the enforcement of the Continental System was evolving into something far bolder.

Spain was already in crisis before Napoleon intervened. Charles IV was widely seen as a weak king. Real power rested with his chief minister, Manuel Godoy, who was deeply unpopular. Godoy was blamed for military defeats, economic hardship, and Spain's humiliating dependence on France.

The king's son, Ferdinand, had become the focus of opposition. Many Spaniards hoped Ferdinand would remove Godoy and restore effective rule. Court politics turned poisonous. Factions formed around the king and the prince, and rumors of coups and arrests spread.

Napoleon did not initially enter Spain with the intention of overthrowing its monarchy. Instead, he saw a chance to insert himself as an "arbiter," using French troops already moving through Spain under the pretext of enforcing the Continental System against Portugal. However, once those forces were in place and Spain's internal crisis deepened, his aims changed. To him, Spain looked unstable and vulnerable; it was ripe for the taking.

Large French forces were already inside Spain under the Treaty of Fontainebleau. In February 1808, French troops seized key Spanish cities and fortresses by surprise or manipulation rather than open battle. Spain, a long-standing ally of France, was caught off guard. The seizures exposed

Napoleon's true intentions and effectively rendered the treaty meaningless. In retaliation, Spain withdrew its forces supporting France in Portugal.

As the crisis intensified, events spiraled. Godoy was overthrown by a popular uprising, and Charles IV abdicated in favor of Ferdinand in March. However, Ferdinand's position was weak, and his father soon claimed he had been forced to step aside.

Napoleon seized the opportunity. In April and May 1808, he summoned both father and son to Bayonne in France. Isolated from Spain and dependent on French support, each hoped Napoleon would rule in his favor. Instead, Napoleon exploited their rivalry and pressured both men into surrendering their claims to the throne. With Spain's royal authority neutralized, he installed his older brother, Joseph, as king of Spain.

The Madrid Uprising

On May 2nd, 1808, the citizens of Madrid rose against the French occupation. Joachim Murat, Napoleon's longtime comrade, commanded French forces in Spain as the emperor's chief military representative. His Imperial Guard units crushed the uprising.

What followed was ruthless retaliation. Cavalry, infantry, and firing squads swept the city. Mamluk horsemen in French service fought through the streets, their unfamiliar dress and curved swords adding to the terror. The violence shocked Spain. Francisco Goya later captured the scenes of May 2nd and May 3rd on canvas as a lasting reminder of the atrocities.

The Second of May 1808 by Francisco Goya.[26]

Joseph Bonaparte was proclaimed king of Spain in June 1808.

Spanish Resistance Spreads

Local insurrections broke out against French occupation in most Spanish cities and across provinces during May and June. Resistance was organized not only through unconventional tactics but also through provincial juntas that claimed authority in the name of Ferdinand VII. The Spanish employed ambushes, sabotaged supply lines, and engaged in hit-and-run strikes before melting back into the civilian population. Despite brutal reprisals when they were cornered, the resistance continued.

When news of the Spanish resistance reached Portugal, they followed suit. Their opposition met brutal counterinsurgency violence, including massacres of residents in towns like Évora.

In June 1808, Spaniards seized five French ships anchored at Cadiz. The French commander in the city was forced to retreat. The overwhelming resistance he encountered in the province of Andalusia led to the Battle of Bailén on July 19th, 1808. Surrounded by Spanish forces and exhausted by heat and constant fighting, a French corps was forced to surrender.

The Battle of Bailén was a turning point. It was the first battle lost on land by an imperial corps of Napoleon. The message reverberated across Europe that the French military was not invincible after all. It stirred up buried hostilities and nationalism in other countries, such as Austria.

Joseph Bonaparte had entered Madrid as king on July 20th, but his rule depended entirely on nearby French troops. Once those forces were defeated or pulled back, Madrid became hostile and dangerous. Joseph fled Madrid for Old Castile on August 1st, 1808. French forces stopped their advances on the freed Spanish cities and retreated to positions across the Ebro River.

This defeat would prompt Napoleon to intervene personally in Spain later in 1808 with a large field army.

British Intervention

Britain saw an opportunity to increase its influence on the continent. Its navy had already assisted Spain by transporting Spanish troops stationed outside the country back to the peninsula. Lieutenant General Sir Arthur Wellesley landed in Portugal with approximately fourteen thousand troops on August 1st, 1808. With his assistance, the main French force in Portugal was defeated at Vimeiro on August 21st, 1808.

Following this victory, Wellesley's superiors arrived and negotiated the Convention of Cintra, which allowed the defeated French forces to evacuate Portugal with their equipment aboard British ships. This controversial agreement provoked outrage in Britain and Portugal. Wellesley was recalled to face an inquiry, though he was eventually exonerated.

Sir John Moore assumed command of British forces in Portugal in October. Additional reinforcements under Sir David Baird were sent from Falmouth to join them. They had orders to actively assist the Portuguese and Spanish forces to reclaim their lands.

Spain was tearing itself apart as it fought the French. Uprisings broke out everywhere, but there was no single authority to direct them. Rival leaders and regional councils competed for influence, and cooperation was limited. Everyone opposed the French, but no one could unite the country behind a common plan.

This disunity made a decisive Spanish response impossible. Some areas fought well and even drove out French forces, but these successes remained local. No unified army emerged that could face the French in a single, decisive battle.

At the same time, the French could not impose control. The Spanish refused to fight on French terms. They attacked garrisons, ambushed columns, and disappeared into the countryside. Towns and provinces changed hands repeatedly. The French could occupy territory, but they could not hold it or force the Spanish into a conventional battle.

Napoleon Takes Command

By October 1808, Napoleon had decided that his presence and leadership at the battlefront were an urgent necessity if a catastrophe was to be avoided in the Iberian Peninsula. The defeat at Bailén, British intervention, and the spreading insurrections threatened to unravel French control entirely. He brought over 200,000 troops into Spain by late 1808, one of the largest concentrations of force he ever commanded personally. He gathered together veterans from his previous successful campaigns and reorganized multiple corps, directing their advance south from the Ebro River.

Napoleon moved fast. He concentrated his army, marched through difficult terrain, and struck Spanish forces before they could unite. Spanish resistance was heroic but poorly coordinated. Columns were defeated one after another, often before they understood the scale of the attack. French pressure was constant, and gaps in Spanish defenses widened rapidly.

By late November 1808, the road to Madrid lay open.

The Battle of Somosierra

The battle for Spain's capital was fought on November 30th, 1808. A combined force under Napoleon's control forged their way through the Somosierra Pass in heavy fighting against Spanish defenders. The Spanish were outnumbered overall but well positioned, entrenched, and supported by artillery.

The heroes of the battle were the Polish light cavalry of the Imperial Guard from the Duchy of Warsaw. They charged uphill with death-defying persistence amid heavy artillery fire from the Spanish defenders. Through successive charges with infantry support, they helped take the battery positions set up by the Spaniards at different points of the pass. Their bravery earned accolades from Napoleon.

The Battle of Somosierra by Louis-François, Baron Lejeune.[26]

Napoleon entered Madrid on December 4th, 1808, and restored French rule in the capital. However, control faded quickly beyond the city. Spanish resistance continued across the countryside, and a stable government never took hold outside major urban centers.

Moore's Retreat

When Sir John Moore heard of the string of Spanish defeats following Napoleon's entry into the war, he attempted a bold maneuver. On December 21ˢᵗ, 1808, his cavalry defeated two French cavalry divisions at the Battle of Sahagún in Spain. Instead of pressing the attack, Moore chose a different course. He threatened French supply lines in the north, hoping to pull French forces away from Madrid and give the Spanish time to recover.

The move worked, but it came at a cost. Napoleon Bonaparte turned north in pursuit, intent on crushing the only British field army in Spain. Moore quickly understood the danger. Outnumbered and far from support, he abandoned the advance and began to retreat toward the coast so his men could evacuate by sea. Napoleon followed closely, driving his forces forward in an attempt to bring Moore to battle before he could escape.

The pursuit became a race rather than a battle. Moore retreated fast through northern Spain in brutal winter conditions. Roads were icy, supplies scarce, and discipline frayed. The British destroyed bridges and supplies behind them to slow the French advance. Skirmishes flared, but Moore avoided a decisive fight.

Napoleon pushed hard at first, driving his troops through snow and mountains in an effort to catch the British before they reached the coast. But as the chase stretched on, the limits became clear. Moore was retreating faster than the French could close the distance, and the terrain favored escape rather than encirclement. At the same time, reports from central Europe began to arrive.

By early January 1809, Napoleon knew he could not afford to remain in Spain. Intelligence from his agents warned that Austria, encouraged and financed by Great Britain, was preparing for war. A new coalition was forming. Napoleon broke off the pursuit, leaving his marshals to continue pressing Moore toward the coast. He returned to Madrid with the main force. Shortly afterward, he departed Spain altogether to prepare for the coming conflict that would become the Fifth Coalition.

In Spain, the British forces made a last stand at Corunna on January 16ᵗʰ, 1809. Moore was mortally wounded during the battle. The general who replaced him decided that immediate withdrawal would be better than continuing the fight. The troops quietly boarded the ships during the night, with the last troops embarking on the morning of January 18ᵗʰ, 1809.

Moore's campaign failed tactically to hold Spain. Strategically, however, it preserved the British army, tied down large French forces, and showed that French dominance was fragile. The French Army gained massive amounts of food, weapons, and other supplies left behind, so the men were able to regain their strength after the hellish forced marches over more than 250 miles of hills, mountains, and snow.

Napoleon's rapid victories briefly restored French prestige after Bailén, but his departure reinforced the perception that Spain was unwinnable by conventional means alone.

The Continuing Conflict

The Peninsular War was far from over. What had begun as an effort to enforce the Continental System had turned into a long and grinding conflict. Napoleon had underestimated Spain's ability to form a resistance and overestimated his ability to impose control. The result was a war that would drain French strength for six years.

Spanish resistance never disappeared, and Britain now backed it with a professional army operating from Portugal. This combination proved far more dangerous than rebellion alone. French supply lines were constantly attacked. Convoys vanished, and garrisons were isolated. Food had to be seized locally, breeding resentment. Desertion and sickness became routine. Losses from hunger and exhaustion often rivaled those from battle.

Spanish and Portuguese fighters refused to fight on French terms. They ambushed columns, sabotaged roads and bridges, and struck quickly before melting away. Territory changed hands again and again. Towns and provinces that had already been occupied were lost, retaken, and lost once more. The French could win battles, but they could not secure the countryside.

The war hardened attitudes on all sides. Spanish resistance became increasingly uncompromising, leaving little room for negotiation or settlement. What might have been a limited occupation turned into a struggle with no clear end.

By 1814, large numbers of French troops were still tied down in Iberia. At times, hundreds of thousands of soldiers were committed to the campaign. Many were veterans who might have been used elsewhere. As losses mounted, they were replaced by younger and less experienced troops. Spain became a steady drain on Napoleon's empire, one that never truly closed.

Consequences

The Peninsular War marked a turning point for Napoleon. His armies suffered losses in Spain that rivaled, and in some cases exceeded, those of his earlier wars. Spanish resistance showed that even the Grande Armée could be worn down by determined opposition.

Abroad, Napoleon's reputation suffered. Brutal reprisals and counterinsurgency violence against civilians shocked allies and enemies alike. By turning on Spain, a long-standing ally, Napoleon also broke the trust he had built through treaties and promises. Respect for him diminished, even among those who had once admired his rise.

At home, the picture was harder to see. Napoleon tightly controlled newspapers and public information. Victories were celebrated loudly, while defeats and setbacks were minimized or ignored. This helped maintain his image as a heroic leader and kept public confidence strong.

However, war had been a constant presence in French life for decades. The French Revolution, years of political upheaval, and then almost nonstop fighting had taken their toll. The Napoleonic Wars demanded ever more soldiers. Families lost sons, husbands, and fathers. Many lost their main source of income. Resentment was inevitable, even if these issues rarely appeared in print.

The Peninsular War did not cause Napoleon's later disasters, but it weakened France at a critical moment. It reduced his margin for error before the War of the Fifth Coalition and the invasion of Russia in 1812. Whether it marked the beginning of his downfall is still argued. What cannot be denied is that Spain proved, for the first time, that Napoleon's military machine could be resisted and that the price of building an empire was beginning to outweigh its glory.

Chapter 8: War of the Fifth Coalition

Austria had been smarting ever since the humiliating defeat at Austerlitz. The territories ceded to France in the Treaty of Pressburg still rankled. The dissolution of the Holy Roman Empire was a wound that hadn't healed. Napoleon's reshaping of Germany threatened Austria's position in central Europe. Vienna watched French influence spread across the German states, and the danger was impossible to ignore.

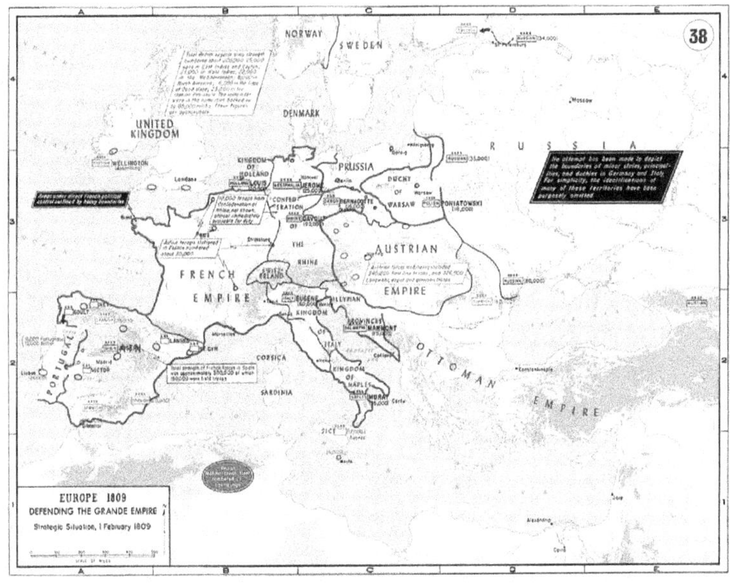

Europe in 1809.[27]

Austria did not remain idle. Archduke Charles, Emperor Francis's brother who was in charge of the military, used the years after Austerlitz to rebuild the army. Drill regulations were updated to encourage flexibility rather than rigid formations. Officers were pushed to think independently and plan beyond rote maneuvers. The army's structure was reorganized, its equipment improved, and its education expanded. By 1809, the Austrian army was no longer the demoralized force that had fled the battlefield four years earlier.

The moment seemed right. France was bogged down in Spain. Men and supplies were being consumed by a war that showed no sign of ending. Troops had been pulled out of Germany to deal with the crisis in Iberia. For the first time in years, Napoleon looked vulnerable.

Emperor Francis was persuaded that Austria should act. Britain supplied the money that made war possible. Other powers offered encouragement but little else. Prussia stayed out. Russia remained neutral under the terms of the Treaty of Tilsit, freeing Napoleon to focus on the west. This new coalition rested on Austrian resolve and British gold.

Napoleon was not taken by surprise. His intelligence network kept him well informed, and he returned to Paris in January 1809 already aware of Austria's preparations. He expected the upcoming war to follow a familiar pattern. Take the enemy capital quickly, break their government, and force a peace. For Austria, that meant another campaign along the Danube and another march on Vienna.

Napoleon gathered veterans from earlier victories but had to fill out his ranks with new recruits. Young, barely trained conscripts would fight alongside experienced soldiers. Napoleon trusted his officers to carry them through. What he did not fully understand was how much the Austrian army had changed since Austerlitz.

The Austrian Offensive

The Austrians didn't bother with a formal declaration of war. On April 10th, 1809, Austrian forces invaded Napoleon's client Kingdom of Bavaria. Napoleon's intelligence was flawed in both timing and location. He expected the Austrian advance to move faster and along usable roads. Instead, bad weather struck early. Cold, rain, and ice turned routes into mud. Supply wagons bogged down, and the advance slowed to a crawl before the armies ever met.

Even so, Napoleon's troops responded quickly. The first week brought several French victories. Napoleon's forces won engagement after engagement, driving toward Vienna. The Austrians fell back, and by May 13th, 1809, French troops occupied the Austrian capital.

Emperor Francis I of Austria and his court had withdrawn to Schönbrunn, the Habsburg summer palace outside Vienna, before the city fell. Taking Vienna didn't end the war. The main Austrian army under Archduke Charles remained intact and dangerous. Napoleon needed to cross the Danube south of Vienna to engage and destroy Austrian forces. However, the Austrians had destroyed all the bridges during their retreat. French engineers would have to construct entirely new crossings under enemy observation.

The Battle of Aspern–Essling

On May 21st, 1809, French engineers managed to build a bridge across the Danube. Meanwhile, Archduke Charles watched and waited. He allowed the French to commit one full corps to the crossing before springing his trap. The Austrians sent a large barge down the fast-flowing river. The makeshift battering ram smashed through the bridge, splitting the French forces. One corps was now isolated on the Austrian side.

Repairs began at once. French engineers worked frantically under fire, but heavy rains caused the Danube to rise by nearly a meter. This complicated reconstruction and left part of Napoleon's army stranded and vulnerable.

In the early afternoon, Archduke Charles launched his assault. He targeted French troops concentrated around the villages of Aspern and Essling. Napoleon and his commanders hadn't expected the Austrians to move so aggressively. Fierce fighting raged throughout the day. Attacks and counterattacks surged back and forth. Neither side gained a decisive advantage despite horrific casualties.

The battle resumed the next morning with renewed intensity. Austrian troops began to waver under French counterattacks. Then Archduke Charles personally stormed into the fighting, carrying their battle standard. His presence on the battlefield rallied his men.

By mid-afternoon on May 22nd, Napoleon was forced to order a withdrawal. His staff urged him to leave. He entrusted the retreat to Marshal Jean Lannes, his trusted friend and a supremely capable commander. During the withdrawal, a cannonball struck Lannes and shattered both legs. He died nine days later. The loss affected Napoleon profoundly.

Napoleon at Marshal Lannes's side after the defeat at Aspern–Essling.[28]

The Battle of Aspern–Essling was Napoleon's first major battlefield setback since he'd taken control in Italy thirteen years earlier. The bloody stalemate at Eylau in 1807 had been claimed as a French victory, but it was really closer to a draw. This, however, was different. The Austrians had won a tactical victory on the battlefield and forced Napoleon's retreat. Many historians consider it a strategic stalemate, though, since Vienna remained under French control and Napoleon quickly rebuilt his position. Still, the psychological impact was enormous. European powers saw that the Grande Armée could be beaten in open battle.

Archduke Charles made what many historians consider a crucial error. He didn't pursue the retreating French Army. His own forces were exhausted after two days of brutal combat. Thousands of dead and wounded littered the battlefield. Perhaps he realized his troops couldn't sustain a pursuit.

Napoleon withdrew to the Marchfeld plain. Vienna remained under French control. He had time to bring in reinforcements and reorganize. His ego had taken a blow, but his strategic mind remained sharp.

The Battle of Wagram

More than a month passed as both armies prepared for the next confrontation. Archduke Charles did not press his advantage. Instead, he watched the French from the Russbach Heights, hoping his brother, Archduke John, would arrive with reinforcements.

Napoleon knew he was being watched. He responded with deception. French troop movements and visible preparations suggested another crossing near Aspern and Essling. Charles reacted by shifting his forces to meet the threat. Only later did he realize he had been misled and pulled his army back to the Russbach Heights. Writing to his brother, Charles admitted that the fate of the Habsburg monarchy would be decided in the coming battle.

By July 4th, 1809, Napoleon's forces had crossed the Danube at a different location. They achieved tactical surprise. The French Army now outnumbered the Austrians. Napoleon positioned his forces on the Marchfeld plain below the Austrian position. He directed operations from a small knoll, the only elevated ground on that flat terrain.

Napoleon was impatient. Late on July 5th, he ordered several probing attacks to test Austrian strength. The French forces were repulsed and suffered unexpectedly heavy losses. Napoleon gained what he wanted, though: intelligence about Austrian positions and defensive preparations. He and his commanders retired that night, convinced the next day would bring victory. Archduke Charles, having repulsed the attacks, went to sleep with the same feeling.

Fighting started around four in the morning on July 6th, 1809. Attacks and counterattacks swept back and forth across the battlefield. The combat raged through small villages, across fields, and in woodlands. Both armies committed everything. Napoleon rode constantly along the line, redirecting divisions whenever the battle threatened to break against him. Hundreds of thousands of soldiers were engaged across miles.

Napoleon during the Battle of Wagram.[29]

By afternoon, Archduke Charles realized his brother wasn't coming. Archduke John had turned back when he heard the Austrian army was about to be defeated, choosing to preserve his corps rather than commit to what he saw as a lost cause. The failure was partly due to delayed orders and communication issues between the two commanders. Some historians argue that John was unfairly blamed for the defeat. However, without those reinforcements, Charles couldn't hold against Napoleon's superior numbers.

Charles ordered an orderly retreat when French troops assaulted the heights. His forces were pushed from their positions. He recognized the war had been lost.

Napoleon didn't launch an immediate pursuit. He expected John's reinforcements to arrive and didn't want to overextend. This caution was uncharacteristic for Napoleon, who had built his reputation on the relentless pursuit of defeated enemies. His preference for quick, decisive battles didn't align well with the evolving nature of warfare by 1809. Attrition and coalitions played an increasing role. Wars were becoming longer and more grinding.

Only when dawn broke on July 7th did Napoleon realize the Austrians weren't coming back. A few days later, after another small engagement, Charles requested a truce.

Aftermath

The Battle of Wagram was the largest battle fought in Europe up to that date. Losses on both sides were staggering. More men had been engaged, and more had been killed or wounded, than even at Austerlitz. Napoleon had shown he was still formidable, but nearly a quarter of the French forces in Austria became casualties during the campaign. This was a far higher proportion than in his earlier wars.

The Fifth Coalition collapsed with the Treaty of Schönbrunn, which was signed on October 14th, 1809. Austria paid heavily. Salzburg was handed to Bavaria. Western Galicia was taken by the Duchy of Warsaw, and France annexed the Illyrian Provinces. Austria was also forced into the Continental System. Emperor Francis I had little choice but to accept Napoleon's terms, though the settlement left a bitter taste in the Austrians' mouths.

Yet Napoleon's triumph concealed troubling signs. He had misjudged his enemy. The Austrian army of 1809 was no longer the broken force destroyed at Austerlitz. Archduke Charles's reforms had produced a disciplined, capable army. They had stopped the French at Aspern-Essling and inflicted severe losses at Wagram. What Napoleon had expected to be a swift campaign had dragged on for more than six months.

The sheer size and diversity of Napoleon's armies created new problems. Conscripts from allied states fought alongside French troops, sometimes under their own officers and sometimes under French command. This created confusion. During one engagement, Saxon troops in white uniforms were mistaken for Austrians and attacked by a French division.

According to Bourrienne, Napoleon worried constantly about plots against him. He believed conspiracies were forming in France, among his allies, and within his client states. The long Austrian campaign, combined with the ongoing war in Spain, strained resources. Experienced soldiers were becoming scarce, and populations were growing weary of taxes, conscription, and endless war.

The cracks were beginning to show. Austria had been beaten, but it was not broken. Britain remained undefeated and continued to fund resistance efforts. Spain and Portugal were still in revolt, tying down more than 200,000 French troops. The Grande Armée was no longer invincible, and Europe was starting to realize it. The French Empire was at its height. Whether it could endure was another question.

Chapter 9: The Russian Campaign: Napoleon's Fatal Mistake

Napoleon directly and indirectly controlled most of Europe by 1812. Family and friends sat on European thrones. New states, such as the Confederation of the Rhine and the Duchy of Warsaw, had been created and were under his influence. France appeared to be surrounded by allies and supporters. However, beneath the surface, pockets of unrest and nationalism were brewing in those countries.

Causes of the Invasion

Russia opposed the Continental System forced on it by the Treaty of Tilsit. In December 1810, the tsar openly withdrew from the treaty. The loss of trade with Britain was hurting Russia's economy significantly. However, Russia's violation of the treaty could have a ripple effect on other European nations. Napoleon felt compelled to act.

Rivalry and mistrust between the two empires grew steadily. Eastern Europe was a constant source of tension, especially in Poland. Napoleon's support for Polish nationalism alarmed Russia, which ruled large Polish territories of its own. The Duchy of Warsaw raised fears in St. Petersburg that Polish subjects within the Russian Empire might one day rise in rebellion.

Napoleon also blocked Russian ambitions to seize Constantinople, cutting off any hope of direct access to the Mediterranean. His marriage in 1810 to Archduchess Marie Louise of Austria added another strain.

Marriages and Affairs

As you may recall, Napoleon had married Joséphine before becoming emperor of France. However, despite their genuine affection for each other, there were tensions from the start. Before Napoleon met Joséphine de Beauharnais, he had a relationship with a French courtesan called Marie-Louise O'Murphy. While Napoleon was in Egypt, he learned that Joséphine was unfaithful. The news humiliated and angered him. He did not divorce her, but the marriage never fully recovered, and affairs on both sides became commonplace.

In 1806, Napoleon fathered a son, Charles Léon Denuelle, with his mistress, Éléonore Denuelle. This proved he could have children. His marriage to Joséphine had not produced an heir. He had adopted Joséphine's two children from her first marriage, but he needed his own heir to continue his lineage. This led to their divorce.

His most serious affair was with Polish Countess Marie Walewska. He met her while organizing state affairs in Poland in the winter of 1807. She influenced him to create the Duchy of Warsaw and even visited him on Elba during his first exile.

In 1810, Napoleon married nineteen-year-old Austrian Archduchess Marie Louise. The marriage was politically motivated. Napoleon was ecstatic when she gave birth to their son, Napoleon Francis Joseph Charles, a year later. Napoleon called him the king of Rome. After Napoleon's exile, his son grew up at his Austrian grandfather's court in Vienna. He died at the age of twenty-one in 1832 from tuberculosis.

There had been talk of a marriage alliance with Tsar Alexander's sister. The Austrian match was seen as an insult.

Napoleon's Planning and Preparation

Napoleon was aware of the dangers a Russian campaign would face. So, he gathered information about historic Russian wars. He read accounts of the Swedish invasion of Russia in 1708–1709. They described difficult geography, the lack of roads and bridges, and scarce local resources. He considered the severe weather conditions his troops would face if they were still in Russia by winter, so he planned his invasion to end before winter set in.

Napoleon hoped to defeat the Russian armies quickly and force the tsar to negotiate a renewed agreement on the Continental System. The campaign would also serve as a warning to the rest of Europe. He planned to move fast, reach Vilna, and destroy each Russian force separately before they could join up. He estimated the operation would be completed within three to five weeks. Many within his command recognized the risk of a longer war, but Napoleon's optimism overruled their concerns.

Napoleon significantly underestimated the distance involved, the inadequate infrastructure, and the massive supply problems. His preparations took more than a year. His armies would have to take everything they required with them. Supply routes and depots were established across Europe right up to the Russian border. In the Vistula River Valley, supply depots would be kept fully stocked. A supply train of nearly eight thousand vehicles would keep the army supplied.

On paper, the supply system looked impressive. In reality, it was incapable of sustaining such a massive army over the vast distances of Russia. All of this preparation did not match the challenge present.

Less than half of Napoleon's 615,000-man army consisted of French soldiers. The rest were drawn from European countries under his control. Many served under duress and were reluctant to fight. Estimates suggest there were more than 200,000 horses and at least 1,372 cannons. It was the largest fighting force ever assembled in Europe at that time.

The Invasion Begins

The army crossed the Neman River on June 23rd and 24th, 1812, without opposition. A Cossack cavalry unit in the vicinity saw the crossing but rode away after firing just three shots.

The Russian commander-in-chief was Michael Andreas Barclay de Tolly, a Baltic German officer. He suspected Napoleon's plan and resolved to draw the invading forces deep into Russia through retreats while applying a scorched-earth policy. He would outwit Napoleon in a war of attrition. Despite opposition from Russian commanders who wanted to fight, Barclay's plan prevailed.

By forced marches, Napoleon reached Vilna on June 28th. He hoped Tsar Alexander might still be there and willing to negotiate, though he likely knew the chances were slim. Alexander and the Russian army had actually left days earlier. Napoleon was disappointed. A quick victory would have better suited his plans. Instead, he faced a choice: press deeper into Russia or turn back.

His army was already showing signs of strain. Shortly after crossing the Neman River, typhus broke out among the troops. Supply wagons and artillery bogged down in mud along roads that were little more than tracks.

They could not keep up. Many soldiers, especially new recruits and allied contingents, were not used to Napoleon's relentless pace. They were tired and hungry. The summer heat and sudden thunderstorms made conditions worse. By the time the army reached Vilna, some five thousand horses, five hundred artillery wagons, and one hundred guns had already been lost.

Napoleon spent ten days in Vilna before pushing on. He would not abandon his goal. Desertion increased, and troops had to plunder food from local civilians. A field hospital was established to treat stragglers suffering from dysentery, fever, and heatstroke.

The Russians refused to stand and fight. Instead, they withdrew in a series of delaying actions near Vitebsk and elsewhere. Each time Napoleon tried to force a major battle, the Russians retreated farther inland under the direction of Barclay. By the time the French reached Smolensk, losses may already have approached 100,000 men. The first major engagement came at the Battle of Saltanovka, after which the Russians fell back once more.

The Battle of Smolensk

Barclay was pressured by Russian commanders to make a stand at Smolensk. Napoleon immediately marched on the city upon receiving this news. By this stage of the campaign, he was becoming aware that a quick return to the Polish border was unlikely. He hoped to defeat the Russians at Smolensk and force a decision that would end the war before winter.

His rapid advance was delayed by a brave Russian rearguard on August 14th. The French troops did not press on the next day either. The day was wasted inspecting troops and finalizing preparations. It also happened to be Napoleon's forty-third birthday. This delay gave Barclay time to strengthen the city's defenses.

The battle lasted from August 16th to August 18th, 1812. It ended with bloody street fighting and heavy losses on both sides. Smolensk was the first major battle of the campaign and a political turning point. The city was set ablaze by Barclay's troops while they retreated under the cover of night toward Moscow. Napoleon captured the city but again failed to destroy the Russian army, reinforcing doubts about his strategy.

Despite the victory, Napoleon was bitterly disappointed that the Russians escaped. The burnt-down city with shelter and provisions destroyed was no longer an option for quarters. Napoleon made up his mind. They had to push on to Moscow.

The Battle of Borodino

Most Russian commanders had opposed Barclay's strategy from the beginning. They considered the continuous retreats a blemish on their nation. After Barclay's withdrawal from Smolensk, Tsar Alexander replaced him with Mikhail Kutuzov, a sixty-seven-year-old veteran who had fought against Napoleon at Austerlitz. The replacement was driven by political pressure, not military failure. Kutuzov realized the brilliance of Barclay's strategy. He knew he had to make a stand to defend Moscow to satisfy the political elite around Alexander. So, he chose Borodino, a village about seventy-five miles from Moscow on the road from Smolensk.

The two armies fought each other for twelve hours on September 7th, 1812. It became known as the bloodiest single-day combat of the Napoleonic Wars. The outcome was tactically inconclusive. Napoleon held the field but failed to cripple the Russian army, which was the campaign's central objective. When Kutuzov noticed the bloodshed was leading nowhere except to great loss of life, he decided to withdraw the next morning. He would carry on with the retreat and scorched-earth tactics employed by Barclay. To pacify those who opposed retreat, Kutuzov suggested that they would take another stand closer to Moscow.

Napoleon, despite repeated requests from his aides and commanders, refused to commit his Imperial Guard to the battle. It was his last fresh reserve, and he would not risk losing it in a battle that offered no guarantee of a decisive result. He was criticized by contemporaries for this decision, and historians have debated it ever since.

After the battle, Napoleon faced a choice. His army was far deeper in Russia than he had planned. Autumn was approaching, though the weather remained warm. He could march on Moscow and hope that taking the old capital would force Tsar Alexander to negotiate.

His troops and horses were exhausted and malnourished. By this point, he had already lost around 150,000 men to disease, desertion, hunger, and battle. Napoleon chose to push on toward Moscow quickly. Retreat was not in his nature. His reputation and that of France were at stake. After Borodino, turning back without pressing forward would make the invasion seem like a failure.

Carnage on the battlefield of Borodino.[80]

Moscow

On the afternoon of September 14th, 1812, French troops entered Moscow. Napoleon waited outside the gates with his Imperial Guard for word about conditions inside the eerily quiet city. When a messenger arrived to inform Napoleon that the city had been abandoned by soldiers and citizens alike, he was shocked and disappointed. The city's governor had commanded a total evacuation of all able-bodied persons. Only some wounded soldiers remained.

As Napoleon and his army rode through the deserted streets, they smelled fire. The last Russian soldiers to leave had been ordered to set fire to the supply depots. Soon, the fires began spreading across the city, driven by winds. Frantic efforts by French troops to put the fires out failed. The Russians had destroyed and removed firefighting equipment.

The destruction of Moscow was a decisive strategic event. At least two-thirds of the city went up in flames, which left French troops without adequate food and shelter. Only stone buildings like churches and cathedrals survived. The hungry French soldiers resorted to pillaging. Undisciplined mobs stripped the churches and cathedrals of valuables while using these buildings for shelter.

Napoleon witnessing the abandoned and burning Moscow in October 1812.[81]

Napoleon was stunned at the tenacity of the Russian people. They chose to destroy their beloved Moscow rather than let it fall into enemy hands. Napoleon realized his forces could not remain in Moscow for the winter. Yet he remained there until October 19th, hoping that Tsar Alexander would negotiate a peace treaty with him. The tsar remained silent, though. It seemed he had no intention of negotiating while Napoleon still occupied Russian territory.

The Retreat

Russian forces were deployed around most of the countryside surrounding Moscow. Napoleon planned to retreat along a different route than the wasteland through which they had arrived. He hoped to reach Russia's fertile southern provinces, where he could get provisions for his starving army. Kutuzov guessed this and deployed his troops to cut off the route.

Napoleon was confident his army could break through the Russian opposition. The Battle of Maloyaroslavets on October 24th was crucial. Although the French held the field, Kutuzov's army barred the way forward, and persistent Cossack attacks forced Napoleon back onto the devastated Borodino-Smolensk-Vilna road. This sealed the army's fate. All available food sources had been exhausted during the march to Moscow.

The French troops retreating from Moscow while being harassed by the Cossacks.[33]

The dejected remnants of the French Army had to cross the Borodino battlefield still strewn with thousands of decaying corpses. But they battled on, driven by one thought: to get out of Russia.

Most losses occurred before winter fully set in. Disease, hunger, exhaustion, and breakdown of logistics destroyed the army. Winter worsened the catastrophe, but it did not cause it. When winter finally caught up with them in mid-November, temperatures dropped severely. Blizzards blinded them. Some men got lost, never to be seen again. Some just dropped dead while trudging through the snow. The retreat became a constant struggle, with Russian troops close behind and Cossacks harassing the column day and night.

Napoleon meant to cross the frozen Berezina River at Borisov, but a sudden rise in the temperature melted the ice. With two Russian forces on their heels and another waiting on the far side of the river, Napoleon organized a distraction while his Dutch engineers built pontoon bridges. The army was saved by the engineers' courage. Of the four hundred bridge builders, only forty survived. Progress was painfully slow, as men, wagons, and guns crowded onto two narrow bridges under constant fire. The operation stretched from November 26th to 29th, 1812.

French troops crossing the icy Berezina River.[88]

On December 5th, 1812, Napoleon Bonaparte left the army in the care of Murat. He had learned that rumors were spreading that he was dead back home. A republican general named Claude François de Malet had exploited the silence from Russia, producing forged Senate decrees announcing Napoleon's death and issuing orders that were being obeyed without question. The plot collapsed within hours when Malet was recognized and arrested.

Still, the damage had been done. The episode revealed how fragile the political order in France had become in Napoleon's absence. Unrest was growing, authority was wavering, and the empire depended entirely on the belief that the emperor still lived and ruled. Napoleon's senior commanders supported his decision to return at once, knowing Paris could not be left to drift. His soldiers, however, felt abandoned as he rode west, leaving them to continue the retreat without him.

The Disaster and Its Consequences

Napoleon entered Russia with more than 600,000 men. Fewer than 100,000 returned. More troops were lost during the extreme heat of the summer of 1812 than during the winter retreat. Disease, starvation, and the collapse of logistics did more damage than the cold weather.

Barclay and, later, Kutuzov outmaneuvered Napoleon with their retreats and scorched-earth tactics despite several French victories. It was impossible for Napoleon to control and direct the enormous numbers of divisions and troops with the communication tools of that era. The diversity of culture, training, language, warfare styles, and reluctant recruits from several nations made coordination nearly impossible. Napoleon's plans and preparations looked perfect on paper, but he had hopelessly misjudged Russian patriotism and Tsar Alexander's character.

The failure of the Russian campaign encouraged the formation of a new coalition against Napoleon. It also marked the irreversible decline of French dominance in Europe. Napoleon retained power for several more years, but his empire would never recover from this catastrophe.

Chapter 10: Wars of the Sixth and Seventh Coalition and Napoleon's Final Defeat

After Napoleon's disastrous retreat from Russia, his reputation no longer scared the rest of Europe. The French military forces were no longer an invincible menace. It would take years for Napoleon to rebuild his strength. Secret meetings and agreements brought together a formidable coalition that even included former enemies.

The Sixth Coalition formed in early 1813. Britain, Prussia, Russia, Sweden, and several German principalities joined together. Britain had been at war with France since 1803. The others declared war between March and August 1813.

Austria was not yet part of the coalition. During the Armistice of Pleiswitz, which halted fighting from June to August 1813, Austrian Chancellor Metternich attempted to mediate between Napoleon and his enemies. Austria offered peace in exchange for major French concessions in Germany and eastern Europe. Napoleon rejected these terms outright. During a tense meeting, he lost his temper and openly insulted Metternich and Austria. The failure of these talks convinced Vienna that compromise was impossible. In August 1813, Austria joined the coalition.

The War Begins

Active conflicts started in the spring of 1813. Meanwhile, Joseph Bonaparte's position in Spain had been deteriorating for months. The Spanish and Portuguese troops in the ongoing Peninsular War, reinforced by British troops under Field Marshal Arthur Wellesley, Duke of Wellington, continued their campaign against the French forces. Joseph's army suffered a final defeat at the Battle of Vitoria on June 21st, 1813, which ended French control of Spain.

Napoleon withdrew twenty thousand troops from the Peninsular War to reinforce his army in central Europe. He swore he would rebuild his decimated army in record time. French forces won victories at Lützen on May 2nd and Bautzen on May 20th and 21st, 1813, against Russia and Prussia. These battles inflicted heavy casualties on both sides.

Napoleon's troops could not finish the war; they did not have enough horses to pursue their fleeing enemy. Napoleon needed time to train troops and replenish the army's equipment and horses.

Prussian morale was low after these losses. After pursuing Napoleon from Moscow, Russian soldiers were tired and wanted to return home. It suited both sides to agree to the Armistice of Pleiswitz. This truce lasted from June to August 1813.

Allied Strategy

The allies in this coalition were better prepared than in previous coalitions. Coordination had improved, and they agreed on a general strategy shaped by Jean-Baptiste Bernadotte, the regent of Sweden and a former marshal of Napoleon. Having served under Napoleon, Bernadotte understood the man's strengths better than most, and he believed those strengths made him dangerous to confront head-on. Now acting in Sweden's interests rather than France's and convinced that Napoleon would not accept meaningful compromise, he urged caution in direct engagements with the emperor himself. Instead, the coalition's three large multinational armies were to wear Napoleon down by attacking his flanks and lines of communication while concentrating their efforts against his marshals whenever they operated away from the main force.

The Autumn Campaign

The truce ended on August 18th, 1813, but it had been dying for weeks. During the pause in fighting, Austria attempted to mediate, hoping Napoleon might accept a compromise that would stabilize Europe. Metternich warned him bluntly that Austria was prepared for war unless

France gave up its grip on Germany. Napoleon refused to yield anything. Convinced that he could still win by force, he dismissed the warnings. Metternich left, persuaded that peace was impossible. Austria soon joined the coalition, and when the armistice expired, the allies were ready.

Before the end of the month, the allies struck. Crown Prince Charles John intercepted and defeated Napoleon's Marshal Nicolas Oudinot, who was on his way to recapture Berlin at the Battle of Großbeeren (Grossbeeren) on August 23rd. Three days later, French Marshal Étienne Macdonald was defeated at the Battle of Katzbach.

Napoleon won the next battle at Dresden on August 27th. However, his subordinates continued to suffer defeats. Marshal Vandamme was defeated and captured at the Battle of Kulm on August 30th. Marshal Ney was defeated at the Battle of Dennewitz on September 6th. These defeats turned the tide against Napoleon.

The allies also severely handicapped Napoleon's forces by attacking their supply lines. When Napoleon pursued the allied forces, they often managed to avoid confrontation.

In October 1813, Bavaria switched support from Napoleon to the allies. In quiet negotiations, Vienna promised that Bavaria would keep its royal title and most of its territory. It would also be recognized as a sovereign state rather than punished as an enemy. It was a clear sign that Napoleon's empire was unraveling.

The Battle of Leipzig

The Battle of Leipzig became the decisive confrontation because Napoleon was finally overwhelmed by numbers and had been deserted by his allies. Surrounded by Russian, Prussian, Austrian, and Swedish armies, he fought for four days as the ring around him tightened. During the battle, Saxon and Württemberg troops changed sides, opening gaps in his lines and shattering his confidence in his German allies.

On the night of October 18th, Napoleon ordered a retreat. The withdrawal funneled his army toward a single bridge over the Elster River. In the confusion, the bridge was blown up too soon. Thousands of French troops were trapped inside Leipzig and captured the following day.

Napoleon defeated at the Battle of Leipzig by Vladimir Moshkov.⁴⁴

The defeat was crushing. Napoleon abandoned Germany and fell back toward France. His empire east of the Rhine was gone.

The Invasion of France

After Leipzig, Napoleon withdrew behind the Rhine and tried to stabilize what remained of his empire. The allies offered Napoleon a peace deal drafted by Metternich. Metternich did not want the French Empire to be destroyed, but he did want the incessant wars to end. He had his own agenda that would keep Napoleon's France as a stabilizing force against future Russian aggression. However, Napoleon was still convinced he could win the war. He refused to accept the terms despite Metternich's warnings that future deals would be increasingly severe.

Several allied armies attacked France in January 1814. Outnumbered and fighting without the support he was used to, Napoleon was defeated at La Rothière on February 1ˢᵗ, opening the invasion of France itself.

Napoleon responded with his last great series of victories. During the Six Days' Campaign in February 1814, he won battles at Champaubert, Montmirail, Château-Thierry, and Vauchamps. These victories showcased Napoleon's tactical genius. He concentrated on one allied army at a time and defeated them separately. Despite these successes, it was not enough. The allies had overwhelming numerical superiority.

As the allied armies closed in on the capital, Napoleon withdrew east with his field army, hoping to get behind the allied armies and force them to turn back by threatening their supply routes. He left Paris with only limited forces, believing the city could hold briefly while he struck elsewhere.

Instead, the allies marched directly on Paris. On March 30th, 1814, they launched a full-scale assault. The Battle of Paris was marked by fierce fighting as regular troops, National Guardsmen, and volunteers defended the city in bloody street battles. Outnumbered and facing destruction, Parisian leaders negotiated a surrender by March 31st.

With the capital lost, Napoleon withdrew to Fontainebleau. A provisional government was formed in Paris, which persuaded the allies to restore the Bourbon dynasty to create stability.

Napoleon's First Abdication

Napoleon's marshals urged him to abdicate to spare France further destruction. Paris had fallen, political support had collapsed, and continued resistance threatened civil war and occupation. After days of reflection, Napoleon agreed to step aside in favor of his young son, hoping to preserve his dynasty and secure peace.

Before the allies could decide, Marshal Auguste de Marmont surrendered his entire force, showing that Napoleon no longer controlled his officers and shattering any remaining leverage. With Paris surrounded and the army divided, the allies demanded Napoleon's unconditional abdication. He complied on April 11th, 1814.

Napoleon's surrender and the end of the First French Empire were sealed by the Treaty of Fontainebleau. In return, Napoleon was made emperor of the tiny island of Elba. He would receive an income of two million francs per year. He was escorted to a waiting ship by allied troops after an emotional farewell to his faithful Imperial Guard on April 20th, 1814.

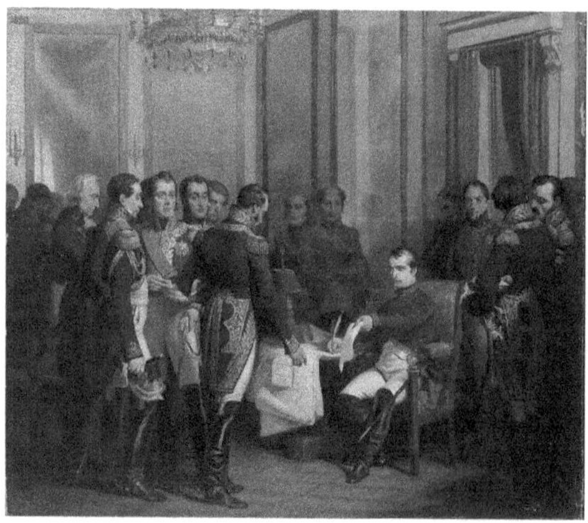

Napoleon signs his abdication at Fontainebleau.[85]

Exile to Elba

In the Treaty of Paris of May 30th, 1814, the Bourbon King Louis XVIII was restored to the throne of France. French territory was reduced to its 1792 limits. The lengthy Congress of Vienna followed, where representatives of European countries met from September 1814 to June 1815 to redraw the map of Europe.

Napoleon watched the aftermath of his exile from Elba. Despite his comfortable palatial residence on a beautiful island with a mild climate, Napoleon hated the situation. His freedom was limited to the island's boundaries. British troops were stationed on the island to monitor him continuously and prevent his escape.

He was permitted to rule the island freely, receive visitors, and implement changes. He created beautiful gardens and renewed the island's infrastructure. He attended local functions and, at times, addressed crowds. He was even visited by his Polish mistress, Maria Walewska. His British watchers were suspicious of the many visitors he received from France. However, Napoleon seemed to have accepted his fate.

In reality, Napoleon's mind was occupied with returning to France from the moment he first set foot on the island. A British author, Sir Walter Scott, later drew on accounts from those who met Napoleon. He wrote that during conversations, Napoleon could appear distracted by his own thoughts. It seemed he was subdued but still planning his future.

Behind the façade, Napoleon built an Imperial Guard of six hundred men, a small army of two thousand men, which included Corsicans and volunteers from Elba, and a small fleet. Napoleon reasoned that the French people and military would join him upon his return to France. He had been informed by his associates that the French people were angry and plotting against their Bourbon monarch. Veterans felt abandoned, liberals feared the return of the old aristocracy, and many resented a king restored by foreign armies rather than by the nation itself.

Napoleon's Escape

Napoleon did not consider his escape from Elba dishonorable. He believed that the Treaty of Fontainebleau had already been undermined, citing unpaid allowances and growing signs that the British intended to remove him further away. On February 26th, 1815, Napoleon openly embarked on the *Inconstant* with his Imperial Guard and volunteers. His personal British minder was away at a conference in Florence. There were no British warships in the vicinity of Elba.

Napoleon's escape from Elba.[36]

Napoleon arrived in France on March 1ˢᵗ, 1815. He took over Cannes and set out on a forced march for Paris. Regiments sent to intercept him were convinced by an impassioned plea from the emperor to join him. French supporters jubilantly greeted his return, and more troops voluntarily joined as they traveled. Troops sent to arrest Napoleon switched sides as soon as they met him.

Napoleon promised the crowds that they would be electing direct representatives to the assembly of his new government. France would embrace liberty, equality, and brotherhood without further wars of conquest and autocratic rule. He promised to completely abolish censorship and ban the slave trade.

When news reached delegates at the Congress of Vienna, they reacted swiftly. On March 13ᵗʰ, 1815, Napoleon was formally declared an outlaw. Planning for a Seventh Coalition against Napoleon commenced immediately. He was not just opposed militarily. He was also branded an enemy of European peace.

The Hundred Days

Napoleon arrived in Paris to a hero's welcome on March 20ᵗʰ, 1815. The Bourbon king had fled Paris shortly before Napoleon's arrival. He left behind depleted coffers and a dysfunctional army. Napoleon immediately set about implementing the liberal changes he had promised. These constitutional reforms won over many of his earlier opponents.

Napoleon knew the next coalition's forces were gathering on his borders. He urgently needed a large enough functional army to oppose them. The Seventh Coalition declared war on Napoleon rather than on France. They were determined to remove him for good.

Britain and Prussia prepared to invade Belgium and attack from the northwest. At the same time, Austria and Russia would gather on the Upper and Middle Rhine. Napoleon surprised them by entering the United Kingdom of the Netherlands on June 14th, 1815. He hoped to defeat each enemy before they could combine forces.

The Battle of Ligny

On the afternoon of June 16th, Napoleon attacked the Prussian positions along the stream near the villages of Saint-Amand and Ligny. French troops advanced into the villages, where fierce fighting quickly developed as both sides committed more forces. What began as a calculated effort to pin the Prussians in place soon expanded into a general engagement.

Late in the day, a powerful French assault broke the Prussian center, forcing a retreat and leaving Gebhard Leberecht von Blücher himself wounded and temporarily unaccounted for. Yet the victory fell short of Napoleon's hopes. The Prussian Army was battered but not destroyed. It withdrew in good order, remaining capable of further action.

The Battle of Ligny.[87]

On the same day, Marshal Michel Ney fought Wellington at Quatre Bras. Ney succeeded in preventing the Anglo-Allied army from marching to Blücher's aid, but he failed to defeat it outright. As a result, both allied armies survived the day. Napoleon had won at Ligny, but it was not decisive enough to end the campaign.

The Battle of Waterloo

Wellington retreated to the heights near his headquarters at Waterloo. Napoleon attacked just before midday on June 18th. Much of the fighting centered on fortified positions such as Hougoumont on Wellington's right and La Haye Sainte in the center, where repeated French assaults failed to break the allied line. Wellington's army held its ground with great difficulty until Prussian reinforcements arrived later in the afternoon.

At the same time, the Battle of Wavre was fought on June 18th and 19th. French forces under Marshal Emmanuel de Grouchy engaged part of the Prussian Army, preventing its full concentration at Waterloo. Even so, enough Prussian troops reached Wellington to tip the balance.

The French fought with determination, but they were outnumbered by the combined British and Prussian forces. Napoleon's final gamble came with the commitment of the Imperial Guard, but their advance was repulsed, dealing a severe blow to French morale. By nightfall, most French units were retreating in disarray. In a single day, Napoleon's final gamble had failed. The Napoleonic Wars effectively came to an end.

The carnage on the battlefield was immense. Around fifty thousand men became casualties, making Waterloo the bloodiest battle since Borodino. Thousands lay dead or wounded across the fields. The evacuation of the wounded took days, and many later died from infection and exhaustion.

The Battle of Waterloo by William Sadler.[88]

Brussels was overwhelmed with casualties. Churches, houses, and public buildings were converted into hospitals, but they could not cope with the numbers. Many of the dead were buried in shallow mass graves, often without identification. Looting of the battlefield began almost immediately.

Elements of the Imperial Guard fought with exceptional stubbornness, but they, too, were eventually forced to withdraw. Thousands of French prisoners were taken and transported to Britain; many of them were held at Dartmoor.

On July 1st, 1815, French forces not present at Waterloo won a small victory over Prussian troops at Rocquencourt. It did little to change the outcome, but it showed that Napoleon's army was not yet completely broken. Two days later, French marshals and representatives of the provisional government signed an agreement at Saint-Cloud, which handed Paris over to the allies and granted pardons to most of Napoleon's supporters.

The Final Abdication and the White Terror

Napoleon left his defeated Waterloo army on June 21st to return to Paris. He discovered that his support amongst the population and the military had cooled greatly. Any plans of raising reinforcements were impossible. He retreated to the palace of Malmaison. Napoleon officially abdicated his throne on June 22nd in favor of his son. The abdication was meaningless, though. The allies were already planning to restore the Bourbon king.

King Louis XVIII was restored to the throne by the Allies on July 8th, 1815. On July 24th, the king, supported by royalists, issued a decree ordering the arrest of Napoleon's known supporters. The king did not consider the Saint-Cloud treaty binding since he had not signed it.

Royalists across France openly took revenge. This period became known as the White Terror. It lasted for the rest of 1815. Officers were executed by firing squads. Marshal Ney, whom Napoleon had once declared the bravest of his men, was executed in December 1815 after a sham trial. Some managed to escape to the United States of America.

Chapter 11: Napoleon's Final Years

By the summer of 1815, the coalition no longer agreed on what should be done with Napoleon. Some Prussian and Russian commanders openly argued for harsh punishment, even execution. Others feared that killing him would turn him into a martyr. In the end, the decision was made collectively. Napoleon would be removed from Europe altogether. British and Austrian voices carried the most weight in this decision.

Napoleon had hoped for a different ending. When the British refused his request for asylum in England, he decided to try for the United States. He traveled to Rochefort, searching for a ship that could carry him across the Atlantic. British warships, however, sealed the coast. There was no escape.

After several days of negotiation, Napoleon boarded the British ship *Bellerophon* on July 15th, 1815. As he left France, crowds gathered along the shore. Some wept. Others shouted "Vive l'Empereur!" The ship sailed north for Torbay, carrying him away from everything he had ruled.

This time, the British took no chances. Admiral Sir George Cockburn was placed in charge of Napoleon's custody under direct orders from Lord Bathurst and the prince regent. Cockburn understood that authority had to be established immediately. Napoleon would be treated with courtesy but not deference. He was no longer an emperor. He was a prisoner.

According to Cockburn's diary, the arrangement tested his patience. Napoleon and his companions still expected to be treated as if the empire existed. Cockburn refused. He ordered his crew to refer to Napoleon only as "general." When Napoleon was rude, Cockburn ignored him. When requests fell outside the rules, they were politely denied.

On August 7th, 1815, Napoleon left England aboard HMS *Northumberland,* bound for the remote South Atlantic island of Saint Helena. The location was chosen for its isolation. It lay far from Europe and the Americas, and it was beyond easy reach of rescue or escape.

This time, there would be no return.

Arrival at Saint Helena

HMS *Northumberland* anchored at the port of Jamestown, Saint Helena, on Sunday, October 15th, 1815, at noon. Napoleon left the ship by boat on Tuesday evening, October 17th. He sat between Admiral Cockburn and the commander of the specially selected troops that would guard him in exile. Napoleon asked Cockburn to delay his transfer until 7:30 p.m. to avoid the crowd gathered on the shore.

The next day, Admiral Cockburn took Napoleon to view Longwood House, the property where he would be living after its renovation and enlargement. On their return journey, Napoleon asked if he could stay at the Briars Pavilion of the Balcombe family rather than in Jamestown for privacy. He was granted his request. Napoleon stayed there until December 10th, 1815, when Longwood House was ready.

Napoleon on Saint Helena.[89]

Life at Longwood House

The isolated dwelling where Napoleon spent his final years is perched on a windswept plateau. The high humidity on the tropical island causes heat, decay, and the rapid growth of black mold. Napoleon soon suffered from respiratory problems. The island, particularly Longwood House, is right in the path of the southeast trade winds. The house remained rat-infested, uncomfortable, and much too small even after additions were made for Napoleon's household of around forty people. A musty odor permeated the interior due to humidity and standing water beneath some floors.

It served the purpose of monitoring Napoleon's movements and outside contact perfectly. Admiral Cockburn had to explain to Bathurst and the prince regent by letter that there was no property on Saint Helena suitable to secure their prisoner's confinement in relative comfort. After renovations, Longwood House was the closest they could achieve.

The property was isolated from the rest of the island and deliberately exposed rather than hidden. No large trees or shrubs screened it from view. A ravine ran along one side of the grounds, opening into a valley where guards could watch Longwood House without obstruction. Sentries came from nearby barracks to patrol the perimeter day and night.

Longwood House in 2014.[40]

When Napoleon first moved in, he revamped the muddy surroundings into a pleasant garden. He added fishponds, lawns, flowers, shrubs, and trees. He walked there every day in the early years despite the windy conditions. He often played tricks on the sentries by hiding from their view. He also did this while out riding.

Napoleon entertained diplomats, select visitors, and occasional travelers with permission from British authorities. Napoleon's friends, the Balcombes, left Saint Helena in March 1818. After this, he became more reclusive.

Governor Lowe and Declining Health

Governor Sir Hudson Lowe took over from Cockburn in 1817. Charged with ensuring Napoleon never escaped again, Lowe enforced strict controls and viewed any personal sympathy as a security risk. Napoleon refused to accept his authority, openly mocked him, and treated him with contempt. Their relationship quickly became hostile, and Lowe moved to remove anyone who appeared too close to the former emperor.

Lowe also faced friction with the British government, the press, and public opinion over his handling of Napoleon's confinement. This broader political controversy complicated his position. He even got rid of Irish ship surgeon Dr. Barry O'Meara, whom he suspected of passing letters to and from Napoleon. O'Meara did not go quietly. His accounts of the conditions at Longwood House were published in England. He described the house as damp, unhealthy, and isolating, and he said Napoleon was subjected to petty restrictions that damaged his health and dignity. These accounts caused a political controversy in Britain over how Napoleon was being treated.

Governor Lowe had two main concerns. First, he received rumors about possible escape plans arranged via the Americas. Second, he was responsible for Napoleon's health. After O'Meara left, the doctors appointed by Lowe were never sure whether Napoleon's complaints were serious or just a ruse. O'Meara had diagnosed Napoleon with hepatitis and wanted him removed from Longwood House. At least one of the later doctors agreed. Lowe was absolutely against this idea. He relented during 1820 and had a new house built, but Napoleon never moved there.

According to Napoleon's staff, he spent hours in a hot bath to relieve his aches and pains as his health declined. A carpenter made a bookshelf that fitted over Napoleon's bath. He would relax there in constantly topped-up hot water for as long as he could.

Over the years, Napoleon gained weight. As his health worsened and he became less active, his legs and feet were constantly swollen. He suffered from respiratory problems and had constant pain in his abdomen. His gums were infected, and he had to have two teeth removed. His always sallow skin was now tinged with yellow.

Death

By April 1821, Napoleon was mostly bedridden and at times delirious. He dictated his last will during this time. His will outlined his wishes for his family and supporters. On Friday, May 4th, 1821, Napoleon's skin was cold. His pulse rate was irregular. His eyes remained half closed throughout the day. The doctor did not expect him to last through the night.

Saturday dawned with bad weather. Napoleon floated in and out of consciousness. He passed away at 5:49 p.m. on May 5th, 1821. Joséphine's name is believed to be the last word he uttered. Outside, a vicious tropical storm lashed the lonely house on the plateau. He died surrounded by his faithful companions who had left their lives behind to follow him into exile. Also present were two priests, the doctor, and some servants.

He was fifty-one years old.

Burial on Saint Helena

The doctor performed an autopsy the next day and recorded that Napoleon had died of stomach cancer. Later, doctors suggested it might have been gastric cancer or ulcer complications. Some people claimed arsenic poisoning, although most experts now think that's unlikely. Still, many questions about Napoleon's death are debated.

Napoleon was placed in his coffin on May 7th. His body rested on a satin lining stuffed with cotton. The coffin was lined with tin, then mahogany, then lead, with another layer of mahogany on the outside. According to some reports, he lay in state at Longwood House until the funeral. As the news spread, the islanders, both civilians and military personnel, flocked to Longwood House to pay their respects. They all attended the funeral.

One of Napoleon's favorite spots was selected for his burial. His reinforced coffin was lowered into a grave on May 9th. The funeral procession and service were led by the French priests of Napoleon's household. It was as dignified and ceremonious as they could manage on the small island.

Return to France

The Bourbon monarchy in France had no wish for Napoleon's remains to be returned despite many requests. In 1840, King Louis Philippe wanted to calm tensions between royalists and Bonapartists and win public support. He sought to reclaim Napoleon as a figure of national pride. Lengthy negotiations with Britain followed since Napoleon's grave remained under British control. Once an agreement was reached, his remains could finally be brought home.

Louis Philippe's son, François d'Orléans, Prince of Joinville, left France on the frigate *Belle Poule* to fetch Napoleon's body. Dignitaries on board *Belle Poule* and the escorting corvette (a small warship) included some of Napoleon's old companions and servants. A chapel draped in black velvet embroidered with silver bees was installed on *Belle Poule* to house the coffin.

British soldiers dismantled the surrounding metal fence, the stone slabs covering the grave, and the masonry in which the coffin was encased. The process took more than nine hours. The outer mahogany casing had to be sawn off, and the lead coffin was soldered apart. After unscrewing the next mahogany casing, they could finally open the tin coffin.

Eyewitnesses described the remarkable preservation of the body. The tin coffin was closed again, placed in its mahogany casing, and covered with the original lead. The reassembled coffin was then encased in a new lead coffin and finally in a new ebony coffin. The lid bore the name "Napoleon" in gold letters. The four sides each had a gilded bronze "N." One side had the words "Napoléon Empereur mort à Sainte-Hélène le 05 Mai 1821."

The island's women handed over several handmade French tri-colored flags and the imperial flag to be flown from the mast of *Belle Poule* on the return voyage. It took forty-three soldiers to load the heavy coffin onto a hearse. Four straining horses draped in black pulled it in heavy rain to the harbor. A large crowd followed.

The *Belle Poule* rushed back to France with its precious cargo. The world and France were coping with unrest and the threat of war in several regions. François d'Orléans had to keep the ship and crew in constant readiness for an attack.

The 1840 Funeral in Paris

The funeral date was set for December 15th, 1840. On December 6th, the casket was transferred to a steamship, *La Normandie*. Later in the Seine, it was transferred to *La Dorade 3* for the final stretch to Paris. The riverbanks and rooftops were packed with crowds along the way. *La Dorade* moored in a suburb of Paris on December 14th. Napoleon's coffin was transferred to a magnificently built giant funeral carriage pulled by sixteen horses.

Napoleon's casket was covered by velvet drapes to obscure it from the view of the thousands who had braved the cold, miserable weather. The obscured view disgusted the author Victor Hugo and most citizens of France. They felt insulted that the state was trying to hide Napoleon from the people at the very moment it claimed to honor him.

Napoleon's coffin was laid to rest in the chapel of Saint-Jérôme under the dome of Les Invalides on December 15th. The chapel was opened to the public from December 16th to December 24th so Parisians could pay their respects. This was only temporary. The grand tomb built for Napoleon took many years to complete. The coffin was moved to its final resting place on April 2nd, 1861, in a small private ceremony.

The French government missed an opportunity to emphasize Napoleon's many reforms and achievements at his Paris funeral in 1840. They were determined to have a military funeral rather than a state funeral because of the continued unrest.

Medical and law students were barred because the government feared they would turn the funeral into a political demonstration, so they marched separately through Paris in a peaceful but defiant show of popular support.

The funeral had mixed reactions. Many people honored Napoleon, but some royalists objected to the ceremonies. There was no mention of his commendable administrative and civil achievements, including the expansion of a modernized education system to all citizens.

Napoleon's final resting place in Paris.[41]

Conclusion

Napoleon is widely regarded as an exceptional military strategist. History books emphasize his campaigns and battles. Friends and enemies wrote memoirs about him, but these are often biased. Napoleon could inspire hero worship, love, or hate. He was a master manipulator and propagandist. But there were also glimpses of human empathy and playful mischief.

The Myths

Some iconic images of Napoleon have interesting origins. For example, the one hand tucked under his waistcoat in paintings and statues was considered a refined pose for a sophisticated gentleman. It was popular during the classical period and made a comeback in the 1700s. Many of the elite adopted it for official portraits.

Napoleon was hated by the British and other enemies. In their propaganda, he was short-tempered and of short stature. Coupled with his French nickname "Le Petit Caporal" (the little corporal), it was a popular theme for cartoons. At five feet seven inches tall, Napoleon was actually taller than the average French male. He was taller than Admiral Nelson!

The term "Napoleon complex" was coined by an Austrian psychoanalyst, Dr. Alfred Adler, a contemporary of Freud. He analyzed it as a way of overcoming an inferiority complex. His theories are widely disputed because they lack any scientific basis.

Some artists who admired Napoleon stopped supporting him when he crowned himself emperor. Beethoven initially admired Napoleon as a symbol of revolutionary ideals. He dedicated his Third Symphony to

Napoleon and titled it "Bonaparte" when he finished it in 1804. When Napoleon declared himself emperor, Beethoven was furious. He crossed out the dedication entirely. The symphony was published as "Eroica" without any dedication to Napoleon.

The Legacy

Napoleon once said on Saint Helena that he would be remembered for his Napoleonic Code rather than his battles. He was right. His influence is still present today. The Napoleonic Code became the foundation for legal systems in many countries. His administrative reforms modernized government structures across Europe. His military strategies are still studied in military academies worldwide.

Too much power breeds arrogance and corruption. Napoleon became a dictator. His empire was filled with nepotism, backstabbing, and suspicion. He curtailed freedoms won in the bloody French Revolution. By 1815, he believed his own propaganda.

Napoleon remains difficult to categorize. This is perhaps why so many books try to understand him. However, it cannot be denied that the man who rose from a minor Corsican nobleman to emperor of France left his mark on history. Napoleon Bonaparte shaped the course of history in ways that still resonate today.

Part 2: The Napoleonic Wars

An Enthralling Guide to Global Conflict, Revolutionary Tactics, and the Empire's Expansion

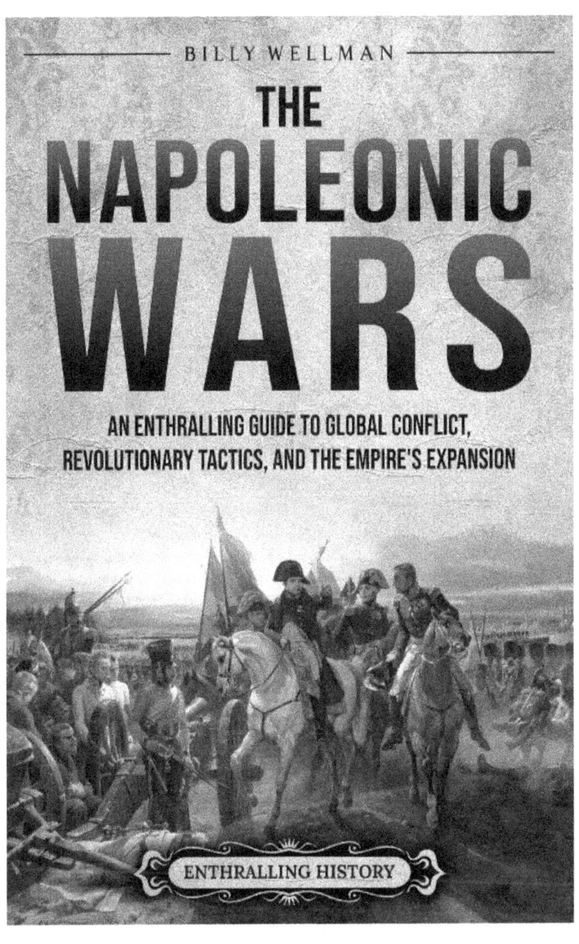

Introduction

The Napoleonic Wars were an important moment in European history and Western civilization. They are a major part of the saga of a military genius named Napoleon Bonaparte. Napoleon ranks with the great masters of military science, and his tactics are still studied in military institutions and universities worldwide. He was more than just a military genius, though. Napoleon was also a lawgiver and a champion of ideas that would transform Western civilization. The Napoleonic Code remains one of the primary legal texts of history, ranking with the Code of Justinian as a powerful instrument of social change. However, what we remember most about Napoleon are not his innovations in law but rather his wars.

The opening years of the 19th century in Europe can best be described as campaign season for the French army. Napoleon was constantly at war with other powers in Europe. His amazing understanding of military science permitted him to outmaneuver armies that were much larger than his time and time again. The French emperor could innovate and adapt quickly. He recognized the need to combine surprise with speed and decisive action to outmaneuver his opponents. Napoleon built a formidable military machine that struck fear in his enemies while also gaining respect at the same time. The Grande Armée was his creation and the driving force behind his outstanding military achievements.

Napoleon was a champion on the battlefield, but he was also successful at the negotiating table. He was able to forge alliances and reach agreements with others. Napoleon also had a unique capability of manipulating Continental politics to be successful.

Napoleon Bonaparte believed that fate and luck were his constant companions. However, that was not always the case. The Peninsular Wars and the Russian campaign of 1812 proved that this man was mortal and did not always make the best decisions. Moreover, his enemies learned from their defeats. This became evident at the Battle of Leipzig (also known as the Battle of the Nations), where the Little Corporal was no longer the master of the fight. He would ultimately lose all he had won, but the path he blazed until the final engagement at Waterloo is still seen as brilliant.

The Napoleonic Wars are an amazing story of the rise and fall of one man. The analysis of these years show us where he made brilliant decisions, how he arrived at them, and what caused him to make mistakes that eventually proved disastrous.

The wars were not spontaneous but resulted from what happened in France in the late 18th century. The Napoleonic Wars followed eleven years of conflicts that pitted Revolutionary France against other European nations. We will briefly examine the French Revolution to see how it influenced the later years of the wars.

Simply put, the Napoleonic Wars testify to the immense genius of Napoleon Bonaparte. The battles he fought and the accomplishments he achieved are worth every minute we take to study them. We will explore these in this work, and we hope readers will benefit from learning about the man and the period in which he lived.

Chapter 1: The Rise of Napoleon

<u>The Lad from Corsica</u>

Napoleon Bonaparte was born in the city of Ajaccio on the island of Corsica on August 15th, 1769. He was the son of Carlo Buonaparte and his wife, Letizia. The boy was part of a large family of minor Corsican aristocrats. At one time, Corsica was the possession of Genoa, but France acquired it the year before Napoleon was born. Napoleon grew up learning French, and he became increasingly acquainted with the new owner of his homeland.

Napoleon was sent to France to receive an education when he was nine. He studied at the Royal Military School in Brienne and then the École Militaire in Paris. He excelled at mathematics and history, but the young man stood out in military subjects. Napoleon had a keen intellect and intensely studied warfare tactics, the construction of fortifications, and military history. His understanding of complex concepts was remarkable for a young man his age.

His years at the École Militaire would be time very well spent. Napoleon learned more about cavalry tactics and artillery at this institution, and he graduated a second lieutenant of an artillery regiment when he was only sixteen years old.[1]

If history didn't play out the way it did, Napoleon could have been a second lieutenant for a long time. One's family was more important in

---

[1] Editors, H. (2023, April 24). Napoleon Bonaparte. Retrieved from History.com: https://www.history.com/topics/european-history/napoleon.

military advancement than actual talent. A young man could become an officer on the staff of a general based on family connections or a good word from an influential friend. It was also possible to purchase a military rank if an individual had the right amount of money. It would have been difficult for Napoleon to rise through the ranks in this system. There was a genuine chance this ambitious young man could have spent his military career posted to a garrison in some remote and forgettable part of France. Fortunately for him, Napoleon entered the military at the right time.

<u>The Three Estates of France</u>

France was in turmoil before Napoleon gained power. The French Revolution kickstarted events that resulted in Europe being at war for over twenty years.

France had a class system that was centuries old. The First Estate was at the top of the pyramid and consisted of the Catholic clergy. (Protestantism was severely repressed by the revocation of the Edict of Nantes in 1685.) Approximately 10 percent of French land was owned by the Roman Catholic Church and was tax-exempt.

The Second Estate comprised the French aristocracy. They were the powerful elite of France and controlled positions of authority in the military and the government. There was a division within the Second Estate. "Nobles of the sword" were those whose titles had been in their families for generations. They had been granted their status for military service or from favors given by the king. "Nobles of the robe" were aristocrats who achieved their status by being administrators, financiers, or judiciary officials.

The last estate, the Third Estate, included more than just the peasantry. It consisted of the commoners, including artisans, farmers, merchants, and anyone who was not part of the nobility or clergy. More than 90 percent of the French population was part of the Third Estate. It was the largest group in French society, and it was the most oppressed.

A medieval adage declared, "The priests pray for all, the lords fight for all, and the peasants pay for all." That was true a thousand years later. The clergy were exempt from taxes. The aristocracy was required to pay poll taxes and the *vingtième* (one-twentieth of annual income, or 5 percent). Neither estate was asked to pay the direct tax, the *taille*. The Third Estate had to pay that and other taxes and levies on their income and holdings.[2]

---

[2] Mark, H. W. (2022, March 7). The Three Estates of Pre-Revolutionary France. Retrieved from

The class structure in France created considerable social tension. The Third Estate rightly saw that they were required to carry the country's burden, and yet the other two estates did not have to pay heavy taxes even though they typically earned more money than them.

Moreover, there were certain privileges that the aristocracy enjoyed that they had maintained for centuries. They were not about to give them up. Some severe problems within the French government aggravated the animosity between the Third Estate and the First and Second Estates.

<u>The Debt Crisis</u>

France was involved in several major wars during the 18th century and had to recover from the Mississippi Bubble, a speculation frenzy that destroyed many people's fortunes. By the 1780s, however, the most significant problem that France was experiencing was a debt crisis brought on by helping a friend.

France became a significant ally of the Americans during the American Revolutionary War, and it was probably because of French aid that the Americans even succeeded. That assistance cost a considerable amount of money. It is estimated that France spent approximately 1.3 billion livres on the war, which added to the already existing national debt. When the war ended, France was left with a debt of over 3.3 billion livres.

This debt had to be repaid by direct and indirect taxes levied on the French people. The tax collection system in France during Louis XVI's reign was inefficient. Royal tax officials collected direct taxes, but indirect taxes were farmed out to the ferme générale ("general farm") and its subsidiary, the régie générale.

The tax system complicated French tax collection. The ferme générale tax collectors were given significant authority to collect taxes and seize property if necessary. They had special privileges and legal protection. They also became incredibly wealthy because they were often corrupt.[3]

The tax system was not meeting the needs of the national budget. Debt service was the largest part of the government expenditures, and by 1780, paying off the debt amounted to 43 percent of national expenses.

<hr>

World History Encyclopedia: https://www.worldhistory.org/article/1960/the-three-estates-of-pre-revolutionary-france/.

[3] Emerson Kent.com. (2024, May 25). Taxation in Pre-Revolutionary France. Retrieved from Emersonkent.com:
http://www.emersonkent.com/history_dictionary/taxation_in_pre_revolutionary_france.htm.

Louis XVI was not blind to the problem. He knew that it had to be resolved. He appointed Charles Alexandre de Calonne to be the controller-general of French finances in 1783 and asked him to look at the situation and come up with an answer to the problem. De Calonne found a system that was in complete chaos. He audited the nation's accounts and records and scrutinized how the money was managed. His final recommendation was to tax the country across the board. This meant that those exempted from taxes or who paid very little would lose their privileges. Louis XVI was confronted with telling the aristocracy they had to pay their fair share. He did not want to do it, but the problem would not go away.

Portrait of Charles Alexandre de Calonne[43].

Additionally, getting loans to cover the debt from European banks was not an option. France was a bad credit risk. Bankers understood how much financial trouble France was in and hesitated to provide funds.[4]

[4] Sparknotes.com. (2024, May 25). The French Revolution (1789-1799). Retrieved from Sparknotes.com: https://www.sparknotes.com/history/european/frenchrev/section1/.

The problems became worse as the 1780s progressed. Finally, in 1788, the crisis came to a head. There was a bad harvest, and the state was not able to collect the money necessary to pay all the bills. The treasury was bare, and the only way to correct matters was to call the Estates General and ask that parliamentary body to come up with a solution to allow France to make ends meet.

<u>The Military of the 1780s</u>

The French military faced difficulties that undermined its effectiveness as a fighting force. The debt crisis cut into military appropriations, depriving all branches of the funds necessary to be a major military presence. Lack of funds meant there was not always enough money for training or replenishing military equipment. The nobility controlled the upper ranks of officers, and soldiers from the middle and working classes resented the lack of an equal chance to advance.

Soldiers and sailors became dissatisfied with the status quo. While they were loyal to the monarchy, they wanted better opportunities for advancement, and the customs of the Ancien Régime were blocking their path to achieve something greater. The French Revolution promised changes, and many in uniform would take advantage of the new, more egalitarian regime.

<u>The Road Leads to War</u>

The French Revolution went from a spark to a bonfire quickly. Traditions, privileges, and laws that had existed for centuries were wiped out in months. France's social and political landscape was radically changed.

The European ruling class was very concerned. It was one thing to be an enlightened despot; a constitutional monarch was something else. That meant sharing power, and the monarchs did not want that at all. They kept a worried eye on what was happening in France as news of the liberal changes spread.

The tension building up between Revolutionary France and the royal crowns of Europe finally broke. The French Legislative Assembly declared war on Austria on April 20th, 1792. An allied army of Austrians and Prussians moved into France to restore the Bourbon monarchy, and a French army was sent to stop the allied force. The two armies would meet at Valmy on September 20th. The allies had a combined force of approximately eighty-four thousand men, and they opposed a French contingent under François Christophe de Kellermann, who had forty-seven thousand troops.

Before the first cannons were fired, it appeared this would be a lopsided victory for the allies. After all, the duke of Brunswick was one of the best commanders of Europe, and he had a nearly two-to-one advantage in troops over Kellermann. Surprisingly, though, the French won. A revolutionary army of volunteers defeated a highly professional opponent. The immediate result of the battle was the abolition of the French monarchy and the creation of the first French Republic on September 22nd.[5]

The Battle of Valmy, painted by Horace Vernet.[48]

How was that possible? The French had been significantly outnumbered. It was more than courage that won the day. The French army that took the field in 1792 was transformed from the royal regiments of 1788. There was a great upswelling of patriotism in France and revolutionary zeal brought on by symbolic gestures, such as the composition of songs like "La Marseillaise."

<u>A Titanic Change</u>

The French Revolution convinced many aristocratic officers to leave France. Their departure created vacancies in the officer ranks, which were quickly filled by energetic men who had talent. The changes in command were extensive. Although 90 percent of the officers before the French Revolution were from the aristocracy, only around 3 percent of those nobles were still in the army in 1794.

---

[5] Hickman, K. (2019, September 4). French Revolutionary Wars: Battle of Valmy. Retrieved from ThoughtCo.: https://www.thoughtco.com/french-revolution-battle-of-valmy-2361106.

The French army was reorganized. There were three distinct army units: Army of the Center, Army of the North, and Army of the Rhine. France also changed the way men were called up for service. Instead of having local levies of troops, Revolutionary France employed *levée en masse*, which was a total mobilization of the population. Conscription generated massive military forces that increased the size of the French army.

Tactics also changed. The French began to use light infantry tactics that prioritized mobility. Light infantry was used more often, and skirmishers were frequently used to start engagements. The army as a whole concentrated on offensive strategies in which they took the fight to the enemy rather than sit back and wait for the enemy to come to them.[6]

An advantage the French Revolutionary Army had was its artillery. Horse artillery was first used at the Battle of Jemappes on November 6th, 1792. Although the equipment and caliber of the cannon were standard for the day, the artillerymen's esprit de corps and efficiency permitted the weapons to be fully utilized.[7]

The French became proficient in siege warfare. Encirclement and scorched earth tactics enabled them to be highly successful in siege campaigns. By using cannons and mortars, the French were able to blast holes through enemy fortifications, allowing infantry units to pour through the gaps caused by the cannonballs and shot.

Engineers were important in the French Revolutionary Army. They ensured French soldiers were well protected in the field with fascines (bundles of brushwood used for protection) and could advance across rivers on quickly constructed bridges.

Lazare Carnot helped to reform the French military during these years. He had the organizational skills to turn the French army into a highly professional fighting force. Carnot instituted the *levée en masse* and merged newly conscripted troops with veterans, allowing the newcomers to learn combat skills rapidly. His efforts gave him the moniker Organisateur de la Victoire ("Organizer of Victory").[8]

---

[6] Jensen, N. D. (2024, May 25). Organization of French Revolutionary Armies 1791-1801. Retrieved from French Empire.net: https://www.frenchempire.net/articles/armies/.

[7] Williamson, M. (2016, August 5). French Napoleonic Artillery in Action. Retrieved from Weapons and Warfare: https://weaponsandwarfare.com/2016/08/06/french-napoleonic-artillery-in-action/.

[8] Napoleonguide.com. (2024, May 25). Lazare Carnot. Retrieved from Napoleonguide.com: https://www.napoleonguide.com/carnot.htm.

The Top of the Class

The military reforms of the French Revolution unlocked a treasure trove of geniuses. The French officer corps was now defined by talent, not titles. Men rose in prominence in the ranks due to their ability to think on their feet and audaciously lead. Napoleon Bonaparte was in a class of very ambitious, highly intelligent young officers. He would rise to the top of the class by the end of the century. Part of his success was admittedly from being in the right place at the right time, but there was more to this young Corsican than just good luck. Napoleon had qualities and skills that made him great.

Initial Success

Toulon was an important French naval base on the Mediterranean coast. Royalist sympathizers had control of the city and turned the port over to an Anglo-Spanish fleet after the British commander, Vice Admiral Lord Hood, agreed to hold the city on behalf of the imprisoned child king, Louis XVII (Louis XVI was executed on January 21st, 1793). It was essential for the revolutionaries to retake the city, and on August 28th, 1793, Toulon was placed under siege by the French government.

Napoleon was given command of the besieging army's artillery after the original commander was wounded. The young captain made the most of his new assignment and conceived a plan to retake Toulon from the allies. The French attacked the forts surrounding the city on December 16th, 1793. They retook the defenses. The Anglo-Spanish forces were forced to leave Toulon, which the French officially retook on December 19th. Napoleon received credit for the victory and was promoted to brigadier general several days after the battle. It was the beginning of a series of successes for Napoleon.

Command of the Army of Italy

Napoleon's next major assignment would be the artillery commander of the Army of Italy. He would assume command of the entire Army of Italy on March 27th, 1796.

The Italian campaign that followed showcased Napoleon Bonaparte's brilliance. He took command of a demoralized army and turned it into a significant fighting force. The young general (he was only twenty-five years old!) used the cavalry, infantry, and artillery efficiently and made mobility, speed, and aggressive tactics priorities. His victories ultimately led to the Treaty of Campo Formio of 1797, which forced Austria to give up northern Italy to France.

<u>Analysis of Napoleon's Achievement</u>

The Italian campaign proved Napoleon's ability as a commander. The Army of Italy was a demoralized unit, and his leadership skills turned things around quickly. Napoleon had something that other generals did not have: charisma. He motivated his men with messages highlighting the honor, rewards, and glory that would come with victories. The commanding general also shared his troops' hardships and endured the same conditions the ordinary private had to suffer.

Napoleon was also brave. He led troops across a bridge at the Battle of Lodi (May 10th, 1796) despite withstanding fire from the enemy. He made decisions quickly and changed course if the circumstances required it. His ability to lead troops in combat conditions was exemplified at the Battle of Montenotte (April 12th, 1796). There, he split his forces and beat two opposing armies.

Bonaparte became the man of the hour in Revolutionary France. He was a general who delivered impressive victories and kept the French Republic safe from its enemies. The Egyptian campaign (1798–1801) was a serious risk, but it allowed Napoleon to use one of his military innovations to win an important victory.

The Battle of the Pyramids (July 21st, 1798) was a major confrontation between Napoleon and the Mamluk rulers of Egypt. He introduced the divisional square in that engagement. The design was straightforward: a division with three brigades was formed into three separate squares. The infantry was on the outside, the cavalry was on the inside, and the artillery was at the corners. There was nothing novel about squares; armies had long used them for defense against cavalry. However, Napoleon used the divisional square as an offensive weapon. The Mamluk army was massacred.

Napoleon was politically savvy. His understanding of the political environment made him capable of making cold-blooded decisions. He ordered French artillery to open fire on a mob of French civilians in the street battle of 13 Vendeemiaire (October 5th, 1795). Several hundred people were killed, but Napoleon's order saved the French government from dissolving.

Charles Monnet's depiction of Napoleon's opening fire on civilians."

However, his loyalty to his troops did not mean he was willing to die with them. Napoleon eventually abandoned his soldiers in Egypt and returned to France to achieve personal political objectives. Both events suggest the man was not above playing politics if it served his purposes.

The end of the 18th century saw France become a republic. It had successfully beaten its military adversaries and was a force to be reckoned with in Europe. The French Revolutionary principles of liberty, equality, and fraternity captured the imagination of people across Europe.

Tensions were growing between the social classes. People were daring to demand rights they once thought they would never have, and tempers were rising. The ruling elite needed to do something to stop the radical ideas from growing; otherwise, they might suffer the same fate as Louis XVI.

Chapter 2: The Reformation of France

The French Revolution brought enormous change to France, but there was still more work to do. Reforms were still required to end practices that had been accepted for centuries without question. France was a major laboratory of political and social improvements, and the reformation efforts continued from the 18th century to the 19th century. Napoleon would be a catalyst for these changes.

<u>The Napoleonic Code: The Beginning</u>

Napoleon became the first consul of France in 1800. He successfully maneuvered his way through the politics and intrigue of the later days of the French Republic and overthrew the Directory with the Coup of 18 Brumaire on November 9th, 1799. He was a very influential person despite his age (he was only thirty-one). He set for himself a task that, when it was completed, would affect France over two hundred years later. This was the Napoleonic Code.

The Napoleonic Code was an ambitious project, and France desperately needed it for several reasons:

- To end the legal confusion.

    France did not have a single code of law, and statutes could vary from one region to another. The Napoleonic Code would create a system of laws that could be applied uniformly across France.

- To enhance a central government.

  A standardized legal code would permit a stronger central government that could curtail regional powers held by the local judiciary.

- To encourage a more robust economy.

  Contract and property law are the basis for a strong economy. There are, of course, other rules of commerce that need to be followed as well. All of this would be part of the Napoleonic Code. In addition, foreign investors would feel more comfortable putting their money into French enterprises if they knew that the economy was stable and following set rules of conduct.

- To codify the French Revolution.

  The French Revolution changed the country, and the reforms needed to be consolidated. The Napoleonic Code would carve these changes into the fabric of French society.

The Process of Codification

An attempt to codify French law was initiated as early as 1790, but the code drafts of 1793, 1794, and 1796 were all rejected. A commission was established in December 1799, and Jean-Ignace Jacqueminot provided an outline that was rejected. Napoleon decided that once and for all, there would be a code for French law. He would use his power and influence as first consul to complete the project.

A final commission was created in 1800. It was chaired by Jean-Jacques-Régis de Cambaceeres, Second Consul of France. The work on the draft of the code was completed in 1801, and it was finally published on March 21ˢᵗ, 1804. Its original title was "Civil Code of the French," and it would be renamed the Napoleonic Code in 1807.[9]

The Parts of the Code

The Napoleonic Code's framework was influenced by an earlier codification of law, the Code of Justinian. The French version distributed French law into four sections:

---

[9] DetailedPedia.com. (2024, May 26). Napoleonic Code. Retrieved from DetailedPedia.com: https://www.detailedpedia.com/wiki-Napoleonic_Code.

1. Persons

2. Property

3. Acquisition of Property

4. Civil Procedure (This would be placed in a separate code in 1806.)[10]

The principles of the Napoleonic Code were impressive and novel for its time. Here are a few examples of what it introduced:

- All male citizens were equal before the law. Privilege based on aristocratic titles was abolished.

- Public institutions were no longer under the control of ecclesiastical authorities.

- People could enter freely into contracts, given certain limitations.

- Criminal law was strictly defined, and rules were established for civil litigation. A person was presumed innocent until proven guilty.

- Property rights were protected.[11]

The immediate impact of the Napoleonic Code on French society was clarity. Instead of a witch's brew of edicts and sometimes contradictory laws, France now had a code that could be followed anywhere in the country. The rules specified in the Napoleonic Code were in clear language that anyone could understand.

Religious dissent was tolerated under the code. This was a significant change. France had been torn apart by religious wars in the 16th century, and there were still problems of religious oppression of non-Catholics. The Napoleonic Code ended that. Freedom of religion was the accepted law of the land. Protestants and other non-Catholic groups were safe.

Of course, there were parts of the Napoleonic Code that modern society would find unacceptable. Men had greater control over their families, and women were still subordinate. Men had equal rights under the law, but these rights were not extended to women. Slavery in the colonies had been abolished during the French Revolution, but the code reinstated it.

---

[10] DetailedPedia.com. Napoleonic Code.

[11] Britannica, E. o. (2024, May 18). Napoleonic Code. Retrieved from Britannica.com: https://www.britannica.com/topic/Napoleonic-Code.

<u>The Lasting Legacy</u>

The Napoleonic Code was the legal template that European and Latin American nations copied during the 19th century, particularly by those countries that had been occupied by the French during the Napoleonic Wars. The Napoleonic Code is still the basis for the legal systems of many modern nations.

There is one interesting fact about the Napoleonic Code. The United States legal system is founded primarily on English common law with one exception. The Napoleonic Code still influences Louisiana, which was once a French possession. There is a difference in the legal standards of practice for lawyers in Louisiana as opposed to the rest of the United States. For instance, in Louisiana, laws like community property and forced heirship dictate that property acquired during marriage is jointly owned and that a portion of a deceased person's estate must go to their children. In other states, property distribution and inheritance can be more flexible and determined through wills.[12]

Napoleon's reform was made against the backdrop of the French Revolution. Radicals wanted a significant transformation of society and were not concerned about the cost. Napoleon was more pragmatic.

He recognized that French society was essentially a center-right culture. Radicals could propose social changes of tidal-wave proportions in Paris that would not take in Lyons or Provence. The French Revolution was extremely violent, and its accomplishments were bathed in French blood. Napoleon accepted the boundaries within which he could make needed reforms and avoided going too far. To him, the Reign of Terror would remain a unique historical moment and nothing more.

<u>Concordat of 1801</u>

The greatest fracture in French society during the French Revolution was the split between the secular government and the Roman Catholic Church. The French Revolution caused the deaths of thousands of clergy and the loss of church property. The radicals tried to make France as atheist as possible, but there were still millions of French who yearned for a reconciliation with the church. This was not a call for a return to

---

[12] DailyHistory.org. (2024, May 26). Why Has the French Civil Code Had a Lasting Influence on Contemporary European Law. Retrieved from DailyHistory.org:
https://www.dailyhistory.org/Why_has_the_French_Civil_Code_had_a_lasting_influence_on_contemporary_European_law.

superstition. The church had been an integral part of the social structure for thousands of communities, and it was sorely missed.

Additionally, a lack of reconciliation meant a large group of Catholics could become serious opponents of the government, which Napoleon did not want. The opportunity for an understanding between the Roman Catholic Church and the state came about thanks to the election of a new pope.

Barnaba Niccolò Chiaramonti was elected pope on March 14th, 1800, and took the papal name of Pius VII. The new pope wanted to return the faithful in France to the church, and Napoleon was tired of religious conflict in his country. The two men commenced serious negotiations in November 1800.[13]

Napoleon entered into the discussions with three objectives: the renunciation of former church property by the Roman Catholic Church, the reinstitution of the church in France with new rules for appointing bishops, and the payment of the clergy's salaries by the state. Pius VII wanted Catholicism to be the official religion of France once again. Of course, it wouldn't be that simple. There would be much back and forth on these points and others.

Fortunately, the pope was willing to be flexible and make significant concessions. His primary concern was to enable Catholics to freely practice their faith in the open and for priests to be able to do their duties unmolested. Pius wanted to ensure the church's future and allow its followers to worship peacefully. In return, Napoleon's secular power in France would be recognized.

<u>The Final Terms</u>

The talks were very constructive since both sides were hoping for an amicable resolution to the dispute. An agreement was finally reached, and the Concordat of 1801 was signed on July 15th, 1801. The following is what they agreed on:

- The Roman Catholic Church was recognized as the religion of the majority of the French citizens. This did not mean that Catholicism was the state religion, but it did concede that most French were practicing Catholics.

---

[13] Coppa, F. J. (2018, May 18). Concordat of 1801. Retrieved from Encyclopedia.com: https://www.encyclopedia.com/philosophy-and-religion/christianity/roman-catholic-and-orthodox-churches-councils-and-treaties/concordat-1801.

- The French government would appoint Catholic bishops, who would then be consecrated by the pope.

- The property lost during the French Revolution was irretrievable; the Roman Catholic Church would not regain possession of any of it, but the state would pay salaries to the clergy.

- The church was allowed to train priests in seminaries and hold public worship. Those who went to Mass could do so freely and without fear of oppression.

The radicals in France who were in favor of a robust secular government criticized the Concordat of 1801 as a betrayal of revolutionary principles. At the same time, French royalists protested the resulting centralization of power within France. Napoleon ignored the protests, and Pius VII quietly accepted the concessions. What was important was that an agreement had been reached between the government and the most powerful social force in France. Devout Catholics were now free to practice their faith and be loyal citizens as well. There would be no Catholic fifth column behind Napoleon's back in the years to come.[14]

The Concordat of 1801 was a sensible balance between a secular state and a religious institution. It was a pragmatic answer to a nagging problem and stabilized French society. The raw emotions of the French Revolution were starting to calm down as church and state were able to agree to disagree and still respect the position of each other.

Economic Changes

Napoleon had other interests he wanted to address that would create a stable French economy. France spent years operating with a financial system that was woefully inefficient, and Napoleon was committed to ending that state of affairs.

He also had a political agenda. The existing financial chaos in France had private financial institutions competing with regional banks. Napoleon wanted greater economic efficiency, and a central bank fit into his overall policy of centralization. His idea would be similar to the British Bank of England but would include achieving national economic and private commercial objectives.

Private capital was used to found the Bank of France, but state funds were also used. The Bank of France (Banque de France) would have a

---

[14] A fifth column is a group of people who undermine a larger group or the nation.

close connection with the French government, and the state appointed the governor and the two deputy governors of this financial institution. The Bank of France was permitted certain privileges. Most importantly, it was allowed the exclusive right to issue banknotes in Paris for fifteen years. The Bank of France's power to issue banknotes would later be extended to the entire country of France.[15]

The Bank of France was able to stabilize the national currency and ultimately standardize the currency in France. Public debt is always a concern for a central bank, and the Bank of France consolidated French public obligations. It allowed international and domestic confidence in France's stability to increase, and the country was able to secure loans with fewer problems than before. The restoration of confidence in French currency and its ability to manage public debt generated considerable prosperity for France in the early 19th century.

The Bank of France played a significant role in the years immediately following its creation. It supported the Napoleonic Wars by extending needed credit and financing military expenditures. Napoleon was later able to wage wars knowing there would be monetary backing for his efforts.

<u>The Lycées</u>

Napoleon's wish to centralize and standardize France also extended to education. Earlier attempts to do that during the French Revolution were not successful, but Napoleon's efforts produced positive results. A central point of his educational reforms was the lycées.

The lycées were secondary schools, and their task was to educate future administrators, professionals, and military officers in France. Beforehand, education was centered primarily on developing the aristocracy. The lycées were boarding schools that accepted students on scholarships and also paying boarders and day students. The curriculum was centered on a humanistic model of education, but it also had courses in science, mathematics, history, geography, and literature, among other areas of study. It was a broad education that would produce a well-rounded graduate.[16]

---

[15] Britannica, T. E. (2024, May 24). Banque de France. Retrieved from Britannica.com: https://www.britannica.com/money/Banque-de-France.

[16] Savoie, P. (2024, May 26). Lycée. Retrieved from Faqs.org: http://www.faqs.org/childhood/Ke-Me/Lyc-e.html.

The lycées were not established just for the sake of educating young minds. The curriculum was intended to promote critical thinking, problem-solving skills, and the intellectual capabilities that military officers needed. Successful graduates would be able to transition into French military academies without a problem and pursue further military education.

Napoleon's changes also included some very useful projects for both the economy and society at large. These included infrastructure, such as better roads, improvement of the ports, and canal work. These all contributed to the growing prosperity of a country that had been wracked by ten years of revolutionary change. All of this benefited France and made Napoleon extremely popular.

Everything Napoleon accomplished, which he did in just a few years, would become a model for others to follow in the years to come. Like the United States Constitution, the Napoleonic Code would be emulated and improved upon. The Concordat of 1801 gave nations ideas on how to manage the sometimes-tricky relationship between church and state. The critical thinking and problem-solving encouraged by the lycées are used today by highly successful educational systems worldwide.[17]

However, there was another side to all this activity. Napoleon centralized France and established standards that would do more than make the nation an economic power. France was capable of financing and conducting military campaigns that might include absorbing territories beyond its borders. Revolutionary ideals were put in their proper place, but they were not entirely forgotten. The French had the means beyond fiery rhetoric to make substantial changes in Europe.

Rulers of other countries became more concerned about what was going on in France and the possibility of these very liberal ideals coming across the French borders. Napoleon needed to be checked, if not stopped entirely. But that was not going to be easy. Napoleon Bonaparte was a phenomenon many had never seen before. If any foreign government underestimated this man, they would find out in a few years just how wrong they were to do so. Napoleon was establishing a modern society in France, but he was also creating a massive military machine that was nearly unstoppable.

---

[17] Globallytaught.com. (2024, May 26). Education Systems Around the World: A Look at 4 Top School Systems. Retrieved from Globallytaught.com: https://globallytaught.com/blog/education-systems-around-the-world/.

Chapter 3: Revolutionary Battlefield Tactics and Warfare

Military reform and innovation were ongoing in France. The reforms made to the ranks of the French Revolution continued into the 19th century. Napoleon fanned the flames of change, and the French military became the most formidable army in Europe as a result.

Nathan Bedford Forrest, a Confederate general during the US Civil War, once made an astute observation describing how an army can succeed on the battlefield: get first with the most. It means that a successful military force must be able to move quickly and deliver maximum force at the right moment. Napoleon understood this concept long before General Forrest was even born.

Napoleon changed the structure of the French army in 1800. He organized the army into corps or corps d'armée. These military units were larger than divisions and were able to operate independently of the main force.

The corps was a small army. It had its own cavalry, infantry, and artillery. The corps was intended to be able to operate by itself, and Napoleon would often have the corps separated from each other by a short distance. They could come together in major battles or be used to fight the enemy on several fronts, which could effectively outmaneuver a larger force. Separate corps could also come to the aid of another corps since they were ordinarily positioned no more than a two days' march from each other.[18]

Napoleon is credited with coining the phrase that an army marches on its stomach. That is true, but it is also correct to say that a long supply train can slow down an army during a march. Napoleon instructed his corps commanders to live off the land as much as possible. In other words, the French military was expected to collect the food and provisions they needed from local areas as they marched through them. This posed a hardship for the civilians living in the area, but it also meant that the army was not slowed down by a cumbersome supply train, nor did it rely on supply depots.

The enhanced mobility of the French army was noticeable in the field. Bonaparte could order forced marches in which his army could cover as much as thirty miles in one day. This speed allowed him to take advantage of any opponent who was trying to collect its forces or regroup. The best example of French speed and mobility happened in the Battle of Ulm. Napoleon was able to quickly surround his enemy and force them to surrender.[19]

<u>Artillery and Cavalry</u>

Both artillery and cavalry were essential to the success of the French. Napoleon emphasized mobility by using lightweight cannons. This enabled the artillery to be brought up quickly and used with devastating effect on an opposing army that was still trying to position its heavier guns. A special group of soldiers known as voltigeurs was organized to support the artillery.

The cavalry units were more than just advanced scouts for the Grand Armée. Napoleon used them as shock troops and employed massive cavalry charges to break the enemy lines and create the chaos necessary to turn the tide of battle in France's favor. The cuirassiers (cavalrymen equipped with a sword, pistols, and a cuirass, a type of armor) were ordered to charge at top speed and demoralize the enemy.

---

[18] Wesson, M. J. (2024, May 28). The Development of the Corps d'armée and Its Impact on Napoleonic Warfare. Retrieved from The Napoleon Series: https://www.napoleon-series.org/military-info/organization/c_armycorps.html.

[19] Mark, H. W. (2023, July 10). Ulm Campaign. Retrieved from World History Encyclopedia: https://www.worldhistory.org/article/2249/ulm-campaign/.

An illustration of cuirassiers.[45]

The cavalry was made even more intimidating by the use of horse artillery. These were cannons that could be moved by horse-drawn teams quickly across the battlefield. They added significantly to the power of the French army.

Psychological Warfare

Sun Tzu, the famous Chinese general and strategist, wrote that the most significant battle is not physical but psychological and that the war is waged in the mind.[20] We do not know if Napoleon read the works of this ancient military strategist, but the French commander certainly used psychological warfare to his advantage.

Napoleon employed propaganda to intimidate his opponents and used disinformation campaigns to make it appear that victory was inevitable and that no one could beat the French army. He controlled the narrative better than his enemies.

---

[20] Powerplace.org. (2023, July 28). Top 51 Timeless Sun Tzu Quotes: Mastering Strategy and Leadership. Retrieved from Powerplace.org: https://powerplace.org/blogs/quotes/mastering-strategy-and-leadership-unveiling-51-timeless-sun-tzu-quotes.

The famous painting of Napoleon crossing the Alps is overly romanticized to make Napoleon appear larger than life.[46]

His battle tactics were often intended to confuse. He feigned a retreat to lure the enemy into traps, and surprise attacks were coordinated to catch opposing armies off guard. Napoleon encouraged personal myths about his invincibility. He wanted to be viewed as unstoppable by his foes and make them doubt their ability to beat him. He was often successful on this front.

The Marshals of France

The French field marshals in the Napoleonic Wars were a stellar group; the closest in quality to them would likely be the German field marshals of the Wehrmacht in World War II. Some of these men had been with Napoleon since the Italian campaign; they hitched themselves to Napoleon's star and were richly rewarded. Historians debate on who was the best of the best in this class. We propose that the following men stand out the most. In order to avoid showing preference, we will discuss them in alphabetical order.

- Louis-Alexandre Berthier

  Louis-Alexandre Berthier did not command massive cavalry charges, but he was a very important player in the Napoleonic Wars. He was Napoleon's chief of staff for almost twenty years and was involved in nearly every major campaign. Berthier managed all logistics and planning for Napoleon's military ventures. He had remarkable administrative skills, and his loyalty to the emperor was unquestioned. He could take Napoleon's notions and turn them into easily understood orders.

  Berthier shined in the Ulm campaign, where his organization of Napoleon's instructions resulted in a total defeat of the Austrian army. However, Berthier was not in favor of gradually stretching the communication lines in the Russian campaign, which restricted the French army's ability to maintain a supply line during the harsh winter of 1812.[21]

- Jean-Baptiste Bernadotte

  Bernadotte was both a skillful administrator and an excellent field commander. He had a unique ability to move through the territory of Napoleonic politics and balance that successfully with military affairs. Bernadotte played a tactical role in the Battle of Austerlitz, which was Napoleon's most significant victory. His efforts at the Battle of Jena were not as impressive, and he was criticized for being unable to sufficiently engage the troops under his command.

  What made Bernadotte stand out was his final opposition to Napoleon. He was elected to be the successor to the king of Sweden on August 20th, 1810, and he formally became king of Sweden as Charles XIV John in 1818. The French occupation of Swedish Pomerania in 1812 and problems with the Continental System caused Bernadotte to switch sides and join the European alliance against Napoleon in 1813.[22]

---

[21] Napoleon.org. (2024, May 28). Louis-Alexandre Berthier. Retrieved from Napoleon.org: https://www.napoleon.org/en/history-of-the-two-empires/biographies/berthier-louis-alexandre/.

[22] Hickman, K. (2020, January 2). Napoleonic Wars: Marshall Jean-Baptiste Bernadotte. Retrieved

- Jean Lannes

Personal bravery and almost reckless courage distinguished Lannes from the other marshals on this list. He was a commander who was not afraid to lead from the front, which constantly exposed him to danger. Lannes could assess the situation quickly and make informed decisions at the right moment. He was one of the marshals who had been with Napoleon throughout his career.

Lannes commanded the left wing of the French army at Austerlitz. He successfully held off Russian assaults, which permitted Napoleon to move over the Pratzen Heights at a strategic moment. Lannes continued to be one of the most dependable field commanders in the Grande Armée and assisted competently in the Spanish campaign.

He died on May 31st, 1809, from wounds suffered at the Battle of Aspern-Essling. Napoleon was overcome with grief when he heard of the loss of his close friend. In a letter to Lannes's widow, he wrote, "I lose the most distinguished general of my armies, my companion arms for 16 years, and whom I consider my best friend."[23]

- Michel Ney

Napoleon referred to Michel Ney as the bravest of the brave. He was another field marshal who was willing to lead from the front. Despite his rank, Ney was devoted to his soldiers. He was deeply concerned for their welfare.

Ney's finest hour would happen during Napoleon's greatest disaster. Ney was placed in command of the rearguard during Napoleon's retreat from Moscow. According to legend, he was the last Frenchman to leave Russia, guarding the retreating troops until the last man crossed the border.[24]

---

from ThoughtCo.com: https://www.thoughtco.com/napoleonic-wars-marshal-jean-baptiste-bernadotte-2360137.

[23] Green, J. (2004, April). Napoleon Bonaparte's "Roland": Marshal Jean Lannes. Retrieved from Warfarehistorynetwork.com: https://warfarehistorynetwork.com/article/napoleon-bonapartes-roland-marshal-jean-lannes/.

[24] Green, J. (2002, April). Michel Ney's Retreat. Retrieved from Warfarenetwork.com: https://warfarehistorynetwork.com/article/michel-neys-retreat/.

Ney pledged allegiance to the restored Bourbon dynasty after Napoleon abdicated. However, he changed sides when Napoleon came back to France from his exile in Elba. Ney fought hard at the Battle of Waterloo, but his desperate cavalry charge, which did not have infantry support, was the final straw in the French defeat. Ney would later be executed for treason by the Bourbons because he returned to Napoleon's side.

• Joachim Murat

Murat was a flamboyant showman and an aggressive field commander. He was always stylishly dressed and stood out from the more conservatively dressed commanders. He also became Napoleon's brother-in-law.

What made Murat noteworthy was his ability to lead the cavalry. He could move quickly and lead cavalry assaults that made a difference in numerous battles. His attacks against the

A portrait of Joachim Murat.[47]

allied forces at Austerlitz were instrumental in sealing the final victory. Unfortunately for the field marshal, his brilliance on the battlefield was not matched by his political decisions. He became the king of Naples in 1808 and lost his throne in 1815. While trying to regain his throne, Murat was captured by the new king of Naples and died before a firing squad.

An interesting feature of Napoleon's marshals is that they performed brilliantly under his command, but when they were given independent commands, these field marshals were not as good. It was Napoleon's ability to lead and inspire that enabled these men to be heroes. Without the emperor, they were not particularly stellar.

European nations worried about the revolutionary ideas coming out of France. Greater attention should have been paid to how France was centralizing itself and, even more importantly, what changes were happening in the French military. In a few short years, France transformed from a traditional army to one full of new technologies and superior strategic thinking. It could take on one enemy or an alliance of foes and have a good chance of winning. Here are some comparisons between France and its major potential enemies: Austria, Great Britain, Prussia, and Russia.

Austria

The French army was comprised primarily of native-born Frenchmen. Every soldier spoke the same language and shared the same cultural heritage. That unity was helpful on the battlefield since orders did not need to be interpreted.

The Austrian army was a diverse mixture of Germans, Flemings, Walloons, and Italians. The military units were consequently split into various ethnicities. The most immediate problem was that a diverse army spoke several different languages, requiring delays in interpreting commands. The quality of the soldiers varied from one nationality to another.

The Austrian army was a professional unit with an excellent heavy cavalry. However, the military tactics of the Austrian army were more conservative than the French. Battlefield flexibility was not a feature of the Austrian forces. There would be dramatic reforms to the Austrian army after the defeat at Austerlitz, but the French had an overall superior quality at the start of the Napoleonic Wars.

Great Britain

The British had overwhelming naval superiority. It proved its ability against the French at the Battle of the Nile and the Battle of Trafalgar. The French navy could not compete with its rival.

At the beginning of the 19th century, the British army was a small but well-disciplined force. It would not engage with the French until the Peninsular War, and its leadership would change dramatically when the duke of Wellington was in charge. Napoleon had plans to invade Great Britain, but the British fleet prevented that.

Prussia

In 1804, the Prussian army was living with a reputation it had won decades earlier. The army had been unstoppable under the command by Frederick the Great, but it had not improved in the years since the king's death. The army was well disciplined, but its military strategy was weak compared to Napoleon's. Prussian tactics were rigid and not effective.

Prussia would pay dearly for not modernizing its military. The French rolled over the Prussians in several battles, notably at Jena. After France soundly beat the Prussians, military reforms were introduced that permitted Prussia to return to its former military greatness.

<u>Russia</u>

Russia participated in the Wars of the Second, Third, and Fourth Coalitions, but then moved to the sidelines until it was invaded in 1812. It was not a modern army when the Napoleonic Wars started.

The regiment was the largest unit in the Russian army. Soldiers were recruited from the peasantry and were roughly treated by officers. Officers were recruited from the aristocracy, which was the general practice of European armies in the 18th century. Their training was not very good.

Russian soldiers were brave and could endure severe hardships, but the army as a whole was lacking. It would take the severe defeat at Austerlitz for Russia to take the necessary steps to modernize its military.[25]

An overall assessment concludes that the French were more than a match for any or all of its enemies on the battlefield. French military innovations under Napoleon made the Grande Armée the best fighting force in Europe.

There was one final advantage the French had over their enemies. The French army was used to winning. Since Valmy, French troops had been on the battlefield with only a few short truces between active engagements. The French did lose a few battles, but they won even more. They were accustomed to being the victors on the battlefield under the direction of Napoleon.

French soldiers were confident of their success, which gave them greater morale than their opponents. The French were often outnumbered in the battles, but they were certainly not outfought. In addition, the French faced enemy troops that had to travel hundreds of miles to reach a common rendezvous point. The French corps moved close to each other and could quickly come together as a result. French soldiers fought under a uniform strategy; allied armies with different tactical maneuvers had to learn how to fight as a single force.

The French military's overall superiority would become evident in the next few years, much to the regret of the enemy.

---

[25] Napoleonistyka.atspace.com. (2024, May 28). Russian Army of the Napoleonic Wars. Retrieved from Napoleonistyka.atspace.com: Napoleonistyka.atspace.com.

Chapter 4: Napoleon's Continental Wars Begin

The Roman Republic existed for hundreds of years. It fell apart when the pressure became too much and tore at the social fabric. The empire ceased to exist when a charismatic leader with an army at his back walked onto the stage. The same happened to the French Republic.

The French Republic spent years trying to be a cohesive entity. However, the National Assembly gave way to the Reign of Terror, which then gave way to the Directory. Napoleon captured the imagination of the French people and led an army that adored him. He was declared counsel for life, but it gradually became apparent that he was more than just a representative of the people. Ultimately, the powers that be in France recognized reality, and Napoleon was crowned emperor of France. The French Republic was officially dead.

<u>The First Consul</u>

All of that didn't happen overnight, though. Napoleon seized control of the French government in the Coup of 18 Brumaire and created the French Consulate, of which he was the first consul.[26]

At the time, France was fighting a war with the Second Coalition. This war saw France pitted against an alliance of Austria, Great Britain, Russia, the Ottoman Empire, Portugal, and Naples. The allies could not

---

[26] Anne S. K. Brown Military Collection. (2024, June 4). Napoleonic Satires. Retrieved from library.brown.edu: https://library.brown.edu/cds/napoleon/time2.html.

communicate properly amongst themselves, and Napoleon took advantage of their confusion. He took his army across the Alps in May 1800 and defeated the Austrians in the Battle of Marengo on June 14th, 1800. Austria was ultimately forced to sue for peace and signed the Treaty of Lunéville on February 9th, 1801, which took Austria out of the war. Great Britain and other allies continued to fight until the British signed the Treaty of Amiens on March 25th, 1802, which led to the war's end.

France was at peace, and Napoleon had the ability to push through some of the reforms he wanted. He did not accept criticism well and did not appreciate any opposition. He declared himself the first consul for life in August 1802, but he wanted more than that. Napoleon drafted a new constitution that included succession if he should have a son, and it was increasingly clear that the type of government Napoleon wanted was not revolutionary but more authoritarian. What he really desired was a crown on his head.

<u>The Empire of France</u>

French military success and the treaties that confirmed their conquests dramatically enlarged France. France came to include Belgium, Luxembourg, Piedmont, Genoa, and the Duchy of Parma. German territory on the left bank of the Rhine was also under French control. And these are just the territorial gains. Napoleon created client states, which included the Batavia Republic, the Italian Republic (later the Kingdom of Italy), and a reconfiguration of the Swiss Confederation.

In Italy, Napoleon dissolved the Republic of Venice in 1797 and made dramatic changes to the political map of Italy. The Cisalpine Republic was created in 1797 from a union of northern Italian states. He carved the Ligurian Republic out of what was once Genoa. The Roman Republic would come into being after the Papal States were invaded, but that political entity did not last long. The Parthenopean Republic was formed in southern Italy, but it also collapsed. Finally, the Cisalpine Republic was incorporated into the Italian Republic. The Kingdom of Italy would later absorb most of these entities, but the political boundaries that had endured for centuries in Italy were gone because of Napoleon.[27]

The changes in Germany were more dramatic. Before Napoleon, Germany had been a hodgepodge of principalities, ecclesiastical states,

---

[27] Marino Berengo, C. M. (2024, June 4). Italy-The Napoleonic Empire 1804-14. Retrieved from Britannica.com: https://www.britannica.com/place/Italy/The-acquisition-of-Venetia-and-Rome.

and imperial cities. Many of these political entities were absorbed into larger ones, such as Bavaria, Baden, and Württemberg. Those states were given extra territory as a reward for being reliable French allies. They continued to be part of the French sphere of influence and provided necessary troops for Napoleon's later campaigns.

The First French Empire at its peak in 1812.[46]

The reorganization included the introduction of the social and legal reforms instituted by the French Revolution and Napoleon himself. The traditional way of governance and doing things was destroyed in a matter of a few years. Europe had not seen anything comparable to what Napoleon did since the Reformation.

Vive l'Empereur!

Napoleon was crowned emperor of France on December 2nd, 1804. It would be easy to say that personal vanity and ambition motivated Napoleon to want the imperial crown, but there was more to it than that. Personal advancement was just one of his motivations.

France was militarily successful, but its government was in shambles. The Directory was corrupt and inefficient. Order and stability were necessary for France to thrive. Napoleon was able to stabilize the government as first consul, and he wanted to continue making changes that he felt would make France better.

It is essential to remember that Napoleon Bonaparte was a true agent of change. The Concordat of 1801 and the Napoleonic Code are examples of his wish to improve French society. Additionally, he believed that he was a protector of the revolutionary ideals that had gripped France. He wanted to be able to spread those principles. The imperial title would permit him to introduce reforms into societies weighed down by antiquated traditions and privileges. However, he also wanted a dynasty, and he wanted to have the glory that came with being emperor. Nevertheless, he would use that position to bring about social change.[28]

Napoleon made one significant move before the Napoleonic Wars began. He sold Louisiana, a vast territory in the North American continent, to the newly founded United States. There is much discussion of how the Louisiana Purchase benefited the United States and gave the country valuable resources. The sale benefited France as well.

A decision had to be made on where France would concentrate its interests. Louisiana was an immense territory, but it would have to be defended. The British were on the northern border, in Canada, and could invade the French territory. All the British needed to do was take New Orleans; the rest of the land would then be more of a burden than a blessing.

Napoleon learned from the French setbacks in the Haitian Revolution, in which thousands of French soldiers died. He realized the Americas were not crucial to France.[29] The British navy was trouble enough without having to defend extensive overseas colonies.

The Coalition Wars

The Napoleonic Wars are also called the Coalition Wars because several coalitions were formed to fight off France. Sometimes, an important power would take a time-out and watch as others struggled to find a way to beat Napoleon.

---

[28] Mark, H. W. (2023, July 6). Coronation of Napoleon I. Retrieved from World History Encyclopedia.com: https://www.worldhistory.org/article/2251/coronation-of-napoleon-i/.

[29] Britannica, T. E. (2024, May 23). Haitian Revolution. Retrieved from Britannica.com: https://www.britannica.com/topic/Haitian-Revolution.

The reasons for each war varied. However, there were common themes in almost all of them. These motivations help us understand the concern Europe had about Napoleon.

- Political and Diplomatic Reasons

    European powers longed for the status quo. The nations did not want one state to dominate the continent. The French Revolution threatened this balance, and it was then substantially challenged when Napoleon scored victory after victory in the wars.

    Napoleon created satellite states that challenged the authority of larger powers, such as Austria. Napoleon went further by putting family members on the thrones of these new states.

    European monarchs believed revolutionary ideas would lead to the creation of republics. Abolishing the monarchy would threaten the power of the ruling classes. There was already a complicated tradition of alliances and royal marriages in place, which meant the European monarchs were somewhat close to each other.

- Economic and Military Concerns

    Napoleon eventually create the Continental System to severely restrict commerce, especially to Great Britain. This system would convince Russia to steer away from allying with France, as the country's economic difficulties gradually outweighed neutrality or forming an alliance with France.

    The military threat posed by the French was quite real. France's mass conscription and novel military tactics triumphed over traditional European ways of fighting wars, and the coalition armies were not prepared to effectively counter Napoleon's military genius.

    France was a social laboratory in the early 19th century. Removing traditional hierarchies, introducing new legal codes, and refining administrative practices made the European social elite consider these innovations as threats to their way of life, encouraging them to join together in alliances.

To summarize, it was a fight between the new and the old. The Ancien Régime was dying, but there were still rulers who wanted to continue a social and political order that benefited them. The reasons for forming coalitions would change over the years, but it appears that the old aristocracy of Europe was terrified of Napoleon and would go to any length to stop him.

A portrait of Napoleon.[49]

The War of the Third Coalition (1805–1806): The Cause

Napoleon's growing influence in Italy and Germany was alarming, particularly to Austria. There was a general worry that Bonaparte would not stop what he was doing and might influence disgruntled subjects into rebelling. There was an isolated incident that further provoked a response.

Louis Antoine, Duke of Enghien, was a member of the House of Bourbon. He wanted to overturn the results of the French Revolution. There was a conspiracy called the Cadoudal Affair, which was uncovered in August 1803. The plotters planned to either kidnap or assassinate Napoleon. The duke was suspected of being part of the plot, and Napoleon ordered his arrest. Even though the Bourbon prince was living in Baden, he was kidnapped by French soldiers and returned to France, where he was tried and eventually executed. His death prompted Austria and Russia to join in opposing Napoleon.

Great Britain declared war on France on May 18th, 1803. Napoleon retaliated by seizing the Electorate of Hanover and organizing an invasion of England. He assembled an army and tried to coordinate an Irish rebellion to distract the British. He had gathered 120,000 men at Boulogne by early spring 1804.

The rest of Europe had been sitting on the sidelines, but the execution of the duke of Enghien, Napoleon's coronation as emperor, and the annexation of Piedmont and Elba in 1805, which was in direct violation of treaties with Austria, alarmed Europeans to the point where other powers were willing to join Great Britain in a coalition against Napoleon.

British Prime Minister William Pitt started to shop for alliances. By August 1805, the Third Coalition had Great Britain, Sweden, Russia, Austria, Naples, and Sicily as members. Napoleon had its German client states of Baden, Württemberg, Bavaria, the Batavian Republic, the Kingdom of Italy, Etruria, and Spain.

The Third Coalition's plan of attack was for Austria to send an army into Italy. A second army would march on Bavaria. Russia was supposed to reinforce the army attacking Bavaria. Unfortunately, the Russians were impeded by poor roads in eastern Europe and moved slowly. They would not be available for an extended period, which helped the French emperor.

The Grande Armée's Quick Step

Napoleon was not waiting for things to happen. He canceled his plans to invade England to respond to the situation in Europe. He ordered an army to advance into Italy to check the Austrians there. Napoleon began moving rapidly with the rest of the army, crossing the Rhine on September 25th, 1805. This surprised the Third Coalition, who thought that Napoleon would not abandon the invasion of England. They were now dealing with a French army numbering close to 210,000 men in central Germany that was headed rapidly eastward. The Austrian army, under Austrian General Karl Mack von Leiberich, had approximately seventy-two thousand men.

Napoleon's advance through Germany demonstrated how quickly the French army could move. He did not have to worry about supply wagons because his troops were living off the land, and the corps were moving semi-independently from each other. Napoleon covered considerable ground, more than an ordinary army of the time could. Within eleven days, on October 7th, 1805, the French were at the banks of the Danube. Mack would have a difficult time responding to this.[30]

---

[30] Mark, H. W. (2023, July 18). War of the Third Coalition. Retrieved from World History

Napoleon was leaving no stone unturned, and he had excellent intelligence. Reconnaissance and a network of spies kept him informed of his enemies' movements, so he had a good understanding of the readiness of the Austrian troops. Armed with this particular, Napoleon was able to make his next move.

The Ulm Campaign

Mack was not as well informed as Napoleon. The Austrian general was still waiting for the Russians to arrive. Mack thought that the French army was not bigger than his. He had no idea that Napoleon was advancing with a force that was nearly three times larger than his own.

Napoleon crossed the Danube unnoticed by Mack. The Grande Armée was screened by its cavalry and moved to the rear of the Austrian force, effectively cutting off any possibility of retreat. Through several engagements, Napoleon gradually forced the Austrians to move to the city of Ulm by October 15th. French artillery started firing the following day, and Mack realized he and his men were surrounded. There was no sign of the Russians. Mack knew the situation was hopeless. So, he surrendered on October 20th. Napoleon had won the campaign without having to fight a major battle.[31]

An illustration of Mack surrendering to Napoleon.[50]

Encyclopedia: https://www.worldhistory.org/War_of_the_Third_Coalition/.

[31] Britannica, E. o. (2024, May 14). Battle of Ulm. Retrieved from Britannica.com: https://www.britannica.com/event/Battle-of-Ulm.

The Third Coalition was defeated, but it was not out of the fight. The Russians, under Mikhail Kutuzov, finally reached the agreed-upon rendezvous point, but they retreated. The road to Vienna was open, and Napoleon entered the Austrian capital on November 13th, 1805. The Austrians and Russians regrouped at Olmutz and had ninety thousand men ready to fight. In addition, Austrian Archduke Charles was coming up from Italy with eighty thousand men. Napoleon had to move quickly, or else he would be overwhelmed by a superior force.

<u>Ready to Deceive</u>

The Coalition army planned to cut off Napoleon from his lines of communication and force him into a decisive battle. Napoleon used a strategy of deception to confuse his enemy. He halted his forward movement and allowed the Coalition to react. Kutuzov advanced, and Napoleon led the Russian commander on by moving several miles southeast of Brunn. He was able to disguise the movement of his troops, and he concentrated nearly seventy-three thousand men behind the Goldbach River.

Napoleon did everything in his power to deceive the Russians into thinking that the French were in a weak position and vulnerable to attack. He used disinformation to paint a picture of low French morale and added to that by openly talking about possibly retreating out of the area. His schemes worked. The Third Coalition forces began maneuvering into position for a battle. The drama would take place at Austerlitz, a town located in what is now the Czech Republic.

<u>Battle of Austerlitz</u>

The Battle of Austerlitz is commonly known as the Battle of the Three Emperors, as Emperor Francis of Austria, Tsar Alexander of Russia, and Emperor Napoleon Bonaparte were present. The French were outnumbered; Austria and Russia had approximately ninety thousand troops in position. The Coalition commanders were confident of a victory thanks to Napoleon's deceptive activity. They would meet in a council of war on December 1st, 1805, to decide what to do the following day.

Emperor Francis and Kutuzov wanted to take a cautious approach. Alexander, on the other hand, was spoiling for a fight. It was finally decided that an attack would be made on the French right flank. Most of the Coalition troops would be deployed in that area. They did not know that Napoleon had deliberately weakened that point in his line to encourage an assault. The Pratzen Heights were strategically positioned, and Napoleon abandoned that high ground to further entice an enemy attack. The battle began the next day on December 2nd.

The Coalition forces took the bait and launched a major assault on the Pratzen Heights. In doing so, they caused their right flank and center to be vulnerable. The Coalition forces captured the Pratzen Heights, but Napoleon ordered a counterattack with his reserves, which overwhelmed the Coalition army. Napoleon turned his attention to the south and forced the Coalition army back. Gradually, the Coalition soldiers panicked, and they abandoned the field. The fight was over. The French had won.[32]

Austerlitz was the most significant victory Napoleon and his army won in the Napoleonic Wars. Austria signed a truce with France on December 4th, and the Treaty of Pressburg, signed on December 26th, ended Austria's involvement. Napoleon had no desire to pursue the Russians, so Alexander and his army were allowed to go home with their tails tucked firmly between their legs. Napoleon had destroyed a larger enemy in only three months.

The War of the Third Coalition showcased Napoleon's Grande Armée and its ability to be a lethal fighting force. If his enemies had not been afraid of him before, they were certainly terrified of him now.

Napoleon Bonaparte had so far proven to be invincible on the battlefield. Fighting on the water was a different story, though.

---

[32] New World Encyclopedia. (2024, June 4). Battle of Austerlitz. Retrieved from New World Encyclopedia.org: https://www.newworldencyclopedia.org/entry/Battle_of_Austerlitz.

Chapter 5: The Battle of Trafalgar: Napoleon's Defeat at Sea

Great Britain was proud of its navy, which was the finest in the world. The nation also relied on its ships as the front line of defense. Great Britain shared no borders with other nations, but the vast ocean guaranteed the country could be attacked from anywhere. The fleet had to be ready to respond to any possible threat.

The Royal Navy had to be in state-of-the-art condition to be ready, which meant keeping up with trends and introducing innovations before other navies. The Napoleonic Wars produced technological changes on the sea as well as on land. The Royal Navy responded accordingly.

A significant development occurred in the naval dockyards, especially those in Portsmouth. Great Britain invested heavily in creating wet and dry docks, which allowed the navy to speed up the repair of ships. In addition, British sailors were trained to do repair work at sea so that fighting vessels were constantly on active duty.[33]

The primary artillery piece used by the Royal Navy was the carronade. This was a smoothbore cast iron cannon that was first introduced in the 1770s. It was a short-range, anti-ship, anti-crew weapon. Its range was about half that of a long gun, and it used a much smaller propellant charge to fire cannonballs and shot. This wasn't a problem because short-range

---

[33] Hicks, P. (2024, June 4). The Royal Navy, 1793-1802. Retrieved from Napoleon.org: https://www.napoleon.org/en/history-of-the-two-empires/articles/the-british-navy-1793-1802/.

broadsides were standard naval tactics. Because this artillery piece was lighter and required a small gun crew, it permitted a ship of the line to carry more guns.[34]

There was a pressing need to construct larger ships that would be able to carry more cannons. A standard warship would have two full gun decks, with the upper deck carrying 24-pounders and the lower deck having 32-pounders. Three gun decks were not uncommon.

The HMS *Victory* is an example of a first-rate ship.[35] It had 104 guns. Other ships, such as the HMS *Royal Sovereign* and the HMS *Britannia*, had one hundred guns. The effect of a broadside from any of these warships was devastating.[36] The Royal Navy did have other kinds of warships and sloops with 12- or 24-pounder guns; these were often used to track down privateers on the open water.

The Royal Navy was using better chronometers during the Napoleonic Wars than other nations, which increased the effectiveness of the fleet. Its battle tactics were also aggressive. An excellent example is the Royal Navy's conduct at Trafalgar, which we will cover in just a moment.

Press-ganging, the kidnapping of men to serve on ships, was a common practice, but there were some advantages for a person to volunteer. The Royal Navy protected a man from creditors if the debt was less than £20. This meant that by joining the navy, a man with debt could avoid landing in a debtor's prison. Parliament passed the Quota Acts to guarantee that the navy had sufficient manpower. Every county had to supply a quota of men to the navy. It was also common practice that a convicted criminal could be given the option of going to jail or serving in the navy. Great Britain did whatever was necessary to get men on board ships.[37]

These men had to be led by good officers and commanders who knew what they were doing. Great Britain conducted several major naval operations during the Napoleonic Wars. Its greatest resource was a man who stood out for his nautical brilliance.

---

[34] A ship of the line was an enormous floating artillery battery. They were the dominant warships of their time.

[35] A first-rate ship is the largest ship in the Royal Navy fleet.

[36] Ernest McNeil Eller, R. L. (2024, June 4). Ships of the Line. Retrieved from Britannica.com: https://www.britannica.com/technology/naval-ship/Ship-of-the-line.

[37] Hicks, P. The Royal Navy, 1793-1802.

<u>Horatio the Great</u>

The Napoleonic Wars produced two men of unique military genius. They never met each other in battle, but both contributed significantly to the art of warfare. The first was Napoleon Bonaparte. The second was a sailor named Horatio Nelson.

The poet Lord Byron called him "Britannia's God of War." Horatio Nelson is considered the greatest naval commander in British history. His seamanship was the stuff of legend, which makes sense. After all, Nelson almost single-handedly frustrated Napoleon's efforts to invade Great Britain.

Nelson was born on September 18th, 1758, in Norfolk and used family connections to join the navy when he was only twelve years old. Sea voyages took young Nelson to the West Indies and the North Sea while he was still a teenager. In a time when talent meant more than years, Nelson was given command of the HMS *Badger*. He was only twenty years old.

In the last years of the 18th century, the Royal Navy was enormous. Over 660 ships flew the Union Jack, which was more than the navies of France and Spain combined. Roughly 100,000 men were in the ranks. That impressive number represented a challenge for ambitious men like Horatio Nelson.[38] All of these ships meant there were thousands of officers trying to advance in their naval careers. It would not be easy for Nelson because he did not have the years of service or aristocratic connections that others enjoyed. He would have to find another way to the top.

Of course, one way to do that is to get into the thick of a battle and risk getting killed. Horatio Nelson was not afraid. Indeed, he was known for his incredible courage and was the kind of officer who led from the front. His personal courage came at a price, though. Nelson lost an eye and an arm, among other injuries, while defending his country.

He became known as someone who inspired loyalty in the officers he commanded. Nelson was particularly close to the captains of the ships in his fleet. He referred to them as his band of brothers, and they looked up to him with love and respect. Nelson's ability to connect with his men and be brave in the face of enemy fire allowed him to advance to the highest ranks in the Royal Navy.[39]

---

[38] Hicks, P. The Royal Navy, 1793-1802.

[39] Setterfield, R. (2019, November 18). Horatio Nelson: From Frail Boy to National Hero.

A portrait of Horatio Nelson.[51]

Excellent Mentors

Two exceptional men shaped Horatio Nelson's outlook on war and battle tactics. The first was his uncle, who helped get Nelson into the navy in the first place. Captain Maurice Suckling coached his nephew on the significance of understanding gun tactics and how crucial good seamanship was for success. Nelson's early years at sea included time in the Mediterranean and service during the American Revolutionary War. He served under Admiral Lord Hood. Thanks to Hood, Nelson received command experience and was exposed to various naval strategies and battle tactics. Surprise and aggression were two primary lessons he

Retrieved from Onthisday.com: https://www.onthisday.com/articles/horatio-nelson-from-frail-boy-to-national-hero.

learned. By the time the French Revolution had broken out, Horatio Nelson had been in the navy for nearly twenty years. Almost half of that time had been spent as the commander of a ship. He was a well-seasoned veteran.

<u>Fighting the Revolutionary French</u>

At the start of the French Revolution, the Royal Navy vessels were the wooden walls protecting Great Britain from any major invasion. The navy also was responsible for protecting trade routes, which were essential for Great Britain's economic survival.

There were encounters with the French during this time. The first was the Battle of Ushant, also known as the Glorious First of June, fought on June 1st, 1794, at the southwestern end of the English Channel. A grain convoy was sailing toward France, and the British fleet under Lord Richard Howe moved to intercept it. Both sides claimed victory; the British sunk seven French ships, but the French were able to get the grain convoy through friendly ports.

A tactical innovation made this battle memorable. Ordinarily, opposing fleets would line up in a row facing each other and proceed to blast away. The British commander Lord Howe did something different. Instead of forming a battle line, Howe ordered his ships to attack the French directly. Every British ship was ordered to engage the enemy ship closest to it, which surprised the French.

Another significant battle was the Battle of Cape St. Vincent, which took place on February 14th, 1797. This was an encounter between the British fleet, commanded by Admiral John Jervis, and the Spanish fleet off Cape St. Vincent, Portugal. Nelson was a principal player in this engagement.

Displaying his trademark audacity, Nelson acted independently and broke out from the British line to attack Spanish ships. He sailed into the enemy squadrons and, at one time, at least according to legend, was fighting seven Spanish vessels. Nelson personally boarded and captured one ship and then boarded and took another. His actions earned him a knighthood, and he became a national celebrity. He was also promoted to rear admiral.[40]

---

[40] Pock, T. (2024, June 4). Battles of Cape St. Vincent and the Nile. Retrieved from Britannica.com: <u>https://www.britannica.com/biography/Horatio-Nelson/Battles-of-Cape-St-Vincent-and-the-Nile</u>.

Battle of the Nile

This engagement, also known as the Battle of Aboukir Bay, was fought from August 1st to August 3rd, 1798. Nelson chased a French fleet carrying an expeditionary force under Napoleon Bonaparte to invade Egypt. He was hot on the tail of the French ships and missed catching up to them several times. The French were able to land in Egypt and anchored in Aboukir Bay.

As soon as Nelson spotted the French vessels, he ordered an attack. He split his fleet into two squadrons, one passing between the French and the shore and the other striking from the seaward side. The French fleet was destroyed, and Napoleon was stranded in Egypt. Nelson had again shown his audacity.

Battle of Copenhagen

The Battle of Copenhagen was fought on April 2nd, 1801, in the harbor of the Danish capital.

The League of Armed Neutrality was an alliance whose members were Denmark, Sweden, Prussia, and Russia. Its intention was to protect the member nations' trade and cut Great Britain off from valuable timber supplies. A British fleet was sent to the Baltic to break the coalition and neutralize the Danish Navy.

There was an attempt to diplomatically resolve the problems, but it went nowhere. Nelson decided to act and launch an attack on Danish and Norwegian ships protected by shore batteries. He was ordered by the British commanding admiral, Sir Hyde Parker, to disengage. A legend of the battle says that Parker placed the signal to Nelson, ordering Nelson to break off the attack. Nelson was blind in one eye and was looking through his telescope using his blind eye. He claimed he didn't see Parker's signal and continued the fight. Eventually, the British admiral was successful and negotiated an indefinite armistice. Once again, Horatio Nelson was the man of the hour.

A Grand Deception

Trafalgar is recognized as one of the fifteen most decisive battles in world history. It was an epic confrontation between the Royal Navy and the combined Franco-Spanish fleet. It had an impact on the Napoleonic Wars, and it was the capstone of Horatio Nelson's career. This battle was not an isolated event but rather part of a strategy that, if it succeeded, might have resulted in Napoleon's invasion and conquest of Great Britain.

A sort of arms race occurred in the early 19th century. The British had naval superiority, and the French were trying to match the size of the Royal Navy. The French were able to come close to that by bullying Spain into an alliance that allowed the French and Spanish fleets to be combined. The possibility of matching the British one on one would help Napoleon in one of his most ambitious military plans.

Napoleon wanted Great Britain out of the way. He considered the British to be a nuisance and a distraction to his Continental plans. Unfortunately for him, the ocean protected the island country. Bonaparte would need to neutralize the British fleet long enough to launch a massive invasion of Great Britain. He had an idea that he was convinced might work.

Napoleon planned to trick the Royal Navy into making Britain vulnerable to attack. What the French emperor had in mind was for the French fleet based in Toulon to run the British blockade of that port and get out into the open waters of the Mediterranean. From there, the French would rendezvous with the Spanish fleet and sail toward the Caribbean. Napoleon gambled that the British would take the bait and chase the Franco-Spanish fleet to the Americas. Eventually, the Franco-Spanish ships would turn and speed back to the English Channel and meet up with French and Spanish squadrons. Napoleon would thus have control of the English Channel for a few days until the pursuing British ships arrived. Those few days would be enough for Napoleon to transport his massive army in Boulogne across the Channel and invade England.

The commander of the French fleet, Vice Admiral Pierre-Charles de Villeneuve, sailed out of Toulon in late March 1805. Nelson, who was commanding ships in the Mediterranean, thought the French were headed toward Egypt. He later found out they were headed toward the West Indies and pursued them, but the French had a three-week head start.

Villeneuve made it to Martinique but then turned around to head back to Europe when he discovered that Nelson had arrived in the Caribbean. Instead of heading straight for the English Channel, the French admiral sailed his ships to Cádiz, Spain.[41]

[41] Encyclopedia.com. (2018, May 23). Battle of Trafalgar. Retrieved from Encyclopedia.com: https://www.encyclopedia.com/history/modern-europe/wars-and-battles/battle-trafalgar.

Villeneuve's ships anchored in the Cádiz harbor, and Nelson established a blockade. Napoleon became angry with Villeneuve and ordered the admiral to break out of Cádiz, sail to Naples, and support French activity in Italy. Villeneuve hesitated and spent the late summer trapped in the Spanish port. He finally received word that he was in danger of being replaced, which prompted him to take action. He ordered his fleet to sail on October 19th, 1805.

Nelson was aware of what Villeneuve was doing and prepared his ships. He ordered a general chase, and on October 21st, the British fleet was only a few miles away from the Franco-Spanish ships. Villeneuve had thirty-three ships of the line, and Nelson had twenty-seven. Despite being outnumbered, Nelson had supreme confidence in the men and officers he commanded. At 11:48 a.m., he hoisted the signals that were later memorialized: "England expects that every man will do his duty."

There was a following message: "Engage the enemy more closely."[42]

The engagement was about to begin.

<u>The Battle of Trafalgar</u>

Horatio Nelson rarely played by the book, and his battle plan was not standard. He would not set his ships in a line parallel to the enemy for broadsides. Instead, Nelson split his ships into two columns and instructed his captains to break through the opposing line perpendicularly. This would make close-quarters combat easier to perform, and that was where the British sailors were best. It would be a tricky maneuver, but Nelson had great faith in his captains.

Nelson led one column in his flagship, HMS *Victory*, and broke through the enemy line. The battle quickly turned into single-ship engagements, and the HMS *Victory* attacked the French flagship, the *Bucentaure*. Nelson's attack on the enemy's flagship disrupted the communications of the Franco-Spanish fleet. The battle raged all afternoon on October 21st. Villeneuve surrendered at 1:45 p.m., and the struggle ended by 4:30 p.m. Nelson had won a stunning victory. It would be his last.

The vice admiral was walking the deck of his ship when he was cut down by a French sniper firing from the *Redoubtable* at approximately 1:15 p.m. The bullet went through Nelson's shoulder and chest. He

<hr>

[42] Royal Navy. (2024, June 4). Trafalgar Day. Retrieved from Royalnavy.mod.uk: https://www.royalnavy.mod.uk/news-and-latest-activity/events/national/171021-trafalgar-day.

received word that the British won the battle, and his last words were, "Now I am satisfied. Thank God I have done my duty." With that, the greatest naval commander in British history died.[43]

Horatio Nelson had given his eye, an arm, and his life in the service of his country. The Franco-Spanish fleet at Trafalgar suffered a terrible defeat. Twenty-two ships were captured or destroyed. The British did not lose one ship.

The consequences of the victory were significant. Great Britain had total control of the sea, and Napoleon's plan to invade Great Britain was destroyed. The French navy would not be a significant factor in the rest of the Napoleonic Wars. Napoleon would turn his attention to mainland Europe. Although the French lost at Trafalgar, they were winning on land. For instance, Napoleon would win at Austerlitz just a few weeks later. His star was still ascending, but he would eventually make a major mistake.

---

[43] Pocock, T. (2024, June 4). Horatio Nelson at Trafalgar. Retrieved from Britannica.com: https://www.britannica.com/biography/Horatio-Nelson/Victory-at-Trafalgar.

Chapter 6: Napoleon's Zenith

The ink was barely dry on the treaty that ended the War of the Third Coalition before another alliance was created to oppose France. The Fourth Coalition included Prussia, Russia, Great Britain, Saxony, and Sweden. Each had their reasons for seeking a fight with Napoleon. The agenda of each reflects the political dynamics that were taking place in Europe and the threat that Napoleon posed to the status quo.

<u>Prussia Steps In</u>

Prussia stayed out of the wars of the Second and Third Coalitions, watching events develop from the safety of neutrality. Not taking sides was a good idea, but it did not sit well with the Prussian upper class and military. These aristocrats and generals believed that Prussia had to play a dominant role in German affairs, and Napoleon's creation of the Confederation of the Rhine disturbed them. They were champing at the bit to reassert Prussian influence in central Europe.

<u>The Curse of Frederick</u>

Frederick the Great was a military genius. He reigned in the 18th century. His battle tactics and strategies in the War of the Austrian Succession and later in the Seven Years' War were admired and studied. Prussia's reputation for martial excellence stemmed from Frederick's achievements. In 1806, this proved to be an albatross around Prussia's neck.

Twenty years after Frederick's death, the Prussian military had changed very little. The generals adhered to the battle tactics of the great king and did not see any reason to change. Frederick's deeds made the Prussians overconfident. They were convinced that a well-disciplined Prussian army was more than a match for a crowd of French conscripts.

The Prussians were making a terrible mistake, though. Prussian soldiers had not been in combat since 1795, while the French regiments had almost constantly fought. If nothing else, the French were seasoned veterans. The Prussians, however, still believed they would be superior on the battlefield, and they also believed in their own legends.

There was also the matter of national honor. Many Prussians, especially those in the officer corps, felt humiliated by not participating in the earlier coalition wars. These people believed they could have made a difference and stopped Napoleon. The Prussians had not paid close attention to the French and were confidently walking into a disaster.

Russia

Russia was still at war with France when the Fourth Coalition was formed. The Russians had been beaten at Austerlitz, so they knew of the strength of the French army. Nevertheless, Russia was concerned about the creation of the Confederation of the Rhine and France's growing influence in Europe. The tsar's government was worried that Napoleon would extend his interests into eastern Europe, an area that was part of Russia's sphere of influence.[44]

There was also a degree of personal prestige. Tsar Alexander I believed Russia should be a principal player in maintaining the status quo of Europe. He felt that Russia needed to counterbalance Napoleon. Moreover, Alexander had aspirations of military glory despite the Russians' humiliating defeat at Austerlitz.

Great Britain's Sterling Assistance

Great Britain had an enormous navy, but its army was considerably smaller. The Royal Navy could control the sea and protect the trade routes of the Fourth Coalition during the war, but there was something else that Great Britain provided, which was a considerable contribution to the war effort: the pound sterling.

The ravages of war did not touch the British economy, and the country's overseas trade thrived. The French navy could no longer stop British ships from carrying goods overseas, and Great Britain had the financial means to conduct a war without suffering significant casualties.

---

[44] Mark, H. W. (2023, July 28). War of the Fourth Coalition. Retrieved from World History Encyclopedia: https://www.worldhistory.org/War_of_the_Fourth_Coalition/.

The British banking system was superior to anything on the Continent. It was able to subsidize its allies without straining the economy. Government loans and taxes were used to finance the costs incurred in the Napoleonic Wars, which, by the end of the conflicts, totaled over £1.6 billion. Great Britain could not provide large armies until later in the war, but its financial support was worth an entire army corps.[45]

The British involvement in the Fourth Coalition continued its hostility with France. That mutual animosity was sufficient for Great Britain to ally against France, and checking Napoleon's expansionism was part of British national policy.

The Others

Sweden played a minor role in the Fourth Coalition. Its primary concern was to counterbalance Napoleon and preserve Sweden's dominant role in northern Europe. Saxony was in the war as an ally of Prussia and would later change sides.

The War Begins

Prussia issued an ultimatum to Napoleon on October 1st, 1806. The Prussians demanded that all French troops on the west side of the Rhine be removed. Furthermore, Napoleon was to recognize the North German Confederation, which Prussia dominated. Napoleon was willing to acknowledge the confederation, but the war party in Prussia was demanding action. On October 9th, 1806, King Frederick William III of Prussia formally declared war on France.

The terms of Prussia's ultimatum suggest that it was worded to leave Napoleon little choice but to ignore it, thereby giving a legitimate reason for Prussia to declare war. In any event, the declaration was strategically a mistake. There were already French troops in Germany. Napoleon could immediately respond. In fact, Napoleon had anticipated the declaration of war, and on October 8th, the Grande Armée crossed over into Saxony. The actual fighting started earlier than the Prussians were expecting.[46]

Prussia underestimated how quickly the Grande Armée could move. Conventional warfare assumed it would take several weeks before major armies could face each other. Prussia would be taking on France without Russia's support, which was still re-mobilizing.

---

[45] Colley, L. J. (2024, June 8). The Napoleonic Wars. Retrieved from Britannica.com: https://www.britannica.com/place/United-Kingdom/The-Napoleonic-Wars.

[46] Mark, H. W. War of the Fourth Coalition.

Napoleon marched his army in three separate columns to southern Thuringia. Each corps was within easy support distance of the other, permitting the French military to be flexible enough to meet the enemy under any conditions. The first contact between the Prussians and the French was on October 9th, 1806, at the Battle of Schleiz, and there was another engagement on October 10th at Saalfeld.[47]

The Prussians followed their traditional military procedures and were caught off guard by Napoleon's quick movement. The Prussians lost their popular commander, Prince Louis Ferdinand, at the Battle of Saalfeld and retreated to Jena.

<u>Battle of Jena-Auerstedt</u>

The war was only five days old when the decisive Battle of Jena-Auerstedt occurred on October 14th.

To take advantage of the field at Jena-Auerstedt, Napoleon had his corps execute a flanking movement north and east. One corps under Marshal Louis-Nicolas Davout outmaneuvered the Prussians and defeated them. Prussian attempts to successfully counterattack failed, and Frederick William III eventually ordered a withdrawal. Marshal Murat's cavalry pursued the retreating Prussians. Thousands of Prussians were either captured or cut down.

The Prussians suffered a total defeat in these two battles. The French pursued the beaten army, preventing it from regrouping to counterattack. Napoleon entered Berlin, Prussia's capital, on October 24th, 1806. Frederick William III still wanted to fight and fled to Königsberg. What was left of the Prussian army was gradually destroyed, as the French marshals, Bernadotte, Soult, and Marat, pursued them. Prussian General Gebhard von Blücher surrendered his command on November 7th, 1806, as Lübeck fell to the French.[48]

The Berlin Decree, issued on November 21st, 1806, highlighted Napoleon's stay in Berlin. This imperial order ordered an embargo on all British trade goods in those territories controlled or allied to the French. The French emperor also used this time to come to an understanding with

---

⁴⁷ Anonymous. (2024, June 8). War of the Fourth Coalition. Retrieved from Resources.saylor.org: https://resources.saylor.org/wwwresources/archived/site/wp-content/uploads/2011/05/War-of-the-Fourth-coalition.pdf.

⁴⁸ Mark, H. W. (2023, June 19). Battle of Jena-Auerstedt. Retrieved from World History Encyclopedia: https://www.worldhistory.org/article/2256/battle-of-jena-auerstedt/.

the Electorate of Saxony. Saxony joined the Confederation of the Rhine and was subsequently made a German kingdom.[49]

The Polish Campaign

The Prussians were eliminated as an effective threat, but the Russians remained. The Russians could not assist the Prussians earlier, but by December 1806, Russian troops had been sent to reinforce what was left of the Prussian resistance. The Russian force numbered nearly eighty thousand men. There were still some logistical problems, and the rapid French advance caused the troops to move before they were ready, but the Russians were on the march. They were under the command of General Levin August von Bennigsen. The fighting to come would take place in Poland and East Prussia.[50]

Poland had endured the humiliation of being gradually partitioned out of existence in 1772, 1793, and 1795. Napoleon entered Warsaw on December 19th to the sound of cheering crowds. The Polish hoped the French emperor would restore the Polish nation.

This was a unique opportunity for Napoleon. He could punish the Prussians by taking the land seized in the partitions and create a client state that bordered Russia. Accordingly, Napoleon established the Grand Duchy of Warsaw, which would be governed by a new French ally, Frederick Augustus, King of Saxony.

Operations against the Russians

Even today, winter is a terrible time of the year to campaign. Napoleon ordered his troops forward to cross the Vistula River and gain ground before winter set in. The French moved forward under poor traveling conditions and fought a Russian force at Pultusk on December 26th. Both sides went into winter quarters after that; they would not meet again until February 1807.[51]

Battle of Eylau

Napoleon fought two battles with the Russians in the Fourth War of the Coalition. The first Franco-Russian confrontation took place in the town of Eylau on February 7th, 1807. The French army comprised

---

[49] Mark, H. W. Battle of Jena-Auerstedt.

[50] Napoleon & Empire. (2024, May 14). Battle of Eylau. Retrieved from Napoleon & Empire.net: https://www.napoleon-empire.net/en/battles/eylau.php.

[51] Mark, H. W. (2023, July 24). Battle of Eylau. Retrieved from World History Encyclopedia: https://www.worldhistory.org/article/2258/battle-of-eylau/.

approximately fifty thousand men, and the Russians had sixty-five thousand.

Napoleon wanted a decisive confrontation with the Russians and planned to strike quickly with an insurmountable force. The Russians might have learned something from the defeat at Austerlitz, though. Despite outnumbering the French, the Russian commander, Bennigsen, took a defensive position. He hoped that the French assault on his lines would expose weaknesses that the Russians could then exploit.

The main battle began on February 8th. The two sides started with an artillery duel that lasted for several hours. Both sides attacked and counterattacked, with the French and Russians giving ground only after a fierce resistance. At one point, there was hand-to-hand fighting in the town's streets. The Russians came close to seizing Napoleon's headquarters; the French emperor was even at risk of being captured. All of this happened during a winter blizzard.

The decisive moment in the battle came with an enormous cavalry charge led by Murat. The chaos that ensued among the Russians permitted Napoleon to re-form his lines. The timely arrival of Russian reinforcements prevented a rout. The battle eventually ended late at night on February 8th. It ended as a draw, with both sides suffering heavy casualties.[52]

The Russians proved they could stand up to the French. Napoleon expected to overwhelm them, but the Russians' use of defensive positions and timely counterattacks prevented that from happening. Moreover, the Russians retreated in good order and would fight the French again.

<u>Battle of Friedland</u>

Eylau was not the smashing victory that Napoleon had hoped to obtain. The Grande Armée needed some time to rest and resupply. Napoleon decided to wait until the regular fighting season began once again. In the meantime, he asked for reinforcements from French allies and called for French conscripts to arrive early. Skirmishes were fought between the French and the Russians in the following weeks. Danzig fell to the French on May 24th, 1807. Reinforcements flowed in, and Napoleon was ready to return on the offensive. He decided that June 10th would be the day to start moving forward. The Russians forced him to change his mind.

---

[52] Mark, H. W. Battle of Eylau.

Bennigsen saw an opportunity. He attacked Field Marshal Ney's corps at Guttstadt-Deppen. The Russians were beaten, and Napoleon decided to cut Bennigsen from his supply base in Königsberg. He used a deceptive tactic; he permitted a messenger to be captured by the Russians. The French soldier was carrying false news that the Grande Armée was about to launch an attack on the Russian rearguard. Bennigsen took the bait and moved his troops to a well-defended position at Heilsberg. On June 10th, Napoleon attacked, but the Russians won a tactical victory. Bennigsen went on the offensive and crossed the Alle River to fight the French on the western bank. He did not realize that he was walking into a trap.

Marshal Lannes led his corps to confront the Russians on the morning of June 14th, 1807, pulling the Russians back long enough to allow Napoleon to bring the rest of the army into position. He ordered an artillery barrage that covered an attack by Marshal Ney's corps on the Russian left flank. Bennigsen ordered a cavalry counterattack, but Ney was reinforced before his line broke. French artillery raked the Russian lines, and the French infantry pressed the Russians up against the banks of the river. Ultimately, Bennigsen ordered a general retreat, and what was left of the Russian army marched (or swam) back over the Alle. Napoleon had won a significant victory.[53]

The Russians fought with considerable courage against superior forces in all of the battles. Their major problem in each engagement was their inability to respond to quick changes on the battlefield. Napoleon's army could move rapidly. One corps could come to the aid of the other before the Russians could effectively respond. There was no doubting the bravery of the Russian soldiers, but changes needed to be made if they could have any hope of defeating Napoleon.

The fighting was over. The allies of the Fourth Coalition could not field an army to meet the French adequately, and a peace treaty had to be hammered out. It was expected that the terms would be to Napoleon's advantage.

Napoleon intended to complete France's domination of Europe at the expense of any remaining rivals. He wanted his new Continental System to be recognized by all of Europe, and he hoped that would be sufficient enough to bring Great Britain to its knees. The Holy Roman Empire,

[58] Mark, H. W. (2023, July 25). Battle of Friedland. Retrieved from World History Encyclopedia: https://www.worldhistory.org/article/2259/battle-of-friedland/.

which had lasted for nearly a thousand years as a dominant presence in central Europe, would be relegated to the dustbin of history. Napoleon wanted a European map consisting of either allies or satellite states.

However, a primary concern was Russia. Despite the losses, Russia was still a significant power and could field large armies. Napoleon wanted to neutralize any possible future threat Russia might pose, making any further coalitions against France impossible.

<u>Napoleon and Alexander</u>

The Russian town of Tilsit would be the scene of the negotiations. Napoleon and Alexander conferred on a raft in the middle of the Nieman River on June 25th, 1807. The meeting between the two emperors was one of mutual respect and an understanding of the needs both had. In retrospect, Napoleon was more than generous.

In return for joining the Continental System, France would aid Russia in its disputes against the Ottoman Empire. Alexander agreed to evacuate Wallachia and Moldavia and give France the Ionian islands and the town of Cattaro (now Kotor, Montenegro). Napoleon compensated for the losses by recognizing the sovereignty of the Duchy of Oldenburg in addition to other small countries in Germany that belonged to Alexander's relatives. The peace treaty between France and Russia was formalized on July 7th, 1807.

A French medallion showing the two rulers embracing each other.[59]

Prussia did not get off easy. Napoleon was in no mood to be kind to the enemy who started the fight. Frederick William III would lose nearly half of his nation. The client states that Napoleon wanted to create included the Kingdom of Westphalia, the Grand Duchy of Warsaw, and the Free City of Danzig. Bialystok became a Russian possession, and Cottbus now belonged to Saxony. Prussia's army was reduced to only forty-three thousand men, and a monetary tribute was later imposed on Prussia. Frederick William III had no bargaining chips and could only agree to the terms. The Franco-Prussian treaty was formalized on July 9th, 1807.

Prussia paid dearly, both politically and economically, for losing the war. Napoleon probably wanted to demonstrate to the rest of the world that while he could be lenient with a former enemy like Russia, he could be ruthless with another.

Napoleon was at the zenith of his power. He had defeated one European rival and destroyed the other. No sane monarch in Europe would try to go up against him. Great Britain remained a French rival, and hostilities continued between the two nations. The Continent, however, belonged to Napoleon.

Chapter 7: The Peninsular War: Napoleon's Struggle in Spain and Portugal

Napoleon was undoubtedly a genius, but he was also a man. He was human, which means he was capable of making mistakes. Bonaparte was at the height of his power when he started making mistakes that would ultimately bring him down. Three major missteps happened between the years of 1806 and 1808.

<u>The Continental System</u>

Napoleon held the British in contempt, but the Battle of Trafalgar ended his plans of invading Great Britain. So, the French emperor decided to take a different tack. He would destroy British trade and bring his enemy to their knees economically.

He issued the Berlin Decree on November 21st, 1806. This was Napoleon's response to the British blockade that seriously restricted commerce in France and other areas of Europe that France controlled. The decree banned British ships from coming into European ports. Napoleon went a step further on December 17th, 1807, with the Milan Decree. This permitted French warships to seize ships that were sailing from British ports or countries that were under British influence. The Milan Decree forbade European countries from trading with Great Britain.[54]

---

[54] History Skills. (2024, June 10). What Was Napoleon's Revolutionary Continental System and

Special agencies were established to enforce the decrees and confiscate any British merchandise that were found in the holds of the ships. It was a 19th-century version of the trade sanctions that are commonly used today.

There was another reason for these restrictions. Napoleon wanted to promote French commerce and develop stronger economic relations with the satellite states of Europe. He wanted to develop self-sufficiency in European economies so they did not rely on British manufacturers. Napoleon used his power to force French-controlled nations and allies to comply. In addition, neutral states, such as Denmark, were forced to be part of the Continental System. Russia was required to be a participant because of the Treaty of Tilsit.

Napoleon was seriously mistaken if he thought that he could do permanent damage to Great Britain with the Continental System. British maritime commerce had been well established for centuries. Although there was some initial inconvenience, and adjustments had to be made, Great Britain still engaged in international trade. British merchants made up for any losses caused by the Continental System by increasing trade relations with the Americas and other parts of the world. Moreover, the British produced high-quality goods, which were still in high demand in Europe.

Widespread Noncompliance

It was easy enough to issue decrees, but the hard part was trying to enforce them. The French no longer had a viable navy, and the British were able to protect any ships flying the Union Jack. Smuggling became a major industry under the Continental System. It is estimated that over eight hundred smuggling vessels were operating in the Mediterranean in 1811. Ports such as Thessaloniki and Malta became principal smuggling hubs. Despite the embargo, Great Britain was able to export £10 million worth of goods to southern Europe in 1809.[55]

The Continental System had a negative effect on Europe, though. European manufacturers had to deal with the shortage of raw materials, and several major Italian industries came close to bankruptcy. The situation became so bad that the king of Holland refused to enforce the

---

How Did It Shape Modern Europe. Retrieved from Historyskills.com: https://www.historyskills.com/classroom/modern-history/continental-system/.

[55] Mark, H. W. (2023, August 3). Continental System. Retrieved from World History Encyclopedia.com: https://www.worldhistory.org/Continental_System/.

Continental System because of its adverse impact on the Dutch economy. Incidentally, that monarch was Louis Bonaparte, Napoleon's brother. The French Emperor forced Louis to abdicate and annexed Holland to France. However, Louis Bonaparte was not the only European ruler who ignored the restrictions. Joachim Murat, who had once been a French field marshal and became the king of Naples, did nothing to stop the smuggling in his own kingdom.[56]

Furthermore, the Continental System damaged relations with other countries. Portugal refused to be part of it, and Russia eventually withdrew. Even France suffered because of the embargo. Ultimately, Napoleon was forced to issue the St. Cloud Decree that allowed southwestern France and Spain to have a degree of trade with Great Britain and reopen French trade with the United States. Unfortunately, significant damage had already been done. The Continental System would lead to other bad decisions by Napoleon that resulted in costly military campaigns.

<u>Family Ties</u>

Napoleon wanted to have people on the thrones of conquered countries whom he could trust; he did not want to be backstabbed by anyone. The only people Napoleon could trust completely were his family.

Also, even though he had an imperial title, Napoleon wanted to spread the ideas of the French Revolution to other parts of Europe. It would be easier for him to implement these ideals if people he could trust were in power. Napoleon likely believed his family members would also introduce a degree of stability that had been absent in the preceding years.

Whenever his motivations were, Napoleon consistently placed his relatives in charge of European countries. His plan was not entirely successful.

Here is a short list of who Napoleon entrusted with nations:

- Joseph Bonaparte was originally made the king of Naples and was later made king of Spain.

- Louis Bonaparte was made king of Holland.

- Jerome Bonaparte was made king of Westphalia.

---

[56] Mark, H. W. Continental System.

- Elisa and Pauline Bonaparte were not major queens, but Elisa was made princess of Lucca and Piombino (a client state in Italy) and later became grand duchess of Tuscany. Pauline became duchess of Guastalla (a town in Italy).

- Napoleon's youngest sister, Caroline Bonaparte, became queen consort of Naples and Sicily when her husband, Joachim Murat, was made the king.[57]

The record of the Bonaparte family as rulers was mixed. There were times when they were competent, and there were times the Bonapartes fell short of the mark. Joseph showed some ability when he was king of Naples, but his time as king of Spain bordered on disaster. He was not able to perform adequately due to the resistance from the Spanish people. Louis was sympathetic to the Dutch people, and he promoted various projects and reforms to enhance their well-being. However, he got into trouble with Napoleon when he resisted the Continental System. As mentioned, Napoleon finally annexed Holland and forced his brother to abdicate. Although Jerome implemented the Napoleonic Code and got rid of the old privileges of the aristocracy, he was in over his head when it came to financial matters. He was criticized for maintaining an opulent lifestyle and had a terrible time trying to balance the budget. Napoleon's sisters ruled over relatively small territories. Elisa had good administrative skills, but she relied too much on French support.

The Continental System and the need to supply troops for their brother's military campaigns created an economic strain on the countries governed by the Bonapartes. While each tried to be accepted by their subjects, it became increasingly difficult as the demands of the Napoleonic Wars became greater.

Nationalism was a major stumbling block for the Bonapartes. They were foreigners and had no viable connection to the countries they ruled. It was the French army that kept these people in charge, and if the army moved on, they found they would not be in power for long. Napoleon's inability to appreciate nationalism's ability to inspire fierce emotions would cause him to make a very expensive error in judgment.

---

[57] Napoleon.org. (2020, December). Napoleon I and His Family. Retrieved from Napoleon.org: https://www.napoleon.org/en/young-historians/napodoc/napoleon-i-and-his-family/.

The Peninsular War

To talk about the Peninsular War, we have to back up in time a bit. In the late 18th and 19th century, Spain was not the imperial power it had been in the 16th and 17th centuries. The War of the Spanish Succession stripped the country of significant European possessions, and Spain gradually became a backwater in European politics.

It still had its empire, though. The Bourbon rulers took steps to develop Spanish possessions in the Americas and make improvements in colonial administration. Efforts were made to revitalize the mining industry, particularly the extraction of silver. The Free Trade Act of 1778 made it easier for Spanish ports in the Americas to do business with other ports. Improvements were made in the education system, and the demands made for tribute on indigenous people were reduced.

Charles III hoped to use the ideas of the Enlightenment to modernize Spain, but his successor, Charles IV, relied too much on his first secretary of state, Manuel de Godoy, whose policies were unpopular.

The Spanish monarchy was concerned about what was going on in France during the French Revolution. They worried that similar problems could surface in Spain. The execution of Louis XVI convinced Spain to join the First Coalition and wage the War of the Pyrenees (1793–1795) against France. That war concluded with the Treaty of Basel. Spain gave its eastern portion of Hispaniola to France. A shift in foreign policy resulted as a consequence of the loss. Spain

A portrait of Manuel de Godoy.[58]

decided to ally itself with the French Republic. The Treaty of San Ildefonso of 1796 made the two countries allies, and Spain agreed to cooperate with France in a war against Great Britain.[58]

---

[58] Britannica, T. E. (2024, April 30). Peninsular War. Retrieved from Britannica.com:

The alliance proved to be a mistake for Spain. The nation was involved in the Anglo-Spanish War from 1796 to 1802, and a British blockade deprived Spain of products from the American colonies. Moreover, the Spanish Navy suffered a terrible defeat at the Battle of Cape St. Vincent. The Treaty of Amiens in 1802 provided a truce, but fighting broke out again in 1804. Once again, the Spanish Navy endured devastating losses; this time, it was at Trafalgar. The second round of warfare ended in 1808, but by that time, even more dramatic events were happening on the Iberian Peninsula.

Napoleon was determined to have the Continental System enforced throughout Europe, and that included Portugal and Spain. Portugal refused to join the Continental System because its economy relied on maritime trade. Napoleon was not accustomed to being turned down, and he issued an ultimatum to Portugal, which the Portuguese rejected. Napoleon responded by invading Portugal on November 19th, 1807. This effectively began the Peninsular War.

Spain did its best as an ally to France and suffered for it. Charles IV was a weak king and relied heavily on his prime minister, Manuel de Godoy. The prime minister's policies were not well received by the Spanish people. Many wanted the son of Charles, Ferdinand, to become the king. This led to internal squabbling, which permitted an opportunity for Napoleon.

<u>An Amazing Act of Treachery</u>

Spain was persuaded to enter a secret agreement with France regarding Portugal. The Treaty of Fontainebleau, signed on October 27th, 1807, was concerned with Portugal and its partition. However, there was something more to this treaty. France needed to push Portugal into accepting its control, and the treaty permitted a French army of twenty-eight thousand men to cross Spain. A reserve of forty thousand troops at Bayonne was included in the event of English intervention. This meant that France could legally enter Spain. The French were successful in Portugal and forced the Portuguese royal family to seek asylum in Brazil. However, there were also French troops in northern Spain.[59]

---

https://www.britannica.com/event/Peninsular-War.

[59] Burkholder, S. H. (2024, June 10). Treaty of Fontainebleau (1807). Retrieved from Encyclopedia.com: https://www.encyclopedia.com/humanities/encyclopedias-almanacs-transcripts-and-maps/fontainebleau-treaty-1807.

The Spanish government was on the brink of collapse. Godoy could not organize any resistance to the French presence in northern Spain and wanted the king to seek refuge in Spanish America, but that did not happen. A rival faction in the Spanish court was able to have Godoy dismissed and forced Charles to abdicate. Charles IV's son was recognized as King Ferdinand VII on March 17th, 1808.[60]

<u>Napoleon Intervenes</u>

Napoleon was concerned that the chaos in the Spanish government might result in a political change that would make Spain more sympathetic to Great Britain. Rather than risk a potential enemy on his border, Napoleon decided to use the Treaty of Fontainebleau to invade Spain under the pretext of helping an ally. France invaded Spain on February 9th, 1808. On March 27th, Marshal Murat entered Madrid.

Portrait of Joseph Bonaparte.[54]

Ferdinand wanted Napoleon to confirm that he, Ferdinand, was the new king of Spain since his father wanted to protest the change. Napoleon convinced both to travel to Bayonne for a conference. Instead of a meeting, Napoleon pressured both into renouncing their respective claims to the throne on May 5th. Napoleon then appointed his brother, Joseph Bonaparte, as the new king of Spain.

<u>Spanish Resistance</u>

Napoleon underestimated the patriotism of the Spanish population. People in Madrid revolted on May 2nd, but the uprising was quickly suppressed. However, the Spanish resistance was not over. The Spanish fought back and forced the French to retreat. The French army was defeated at Baylen, which marked the first major defeat of Napoleon's army in a land battle. The Spanish success story continued, and they were able to force Joseph Bonaparte out of Madrid in August.

---

[60] Britannica, T. E. Peninsular War.

Napoleon decided to personally intervene in the situation. He led an army of approximately 300,000 men into Spain and crushed the Spanish resistance. One would think that would have settled the matter, but a new player was about to enter the game, and he would prove to be Napoleon's greatest nemesis.[61]

Sir Arthur Wellesley (Duke of Wellington)

Napoleon's battlefield success was due partly to the quality of the commanders he faced. Those generals were typically nothing special and rarely posed a threat to the French emperor. Napoleon's advantage in this arena would gradually erode as the performance of his enemies improved. The change started in the Peninsular War when a British general came into the picture.

Sir Arthur Wellesley was a career officer who served in Europe and India. He was particularly successful in battles on the Indian subcontinent and even developed some of the strategies that he would later use in the Napoleonic Wars there. His better qualities were common sense, attention to detail, care of his soldiers and their provisions, and maintaining good relations with civilians. He was also capable of making firm decisions at the right moment. He is commonly known as the Duke of Wellington, and his moniker was the Iron Duke. He became the worst nightmare the French ever had.[62]

The Duke of Wellington.[55]

Great Britain decided to help the Portuguese and Spanish in their resistance against France. An expeditionary force of fourteen thousand men under Wellington, who at the time was a lieutenant general, landed in Portugal in August 1808.

---

[61] Pisa, J. d. (2011, October 5). Napoleon's Nightmare: Guerilla Warfare in Spain (1808-1814). Retrieved from Smallwarsjournal.com: https://smallwarsjournal.com/jrnl/art/napoleon%c2%b4s-nightmare-guerrilla-warfare-in-spain-1808-1814.

[62] Jacques Godechot, E. P. (2024, April 30). Arthur Wellesley, 1ˢᵗ Duke of Wellington. Retrieved from Britannica.com: https://www.britannica.com/biography/Arthur-Wellesley-1st-Duke-of-Wellington.

Wellington wasted no time in taking the fight to the enemy. On August 17th, Wellington defeated the French at the Battle of Roliça and followed that up with a victory at Vimeiro on August 21st. He was clearly on the offensive, but Wellington was checkmated by his own commanders.

Wellington's supervisors negotiated the Convention of Cintra, which allowed the French to leave Portugal. There was an outpouring of public rage in Great Britain about this agreement, and Wellington had to return to Great Britain to face court-martial. Fortunately for Britain, he was acquitted.[63]

Wellington would later be reinstated, but in the meantime, the Peninsular War was entering a stage of immense tragedy for the Spanish people.

Unconventional Warfare

The Grande Armée was used to fighting conventional battles that followed certain rules. What happened in the Peninsular War was entirely different. The French were not always facing organized columns of soldiers. Instead, they had to deal with bands of guerrilla fighters who did not follow the conventions of civilized combat.

Guerrilla bands were formed not long after the French invasion. The French tried to quell these attacks, but it only resulted in the guerrilla bands getting larger. The guerrilla bands attacked those targets that had the best chance of disrupting French supply lines and gathering loot. The attacks on couriers forced the occupiers to provide military escorts for messengers.

Every retaliation served to stiffen the resistance of the Spanish. The French soldiers could not be sure if and when they were going to be attacked. More and more French troops had to be sent to Spain to fight. The civilian population of Spain suffered from the attacks and the retaliations, but they appeared united in their desire to rid the country of the French. So much time, effort, and resources were expended that Napoleon began to refer to the entire Iberian Peninsula as the "Spanish Ulcer."[64]

---

[63] National Army Museum. (2024, June 10). Peninsular War. Retrieved from Nam.ac.uk: https://www.nam.ac.uk/explore/peninsular-war.

[64] Mark, H. W. (2023, August 7). Peninsular War. Retrieved from World History Encyclopedia: https://www.worldhistory.org/Peninsular_War/.

<u>British Efforts</u>

The conventional war between British and French soldiers continued, but the results were inconclusive. The British were forced to evacuate Spain at Corunna on January 16th, 1809, but they were not finished in the Iberian Peninsula. Wellington returned to the warfront in 1809 and was able to drive Field Marshal Jean-de-Dieu Soult out of Portugal. Wellington then moved into Spain and scored a victory at the Battle of Talavera. Wellington had to retreat because of logistical problems and because he needed to secure his supply lines. However, he demonstrated that the British were still in the conflict and that the French did not have absolute control over the peninsula.[65]

Wellington secured the position of the British army thanks to defensive fortifications he ordered to be constructed near Lisbon. The Lines of Torres Vedras were constructed between October 1809 and October 1810 and were a network of forts and redoubts with trenches and roads that extended for approximately fifty miles. It took advantage of the terrain around Lisbon region. When Marshal André Masséna tried to capture Lisbon with over sixty thousand men, he was effectively stopped by these defenses and had to fall back.

The Peninsular War continued, but there were no major developments during the following few years. Tens of thousands of French troops were tied down by activity in Spain and Portugal, depriving Napoleon of badly needed soldiers. The Peninsular War's manpower requirements would affect Napoleon's execution of what was not only his greatest military campaign but also the worst disaster of the Napoleonic Wars.

---

[65] Jacques Godechot, E. P. Arthur Wellesley, 1st Duke of Wellington.

Chapter 8: The Culture of the Time

Before we talk about the final major campaign of the Napoleonic Wars, let's take a look at the culture that blossomed. Wars are disruptive, but they do not force society to a dead stop. Creative people continue to paint, compose, and perform artistic works for the enjoyment and improvement of others. The Napoleonic Wars coincided with the Romantic movement. It was a time of creative experimentation and a move away from older music, art, and poetry styles.

There were giants of the arts during this time. They dared to challenge conventional practices and generated cultural masterpieces that are still enjoyed today. Let's examine several of these highly creative people and take note of how they improved society.

<u>Characteristics of the Romantic Movement</u>

Several popular themes can be found in the Romantic movement. The Romantics considered nature a source of inspiration and beauty. The Romantic movement also centered on the individual and personal expression. Introspective behavior and rebellious spirit were integral themes, as the main characters were often developed as being distant from society. Mythology and the supernatural could be found in various artistic works of this time as well.

The Romantic movement began before the Napoleonic Wars and continued long after the guns fell silent. Nevertheless, the wars sparked the creative forces that changed the cultural world. Emotion and passion replaced sedate parlor musings, and the vortex of war provided the energy to create astounding original pieces.

<u>Music</u>

The master of music in the Romantic movement was Ludwig van Beethoven. Earlier composers wrote works that were soft and gentle. Beethoven's music booms like an artillery barrage across a concert hall. His symphonies can start slow and smooth and end with a thunder blast of trumpets. Beethoven was already an established composer when the Napoleonic Wars began, and he would compose some of his greatest works during those years.

<u>The Eroica Symphony</u>

Beethoven initially was a fervent supporter of Napoleon because he believed that the French leader was an advocate for the ideals of the French Revolution. Symphony No. 3 was initially composed to honor Napoleon, but Beethoven was infuriated by Napoleon's coronation as emperor. So, he renamed the musical score the Eroica Symphony.

The symphony's title page with Napoleon's name erased.[56]

This composition was a revolutionary piece. The work has more emotion than earlier writers, such as Mozart, would have used. Beethoven attempted to capture the mood of the time with dramatic and not sentimental music. It was a surprising break from tradition and was well received.

<u>The Fifth Symphony</u>

Beethoven wrote the Fifth Symphony between 1804 and 1808 when war was raging in central Europe and Napoleon was conducting decisive campaigns in Germany and Austria. This symphony also reflects the heightened energy of the Napoleonic years. Vienna was Beethoven's home at the time, and it was threatened by the French army. The bold character of the music is symbolic of the resolve of the Viennese in the face of an ominous threat.

The composer was disappointed with Napoleon and how the French leader had changed. However, this did not mean that Beethoven turned his back on the Bonaparte family. Beethoven's notoriety was so great and his music so splendid that Jerome Bonaparte, King of Westphalia, offered the composer the position of *kapellmeister* at the Westphalian court.

By 1814, Beethoven was a confirmed German nationalist and was opposed to Napoleon. He created a short orchestral work in celebration of Wellington's victory at Vitoria in 1813. Any illusions that Beethoven had about Napoleon being a champion of liberty were gone.[66]

There is a fascinating personal note to Beethoven's efforts during these years. The composer grew more and more deaf. He could not hear the music that he was creating, but it was still magnificent. How was it possible that a deaf man could write music that he could not even hear?

The answer is more intellectual than physical. The composer lost his hearing, but he did not lose his mind. Beethoven had been exposed to music since he was a toddler. Musical notes and the sounds of various instruments surrounded his days. He could no longer hear the sound, but Beethoven remembered how certain chords sounded. He used his memory to create some of the most incredible music we have ever heard.

<u>Art: Getting the Message Out</u>

The *Coronation of Napoleon* is a massive painting that is currently in the Louvre Museum. It shows Napoleon crowning his wife Josephine as various dignitaries, including the pope, are watching. In the stands above Napoleon's mother, in the center of the painting, we see somebody who is busy sketching something on paper. That is the artist of the work, Jacques-Louis David.

---

[66] Lee, A. (2018, March 3). Beethoven and Napoleon. Retrieved from Historytoday.com: https://www.historytoday.com/archive/music-time/beethoven-and-napoleon.

Coronation of Napoleon *by Jacque-Louis David.*[67]

David is an interesting person in art history. He was influenced by the neoclassicist style of painting and is famous for his *Oath of the Horatii* and the *Death of Socrates*.

He was a member of the Royal Academy and a favorite painter of the Bourbon aristocracy. That did not stop him from switching sides at the start of the French Revolution. David was a Jacobin who supported Robespierre. His work, the *Death of Marat*, was an icon of the French Revolution.

David was already an established artist at the time of the Napoleonic Wars, and he is technically not part of the Romantic movement. However, his role during the Napoleonic Wars was significant in the art world. David was Napoleon's personal artist.[67]

<u>Artistic Propaganda</u>

Napoleon recognized the value of propaganda and how crucial visual representation could be in shaping public opinion. David's representations of Napoleon, particularly the work *Napoleon Crossing the Alps*, depict the emperor as a heroic figure. Later works show Napoleon with a crown of golden laurels, connecting him to the classical rulers of Rome.

---

[67] The Open University. (2024, June 10). 3 Gros and the Napoleonic Propaganda Machine. Retrieved from Open.edu: https://www.open.edu/openlearn/history-the-arts/history-art/napoleonic-paintings/content-section-3.1

Interestingly, while David was an ardent revolutionary during the French Revolution, he quickly transferred his allegiance to the French Empire. Perhaps the painter was as much a businessman as he was an artist. He knew where his commissions were, and he gravitated toward the money.[68]

Painting the Nightmare

Francisco Goya's artistic career before Napoleon came to power was comparable to David's. He was a court painter for the Spanish Bourbons and painted beautiful pictures of the Spanish royalty and the aristocracy. His life did not seem to have any ripples in the water, but the Spanish invasion of 1808 changed Goya's perspective dramatically.

Goya saw the devastation of war, and he could not turn away. His work *The Second of May 1808* depicts the street fighting that occurred in Madrid when the population rose in revolt. A second painting, *Third of May 1808*, is a depiction of when the French executed Spanish insurgents to suppress the uprising. Goya's message to the viewer in both works was an antiwar statement that showed the violence and inhumanity of war.

Second of May 1808.[69]

[68] The Clark. (2024, June 10). David & Napoleon. Retrieved from Clarkart.edu: https://www.clarkart.edu/microsites/jacques-louis-david/david-napoleon.

Goya did not hesitate to depict the horror of warfare. He departed from the royal court's urbane sensitivities to show the brutal aspects of revolt and depression. Human suffering was a theme that the Spanish painter concentrated on.

The Disasters of War

The most significant contribution Goya made to the art world was *The Disasters of War* series. This was a collection of eighty-two etchings Goya created between 1810 and 1820.

The first forty-seven etchings concentrate on episodes during the Peninsular War and the consequences of the fighting. Plates 48 to 64 are a record of the Madrid famine of 1811-1812. The final group of etchings depicts his disappointment in the Bourbon restoration, which opposed all the state and religious reforms that had taken place in the prior years.

Goya challenged the viewer to confront the realities of war and not be seduced by glamorous depictions of valor. One can see starvation, humiliation, atrocity, and inhumanity in *The Disasters of War*. He did not use his art as a means of propaganda but as a way to send a message that war was not the answer.[69]

A Spanish civilian about to decapitate a French soldier.[59]

The prints were so dramatic and overwhelming that they were not published until 1863.

---

[69] Franciscogoya.com. (2024, June 10). The Disaster of War, 1810-1820 by Francisco Goya. Retrieved from Franciscogoya.com: https://www.franciscogoya.com/disasters-of-war.jsp.

Francisco Goya is remembered primarily for the works he created during the Peninsular War. A later artist who was greatly influenced by Goya's work was another Spaniard, Pablo Picasso. Picasso shared Goya's indignation at inhumanity and respected the earlier artist's freedom of tone and creation. While Picasso studied the works of other Spanish artists, he was so inspired by Goya's work that he was given the nickname "Little Goya."[70]

The Disasters of War had an effect on Pablo Picasso. The stark scenes that Goya depicted inspired Picasso to create his masterpiece, *Guernica*, which was another plea to bring an end to violence.

<u>The Poet's Quill</u>

War was the most important fact of British life from 1793 to 1815, and it became the principal poetic subject, according to Betty T. Bennett, a distinguished professor of literature.[71] Great Britain did not suffer material damage comparable to Spain or Germany, but the war affected the psyche of the British people. A sense of disillusionment, a feeling that the revolutionary ideals of the late 18th century would never materialize or that war could be dignified, crept into the spirit of the British.

William Wordsworth created some of his best works before the Napoleonic Wars started, but he did compose poems during the war years. His work, *Elegiac Stanzas*, was composed in 1805 in memory of his brother who drowned in a shipwreck. It speaks of the loss and mourning that were prevalent in a society that had to accept the loss of young men to war. It also shows the fragility of life and the unpredictability of life's twists and turns.

Wordsworth used the Romantic movement's theme of nature as a place for consolation. However, a sense of grief permeates the lines of his poem:

"I have submitted to a new control:

a power is gone, which nothing can restore;

a deep distress hath humanized my Soul."[72]

---

[70] Musee Goya Castres. (2024, June 10). Goya-Picasso: A Cross-View. Retrieved from museegoya.fr: https://www.museegoya.fr/en/goya-in-piccaso-s-eye.

[71] Bainbridge, S. (2016, June 2). Romanticism and War. Retrieved from Oxford Academic: https://academic.oup.com/edited-volume/43514/chapter/364255284?login=false.

[72] Wordsworth, W. (2024, June 19). Elegias Stanzas Suggested by a Picture of Peele Castle in a Storm, Painted by Sir George Beaumont. Retrieved from Poetryfoundation.org:

<u>A Disillusioned Pilgrim</u>

The Grand Tour of Europe was once part of the education of a young English aristocrat. The Napoleonic Wars prevented that, but Lord Byron still traveled through Spain and Portugal. He was shocked at the devastation he saw, and the poet rebelled against any romantic notions of heroism that people had. His work, *Childe Harold's Pilgrimage*, part of which was published in 1812, evoked a revulsion to what war was like. Canto I contains particularly sharp lines.

"Let their bleached bones,

and blood's un-bleaching stain,

long marked the battle-field with hideous awe: thus, only

May our sons conceived the scenes we saw."[73]

The great British victory at the Battle of Waterloo did not impress Lord Byron at all. In a later work, *Don Juan*, Byron attacks the Duke of Wellington:

"And I would be delighted to learn who,

Save you and yours, have gained by Waterloo?"[74]

National identity was also a theme used by poets during the Napoleonic Wars. The Italian poet Ugo Foscolo's *Dei Sepolcri* is concerned with national identity and cultural ties to the past. The poet saw the St. Cloud Decree as an insult to Italian culture because it regulated burial practices in Italy. Foscolo believed that tombs and monuments of the dead could inspire the living and remind people of their country's glorious past.

"Only those who leave no legacy of affection

find little joy in their earn; and if they gaze

after their obsequies, they see their spirit wander

among the laments of Achaean temples,

of a thousand

---

https://www.poetryfoundation.org/poems/45516/elegiac-stanzas-suggested-by-a-picture-of-peele-castle-in-a-storm-painted-by-sir-george-beaumont.

[73] Lord Byron. The Works of Lord Byron Vol. 2. https://genius.com/Lord-byron-the-works-of-lord-byron-vol-2-to-inez-annotated.

[74] Collinson, A. (2015, May 11). In Literature and Song: The Legacy of the Napoleonic Wars. Retrieved from Ageofrevolution.org: https://ageofrevolution.org/in-literature-and-song-the-legacy-of-the-napoleonic-wars/.

desolate Greek shades."[75]

Foscolo took a risky step in this poem and criticized the French emperor:

"And you, Hector, will be honored in tears,

were holy and lamented is the blood

shed for one's country, and as long as the Sun

shines upon human suffering."[76]

<u>Deal with the Devil</u>

Johann Wolfgang von Goethe is one of the giants of the modern literary world. His epic work *Faust* was published in two parts; the first was made public in 1808. Although the author does not directly confront the Napoleonic Wars, *Faust I* is interwoven with character references that mirrored current events.

The main character, Dr. Heinrich Faust, makes a deal with the devil, giving his soul in return for unlimited knowledge, power, and pleasure. Faust has enormous ambition, similar to what Goethe perceived in Napoleon. Goethe believed that Napoleon's genius bordered on demonic. Faust's desire to satisfy personal ambitions reflects the changes brought about by Napoleon. What is interesting to notice is the respect that Napoleon had for Goethe. He tried to persuade Goethe to relocate to Paris, but the author politely declined the invitation.[77]

The culture of the Napoleonic Wars suggests a growing fatigue settled in Europe. The hopes for positive change slowly crumbled, as reality and the tumult of war made people more cynical. The conflicts kept dragging on, and only a few months of tranquility separated one war from another. A cataclysmic event was forming, and it would become real in 1812.

---

[75] Foscolo, U. (2024, June 11). Ugo Foscolo-Opere Omnia. Retrieved from Foscolo.letteraturaoperaomnia.org:
https://foscolo.letteraturaoperaomnia.org/foscolo_dei_sepolcri.html.

[76] Foscolo, U. Ugo Foscolo-Opere Omnia.

[77] Keene, R. (2024, June 10). Napoleon and Goethe: Touchstone of Genius. Retrieved from Thearticle.com: https://www.thearticle.com/napoleon-and-goethe-touchstone-of-genius.

Chapter 9: The Invasion of Russia: Napoleon's Catastrophic Campaign

The Continental System was a bad public policy that was riddled with holes. It was almost impossible for France to enforce the rules, given the expansive coastline of Europe. Nevertheless, Napoleon was committed to it. The obsession to bring Great Britain to its knees through economic pressure resulted in the Peninsular War, which would cause other problems for the French emperor. His determination to uphold the Continental System eventually led to his greatest mistake.

<u>War of the Fifth Coalition</u>

France was the dominant power in Europe in January 1809. France's control over the continent was nearly complete despite the distractions of the Peninsular War. Austria had already been humiliated by Napoleon and lost considerable amounts of territory. The Habsburgs wanted to regain some of their foreign possessions. The Austrian army had been reformed, and the government was willing to take a chance.

Consequently, Emperor Francis I ordered the Austrians to invade Bavaria on April 10th, 1809. It was a mistake because Bavaria was an ally of France, and Napoleon was obligated to come to its defense. This began the War of the Fifth Coalition.

Austria hoped that Prussia would help, but the Prussian army was too small and was unwilling to risk a defeat. Great Britain sent financial subsidies to Austria, but it was clear that the main force confronting Napoleon would be Austria this time around.

<u>Changes to the Army</u>

The Austrians had worked to modernize their army. Archduke Charles, commander in chief of the Austrian military, introduced several reforms. These included reorganizing the army into lines and reserve corps that resembled Napoleon's organization of troops. Additionally, Charles introduced mass conscription that supplied fresh troops. Austria was able to field the largest army it had ever seen.

Fighting against Napoleon was a gamble that Emperor Francis I was willing to take. The Peninsular War caused the French to direct hundreds of thousands of soldiers to the Iberian Peninsula. It appeared that the odds were slightly in favor of the Austrians.

However, Napoleon was aware of the Austrian buildup and prepared for the possibility of war. He ordered a counterattack after the Austrians invaded Bavaria. After several battles, the French met the Austrians at Eckmuuhl on April 22nd, 1809. The Austrians were doing a better job of fighting than before, although they lost that battle thanks to Napoleon arriving just in time. Napoleon captured Vienna on May 13th, but the Austrian army was still in the field and, while bloodied, could fight on.

<u>A Rude Surprise</u>

Napoleon wanted to finish off the Austrian army that Archduke Charles was leading, so he marched the French army out of Vienna to find it. The retreating Austrians had destroyed the Danube's bridges. Napoleon was forced to move downstream and build a pontoon bridge to the island of Lobau on May 20th. Another bridge was constructed from that island to the other side of the Danube, and French troops moved across and occupied Aspern and Essling.

Archduke Charles did not contest the crossing. He wanted to attack part of the French army that crossed over and defeat it before the rest could come to its rescue. The Austrians attacked on May 21st, and the French were able to beat them back. Archduke Charles resumed the offensive on May 22nd. An attack by the Austrian reserve, led by Archduke Charles himself, got on the left side of the French and forced Napoleon to retreat to a defensive position. The Battle of Aspern-Essling ended in Napoleon's defeat.

The victory was a significant boost to Austrian morale. Unfortunately, Archduke Charles did not follow up on the success. Napoleon would strike back a few weeks later.[78]

<u>Wagram</u>

The French and Austrian armies were now on opposite sides of the Danube. Napoleon would not concede and began to gather more troops for a second attempt to destroy the Austrian army. It took several weeks, but by the beginning of July, he had nearly 170,000 soldiers and 600 artillery pieces ready. The Austrians were able to assemble 140,000 men and 400 cannons. The French started to cross the river on July 4th, 1809.

The Battle of Wagram commenced on July 5th. There was heavy fighting, and the French made some gains, but the Austrians were in defensive positions that could not be breached. Both sides suffered heavy casualties on the first day.

Napoleon gave a demonstration of shock and awe on July 6th. His artillery was positioned in grand batteries, and the engagement started with an enormous artillery duel in which more than one thousand cannons opened fire on each other. This was followed by a massive coordinated attack by the French, with Marshal Davout attacking the left wing of the Austrians and Marshal Masséna targeting the right.

A central assault by the French broke through the Austrian lines, while, at the same time, French cavalry charged into the Austrian reserves. Under enormous pressure from the advancing enemy, Archduke Charles ordered a retreat.

Wagram was an enormous battle in which 300,000 troops fought each other. It is also noted for the use of massed artillery that resulted in a total of nearly seventy-seven thousand casualties. The losses seriously weakened Napoleon's army, but the Austrians could not press further. Peace negotiations between Austria and France started, resulting in the Treaty of Schönbrunn, signed on October 14th, 1809.[79]

The treaty was an embarrassment for Austria. Additional territory was carved out of the Austrian Empire and given to France and French allies. Joseph Bonaparte was formally recognized as the king of Spain, and

---

[78] Hickman, K. (2015, March 10). Napoleonic Wars: Battle of Aspern-Essling. Retrieved from Thoughtco.com: https://www.thoughtco.com/napoleonic-battle-of-aspern-essling-2361108.

[79] Frithowulf, H. (2024, February 29). Battle of Wagram: Napoleon's Masterstroke. Retrieved from Malevus.com: https://malevus.com/battle-of-wagram/.

Austria was forced to pay a large indemnity. Moreover, the Austrian army was reduced to 150,000 men, and Austria was to become part of the Continental System. One Austrian concession was more personal, though.[80]

The Divorce

Napoleon's relationship with his wife Josephine was complex. Both were unfaithful, but Napoleon was deeply in love with his wife. The main problem was that Josephine could not produce an heir. By 1809, she was past her childbearing years. Napoleon needed a male successor to continue his dynasty. Josephine could no longer fulfill that need for him.

Napoleon formally divorced Josephine on December 15th, 1809. He made it clear that the divorce was necessary for the good of France. He was generous and permitted his former wife to keep her title as empress. She was given a residence at Château de Malmaison and a substantial financial settlement. Both maintained a friendly relationship despite the divorce.

The Austrian Marriage

The Habsburgs had a reputation for using marriages as a diplomatic tool. They saw an opportunity to gain better relations with France by marrying Napoleon to Emperor Francis I's daughter, Marie Louise. Negotiations between France and Austria began in January 1810. A marriage contract was agreed upon on March 9th, 1810, and Marie Louise married Napoleon by proxy on March 11th, 1810. A civil marriage occurred on April 1st, 1810, when Marie Louise arrived in France, and a religious ceremony was held on April 2nd.[81]

Marie Louise was very young (she was eighteen years old at the time of the marriage), but she understood her duty. On March 20th, 1811, she gave birth to a healthy boy who was named after his father. Napoleon now had the heir he had so desperately wanted.

[80] Britannica, T. E. (2024, June 11). Treaty of Schonbrunn. Retrieved from Britannica.com: https://www.britannica.com/event/Treaty-of-Schonbrunn.

[81] Napoleon.org. (2010, March). The Marriage of Napoleon I and Marie-Louise of Austria. Retrieved from Napoleon.org: https://www.napoleon.org/en/history-of-the-two-empires/timelines/the-marriage-of-napoleon-i-and-marie-louise-of-austria/.

Empress Marie Louise with her son, who was given the title "King of Rome." Portrait by Jacques Franque.[60]

Eyes on Russia

Napoleon was the master of Europe, and Great Britain was the only nation strong enough to continue fighting him. Nevertheless, the French emperor was tired of fighting coalition wars. He successfully reduced the military power of Prussia and Austria, but there was one final country that could field a sizable army against him: Russia. Napoleon needed to neutralize any potential threat from the east and bind the Russian Empire closer to France.

However, Russia was not cooperating. It had agreed to be a part of the Continental System, but those trade restrictions hurt the Russian economy. Tsar Alexander turned a blind eye to the violations, allowing Russians to blatantly trade with Great Britain. Despite declarations of friendship, Napoleon and Tsar Alexander did not trust each other.

Napoleon continued to worry that Russia would eventually disregard the Treaty of Tilsit and become an ally of France's enemies. Bonaparte finally concluded that a preemptive strike of massive proportions would be the best way to put Russia back in line.

<u>A Massive Force</u>

Napoleon organized one of the largest military forces in European history to teach Russia a lesson. He gathered an army of nearly 600,000 men from all parts of the French Empire, including France, Italy, Poland, and his German allies. His invasion force was divided into three primary groups.

- The Northern Army Group would be under the command of Marshal Étienne Macdonald and would concentrate on the Baltic region.

- The Central Army Group was under Napoleon's direct command, and its target was Moscow.

- The Southern Army Group was commanded by Karl Philipp, Prince of Schwarzenberg, and was assigned to secure the southern flank from any Russian attack.

An immediate challenge for this military force was language barriers. The logistical planning for the invasion was staggering.

The invasion of Russia would be greater than any of the previous campaigns of the Napoleonic Wars. Feeding and supplying the troops was a monumental task. The French had 20 train battalions, with 7,848 carriages and wagons tasked with providing 40 days' worth of supplies for the army. In addition, auxiliary supply convoys were created to carry enough medical supplies, flour, and bread to supply 300,000 men for 2 months.

Supply depots were established at Danzig, Magdeburg, and Breslow. The Central Army Group had sufficient provisions for the Northern and Southern groups and confronted supply problems brought on by prioritizing supplies for the Central Group and Russian raids.[82]

The Grande Armée crossed the Niemen River on June 24th, 1812. Napoleon expected a relatively short campaign, and the initial stages of the invasion went smoothly.

---

[82] Thenapoleonicwars.net. (2024, June 11). Napoleon's Invasion of Russia. Retrieved from Thenapoleonicwars.net: https://www.thenapoleonicwars.net/invasion-of-russia.

Napoleon also anticipated an immediate confrontation with the Russian army. He was disappointed.

Challenges of Fighting in Russia

Napoleon grossly underestimated the size of Russia. The nation was vast, stretching for thousands of miles. The French also discovered that the road system was so primitive that a storm could turn the road into a muddy swamp in minutes. Alexander had ordered a scorched earth policy, and where there once had been acres of wheat flowing in the breeze was nothing but burned stalks.

Bonaparte had hoped one or two significant battles would determine the outcome. In his defense, that happened in the other coalition wars; a major engagement would result in a smashing victory, and peace negotiations would commence. Tsar Alexander did not play by Napoleon's rules. Instead, the Russians kept moving back, denying the enemy an opportunity to fight.[83]

Napoleon was aware of what the enemy was doing, but he continued to advance. He hoped that by capturing Moscow, he could convince Alexander to enter peace negotiations. It was a mistaken assumption. Alexander had matured since the defeat at Austerlitz. This time, he listened carefully to his commanders in the field and agreed with the strategy of retreating. The supply lines of the French were being stretched to the limit, and Russian attacks on the columns were wearing down the invaders' morale.

Finally, there was a battle between the French and the Russians. It took place at Smolensk from August 16th to the 18th. What was notable about this encounter was the French artillery bombardment of the city. Approximately 84 percent of the buildings were destroyed, and only one thousand inhabitants remained. The retreat strategy had now run its course. The Russians began to organize to resist the French in a pitched battle.[84]

---

[83] Historyskills.com. (2024, June 11). Napoleon's Catastrophic Invasion of Russia: A Military Miscalculation of Epic Proportions. Retrieved from Historyskills.com: https://www.historyskills.com/classroom/modern-history/napoleon-s-russian-invasion/.

[84] DetailedPedia.com. (2024, June 11). Battle of Smolensk (1812). Retrieved from Detailedpedia.com: https://www.detailedpedia.com/wiki-Battle_of_Smolensk_%281812%29.

<u>Borodino</u>

Borodino is approximately eighty miles west of Moscow. The area has natural defensive features, including a river and, more importantly, ridges that could be fortified. The Russian commander, Marshal Mikhail Kutuzov, chose this as the place to make their stand.

Several fortifications were constructed to strengthen the Russian defensive line. The Raevsky redoubt, placed in the center, and the Bagration flèches at the southern end of the Russian line were the most prominent. The artillery reinforced the defense, and the Russians had more than six hundred cannons.

The French arrived at the battlefield, which began on September 7th. French artillery bombarded the Russian positions and created significant gaps. A major French attack occurred on the Bagration flèches, but the fiercest fighting occurred at the Raevsky redoubt. The redoubt changed hands numerous times during the battle.

Both sides had attacks and counterattacks. Historians have criticized Napoleon for not sending in his Imperial Guard despite being begged to do so by his marshals. His reluctance permitted the Russians to stiffen their lines. The fighting got more intense, and both sides took heavy casualties. The Raevsky redoubt was finally captured, and the Russians retreated. The battle was technically over.

The Battle of Moscow by Louis-François, Baron Lejeune.[61]

September 7th, 1812, was the bloodiest day of all the Napoleonic Wars. Both sides were too exhausted by the end of the day to continue the fighting. Napoleon had tactically won the battle, but the Russian army was able to retreat in good order. They would fight another day.

Napoleon and his army achieved a primary military objective on September 14th, for that was the day when the French entered Moscow. Napoleon wanted the city, and it cost him thousands of veterans to obtain it. He entered the city and received a major surprise.

Moscow was abandoned.

The citizens had fled the city. Napoleon quickly discovered that the Russian scorched earth policy did not just apply to wheatfields. Arsonists set fire to Moscow starting on the night of September 14th. Within a few days, Napoleon was in control of a burned-out city.

Attempts were made to reach the tsar to start peace negotiations, but Alexander was uninterested. Napoleon waited several weeks, but there was no response from St. Petersburg. Supplies were beginning to run short, and the French emperor realized he had to evacuate the city. On October 19th, 1812, the Grande Armée marched out of Moscow. It would face a determined Russian army with an ally that even Napoleon could not defeat.

The Russians harassed the retreating French army. Napoleon intended to lead his troops over the ground that had not been devastated by the war. Kutuzov was not going to let that happen. On October 24th, 1812, the Russians engaged the French in the town of Maloyaroslavets. The French won, but the Russians retreated toward Kaluga and blocked Napoleon's intended route. The French had to retreat northwest through Smolensk, which meant that Napoleon was moving over the route they had used to approach Moscow. The land had already been devastated, making living off the land difficult.

General Winter

Russia has long relied on the weather to help repel invasions. King Charles XII of Sweden learned that in the 18th century. Hitler would discover what a menace General Winter would be in the 20th century. The first snowstorm the French endured occurred on November 6th, 1812, and it would not be the last.

The winter weather was brutal. Temperatures fell as low as -22°F, and the soldiers suffered from frostbite because they had not been issued winter clothing. The horses also suffered because they did not have horseshoes suitable for the ice and snow. The French had already suffered a large number of casualties from the battles, and now the Grande Armée was losing men to starvation and hypothermia. And still, the Russians kept harassing them.[85]

A depiction of what the French forces faced during the harsh Russian winter.[68]

Crossing the Berezina River

The Grande Armée still trudged on despite the terrible conditions. The Berezina River blocked the western progress, and the army was required to cross it. The Russians had already moved ahead and captured the bridge spanning the river and destroyed it once they gained control of the west bank on November 23rd, 1812. The French built two pontoon bridges despite being under heavy attack. They crossed the river from November 26th to the 29th, but they lost thousands of men in the process and most of the army's baggage.

Napoleon Leaves

All was not well back in Paris. General Claude François de Malet spread a rumor that Napoleon was dead and attempted a coup d'état on October 23rd. It was unsuccessful, and the general was executed, but Napoleon was greatly disturbed when the news reached him. He was so

[85] Napoleon.org. (2024, June 11). Napoleon's Russian Campaign: The Retreat. Retrieved from Napoleon.org: https://www.napoleon.org/en/history-of-the-two-empires/timelines/napoleons-russian-campaign-the-retreat/.

worried that this would not be the only attempt to overthrow him that he decided to return to France. He set out for Paris on December 5th and was in the French capital before Christmas.

Meanwhile, the French army entered Vilna under the command of Marshal Murat. The soldiers' morale was extremely low because of Napoleon's departure, and there was worse to come. The army experienced an outbreak of typhus that killed thousands of men. Murat decided to leave Vilna. On December 12th, Kutuzov and his troops marched into the city. The last French soldiers crossed the Nieman River and left Russia behind on December 14th, 1812. The campaign was over.

The retreat would have been worse had it not been for the efforts of Marshal Ney. He was in charge of the rearguard, and he fought off attacks by Russians and Cossack partisans every step of the way out. His last action was at the Nieman River, guarding what was left of the army from the final assaults. Ney's stubborn courage and command of soldiers under horrible circumstances solidified his reputation as one of France's best marshals during the Napoleonic Wars.

The Butcher's Bill

The casualty figures of the Russian campaign were grim. Approximately 563,000 men were killed, wounded, or missing by the time the French forces left Russia. In addition, nearly 200,000 horses and more than 1,000 artillery pieces were lost in the effort.[86]

The Russian campaign was an unprecedented disaster. The French were accustomed to winning great victories and wars. Now, their military ranks were devastated. In addition, French allies lost men in a campaign that was a hopeless venture. Other European countries noticed the decline of France.

Prussia and Austria were still smarting from past humiliations. A defeated Napoleon presented a possible opportunity to regain lost territories and prestige. Great Britain was willing to provide financial support, and the Russians were in high spirits because of their victory. What was once considered impossible, that Napoleon could be brought down, was beginning to look possible. The year 1813 was going to be a challenging one for Bonaparte.

---

[86] New World Encyclopedia. (2024, June 11). French Invasion of Russia. Retrieved from New World Encyclopedia.com:
https://www.newworldencyclopedia.org/entry/French_invasion_of_Russia#Retreat_and_losses.

Chapter 10: The War of the Sixth Coalition and the Abdication

France was left staggering after the Russian disaster. Approximately 300,000 French soldiers, including many seasoned veterans, died in the campaign. The Continental System was a complete failure, and France was experiencing economic problems brought on by the war and the constraints on markets. The most significant result of the Russian campaign was the damage to Napoleon's image. The French emperor was no longer invincible; he was vulnerable and human. A mystique that served his purposes for years vanished, and it did not go unnoticed in the other countries on the Continent.

The former enemies of France saw that the country was now crippled. The French Empire and its satellite states were shaken to the core. Ministers in various capitals were starting to wonder if there might be a way to end the Napoleonic era and the wars that resulted from it.

Prussia and Austria were technically allies of France, but they were looking for revenge and the possible return of lost territory. Russia had paid a price for its victory in 1812, but national pride and morale were incredibly high. The Russian army knew it could beat Napoleon, and it was hoping for more opportunities to do so. Great Britain relished the idea of finally ending a problem it had faced for years. It would take some sophisticated diplomacy and maneuvering to bring about another coalition.

<u>Enter Metternich</u>

Prince Klemens von Metternich was Austria's foreign minister and perhaps the most talented diplomat of his time. He was a conservative who hoped to restore stability to Europe.

Metternich did not necessarily want to return to the status quo, though. The old regimes of the 18th century could not be fully restored; revolutionary ideas were now laws. What the Austrian prince wanted was a balance of power in Europe. One nation should not be dictating terms to everyone else. Instead, balancing one power against another would make negotiating more acceptable than war.

<u>Realignment</u>

Prussia was required to provide troops for the Russian campaign. After Napoleon's defeat, the Russian army marched into Prussia and captured Königsberg on January 4th, 1813. Before this, the commander of the Prussian contingent, Lieutenant General Johann Yorck von Wartenburg, signed an armistice with the Russians on December 31st, 1812. King Frederick William III of Prussia initially denounced the armistice, but there was a wave of public enthusiasm in favor of renouncing all ties with France.

Frederick William III decided not to go against popular sentiment, and on February 28th, 1813, he signed the Treaty of Kalisz with the Russians. This treaty stipulated that Prussia and Russia were in an alliance, and neither would negotiate with Napoleon independently of the other. Together, Russia and Prussia invaded Saxony in March 1813.

Austria's alliance with France formally ended in February 1813, and the nation took a stance of armed neutrality. Austria was initially reluctant to enter any coalition against Napoleon. This hesitancy was understandable, given Austria's recent history of losing to the French.

Great Britain sought any chance to eliminate Napoleon, so it actively recruited allies. It persuaded Sweden to enter a military alliance on March 3rd, 1813, and the two nations formally declared war against France.

The genesis of a new coalition was beginning to take shape. Russia formally declared war against France on March 13th. Great Britain was willing to provide financial subsidies, and that financial assistance was slowly changing people's minds about entering a new war.

<u>Napoleon on the Offensive</u>

Napoleon was not napping while all this was going on. At the start of 1813, he realized he needed an almost complete overhaul of the French army and went to work to bring the troop level back to a normal size. On January 11th, 1813, Napoleon called up the conscription class that should have been summoned in 1814 as a contingent numbering 150,000 men and raised an additional 100,000 men from earlier conscription classes. He withdrew troops from Spain, although he left 150,000 soldiers on the peninsula. Extra troops were also raised, but these were inexperienced soldiers who needed training. The veterans who had been counted on in the past were now buried under the snow in Russia. Nevertheless, by April 15th, 1813, Napoleon had 226,000 soldiers under his command and marched out of Paris, heading toward Germany.

Metternich tried to broker a peace and met with Napoleon in April 1813. The Austrian diplomat asked Napoleon to return Illyria to the Austrian Empire, partition the Grand Duchy of Warsaw, and dissolve the Confederation of the Rhine. Metternich warned Napoleon that Austria would intervene against the side that did not agree with these proposals. Napoleon rejected the terms.

Napoleon left his wife as acting regent in Paris and took command of his Army of the Main. He crossed the Saale River on May 1st, 1813, and moved to aid Saxony. He confronted the Russian-Prussian army at Lützen on May 2nd and again from May 20th to the 21st at Bautzen. Both battles resulted in French victories.

These military successes once again demonstrated Napoleon Bonaparte's military acumen. He was not leading an army of battle-hardened veterans as in earlier campaigns, but he was still able to win. Moreover, he was taking the fight to the enemy, and by the end of the month, the coalition forces wanted an armistice. Napoleon agreed to pause the fighting, and the Plaaswitz Armistice, signed on June 4th, provided a temporary peace that would last until August 18th, 1813.[87]

<u>Metternich the Mediator</u>

Metternich continued his role as a peace broker and met with Napoleon on June 26th in Dresden. Metternich informed Bonaparte of the pending conditions and warned that Austria would join the coalition if

---

[87] Mark, H. W. (2023, September 4). War of the Sixth Coalition. Retrieved from World History Encyclopedia: https://www.worldhistory.org/War_of_the_Sixth_Coalition/.

those conditions were not accepted. The terms included the following:

- France surrendering the Illyrian Provinces to Austria
- France recognizing the independence of the Confederation of the Rhine
- The removal of all French troops from Germany and Italy
- France abandoning the Grand Duchy of Warsaw
- France restoring independence to Hesse-Kassel, Hanover, and the free cities of Hamburg and Lübeck
- The return of the Papal States, Piedmont, and all German possessions of the House of Orange to previous owners
- France restoring the 1806 borders to Prussia

This meeting took place at the wrong time for Metternich. Napoleon had previously won battles against the coalition and was confident of further military success. The emperor rejected the conditions outright.

In retrospect, those conditions were a little bit cynical. Metternich probably knew that France would reject them and that hostilities would continue with Austria fighting on the side of the new alliance. The situation was one of 19th-century realpolitik. Austria had been France's ally in 1812. By 1813, the situation had changed dramatically, and Metternich saw the possibility of regaining land and reputation while buying some time for Austria to rearm.[88]

<u>The Treaties of Reichenbach</u>

June 1813 saw other significant diplomatic movements. On June 14th, 1813, Great Britain signed a treaty with Prussia, agreeing to provide a financial subsidy of £666,666 to Prussia. The following day, Great Britain signed another treaty with Russia, which promised a subsidy of £1,333,334. The money promised would fund 80,000 Prussian soldiers and 160,000 Russian soldiers. A final treaty was signed on June 27th, 1813. This time, it was between Prussia, Russia, and Austria. Austria agreed to formally enter the war against Napoleon.

---

[88] Cheikh, M. (2020, September 24). Were Metternich's Peace Ouvertures in 1813 Genuine? Retrieved from Thenapoleonicwars.net: https://www.thenapoleonicwars.net/forum/napoleon/were-metternich-s-peace-ouvertures-in-1813-genuine.

The members of the Sixth Coalition met at Trachtenberg on July 2nd to prepare a war strategy. It was decided that half a million men would be deployed in three army groups to oppose Napoleon. These were not divided by nationality; each army would be multinational, assuring that there would be cooperation between the member nations.

The plan was a departure from the standard way of dealing with Napoleon. Confrontation with Bonaparte was to be avoided. The Sixth Coalition would concentrate on defeating the French marshals instead. There would be better coordination between the allies than before, and the supply lines of the French army would be disrupted whenever possible.

Crown Prince Charles John of Sweden was the Trachtenberg Plan's principal architect. He was formally known as Jean-Baptiste Bernadotte and had once been one of Napoleon's most reliable marshals. The crown prince was now a principal advisor to the coalition and understood Napoleon's strategies and his frame of mind. Charles John would be invaluable in the months to come.

Portrait of Charles XIV John after he became king of Sweden and Norway.[68]

The Prague Congress

As a final effort to mediate peace, the Prague Peace Congress met in July and August, but nothing came of it. The armistice expired, and fighting began again. The coalition's plan of action was working, and French Marshal Nicolas Oudinot was beaten on August 23rd at Grossbeeren, and Marshal Macdonald was defeated at Katzbach on August 27th.

Dresden was a major supply depot in base operations for Napoleon's army. The coalition wanted to capture it, but Napoleon found out what the coalition planned to do and quickly moved reinforcements to Dresden, starting the march on August 23rd. His army was able to cover 120 miles in only four days.

Napoleon engaged with the Sixth Coalition from August 26th to the 27th in the Battle of Dresden. The weather conditions were terrible, and Napoleon used artillery to force the coalition armies to leave the battlefield. It was technically a victory for Napoleon, but he could not follow up on the success, and the coalition forces were able to retreat in good order.[89]

<u>The Battle of Leipzig</u>

The Battle of Leipzig is also known as the Battle of Nations and was fought from October 16th to October 19th, 1813. This was the most pivotal battle of the War of the Sixth Coalition.

The Sixth Coalition armies were able to coordinate their activity, and they attacked in multiple directions. The military force was close to 380,000 men, which outnumbered the 225,000 French troops. The battle line stretched between twelve and twenty-five miles, and over two thousand artillery pieces were deployed by the fighting armies.

The Sixth Coalition gradually encircled the French army and applied pressure on all sides. Napoleon took a central position, allowing his army to respond more effectively to attacks. The French emperor ordered several counterattacks to try to break out of the encirclement, and he fortified positions around Leipzig, which slowed down the coalition's movements.

The decisive moment came on October 18th. The Saxon troops fighting for the French defected. They went over to the coalition, which damaged the morale of the French forces. Fresh reinforcements strengthened the Sixth Coalition and allowed them to pressure the French lines significantly.

The French were forced to retreat on October 19th, and a premature explosion intended to destroy the only bridge over the Elster River caused the death of thousands of French and the capture of thirty thousand French soldiers. What was left of the Grande Armée finally made it across the river and were in full retreat toward the Rhine.

Leipzig was the bloodiest battle fought in the Napoleonic Wars. There were somewhere between 80,000 and 110,000 casualties. The French lost 325 artillery pieces, and over fifty generals were among the casualties.

---

[89] Britannica, T. E. (2024, May 14). Battle of Dresden. Retrieved from Britannica.com: https://www.britannica.com/event/Battle-of-Dresden.

The Battle of Leipzig by Vladimir Moshkov.[64]

Napoleon was finished in Germany. His allies were beginning to desert him, and his enemies were now unified in using a well-thought-out plan to defeat him. The worst was yet to come.

Invasion of France, 1814

While things were falling apart in Germany, the Peninsular War became a disaster. The Duke of Wellington won the Battle of Vitoria on June 21st, 1813, and following that success, Madrid was taken. The French retreated north toward the Pyrenees with the British in pursuit. The last French stronghold in Spain, San Sebastian, fell in September 1813. Wellington then crossed the Pyrenees. His army was now in southern France.

The French opposition to the Sixth Coalition was falling like a house of cards. Napoleon achieved some victories, most notably during a six-day campaign in February 1814, but these achievements were little more than delaying actions. The Sixth Coalition armies entered Paris on March 31st, 1814. Although Napoleon wanted to continue, his marshals knew victory would be impossible. The only honorable thing for the French emperor to do was to abdicate. On April 6th, 1814, Napoleon gave in to the coalition's demand for an unconditional abdication. The Treaty of Fontainebleau was signed on April 11th, and Napoleon was forced into exile on the island of Elba off the Italian coast.

The Congress of Vienna

The Sixth Coalition succeeded where others had failed. Napoleon Bonaparte was no longer the dominant force in Europe. The guns fell silent, and Europe was at peace. However, the European powers faced a significant challenge. The Napoleonic Wars had been a period of conflict and enormous change. It was essential to establish a lasting peace and normalcy.

In Vienna, a conference of the major powers was held on November 1ˢᵗ, 1814. Klemens von Metternich chaired the conference. The Congress of Vienna impacted European politics for the next century.

The representatives were not interested in preserving any of the new liberties created by the Napoleonic Wars. They wanted to restore a sense of stability and peace to Europe. Essentially, the representatives were looking to achieve some form of *status quo ante.*

Five major European countries played deciding roles in the Vienna Congress.

- Austria was represented by Prince Klemens von Metternich.

- Russia was represented by Tsar Alexander I.

- Prussia was represented by Prince Karl August von Hardenberg.

- Great Britain was represented originally by Foreign Secretary Viscount Castlereagh and then later by the Duke of Wellington.

And the fifth? Well, it was France. Charles Maurice de Talleyrand-Périgord, the French foreign minister, represented France's interests at the congress. Despite being defeated, France played a prominent role in the Congress of Vienna thanks to Talleyrand's diplomatic skills.

<u>Redrawing Europe</u>

Napoleon had changed the borders of European countries, and now, the Congress of Vienna was going to redraw the map. It did not mean that the borders would be returned to their respective positions before the Napoleonic Wars. There was going to be a new Europe.

A new Kingdom of the Netherlands was one territorial change. This new state would include Belgium and serve as a buffer between Germany and France. Switzerland was recognized as a permanently neutral country, and it was another buffer state, this time between France and Italy.[90]

The question of what to do with Germany was addressed. Reestablishing the Holy Roman Empire was out of the question; that empire was relegated to the history books. The Confederation of the

---

[90] Britannica, T. E. (2024, June 12). Congress of Vienna summary. Retrieved from Britannica.com: https://www.britannica.com/summary/Congress-of-Vienna.

Rhine also did not continue. The German Confederation, an association of thirty-nine German states, was created in its place. It would be under the control of Austria and was primarily established for mutual defense.

For whatever good intentions the Congress of Vienna had, the major players had agendas that included gaining territory. Austria received control of Lombardi and Venetia and land in the Balkans. Prussia received two-fifths of Saxony and extensive new territories in Westphalia and the left bank of the Rhine. Russia insisted on Polish territory, which caused some friction because Austria and Great Britain were concerned about Russia acquiring too much power. In the end, Russia received two-thirds of what was the Grand Duchy of Warsaw.[91]

In other land distributions, the German state of Hanover was enlarged, Piedmont gained possession of Genoa, the Papal States were restored to the pope, Denmark lost Norway to Sweden but got Lauenburg as compensation, and Swedish Pomerania was transferred to Prussia. Great Britain's colonial holdings increased, as the British received Malta, the Cape of Good Hope, and Ceylon. France was reduced to its original borders of 1792.[92]

Monarchies were restored. The Bourbons were placed back on the throne of France, and Ferdinand VII was once again the king of Spain. The sovereigns in Portugal, Naples, and Sardinia were restored. France lost territories taken during the French Revolution and the Napoleonic era, but it did not fare all that badly, primarily because of the efforts of Talleyrand.

The French foreign minister was a political chameleon. He was a Roman Catholic bishop before the French Revolution. He became an ardent revolutionary but later switched sides when Napoleon Bonaparte came to power. Napoleon had mixed feelings about the man but recognized Talleyrand's diplomatic skills. After Napoleon abdicated, the French king, Louis XVIII, made Talleyrand his foreign minister. Talleyrand's ability to play one side against the other during the Congress of Vienna prevented France from having to concede even more territory.[93]

---

[91] Schneid, F. C. (2024, June 12). Congress of Vienna. Retrieved from Encyclopedia.com: https://www.encyclopedia.com/history/encyclopedias-almanacs-transcripts-and-maps/congress-vienna.

[92] Britannica.com. (2024, June 12). Decisions of the Congress. Retrieved from Britannica.com: https://www.britannica.com/event/Congress-of-Vienna/Decisions-of-the-congress.

[93] Godechot, J. (2024, May 13). Charles-Maurice de Talleyrand, Prince de Benevent. Retrieved

Other issues, such as the free navigation of international rivers and a declaration advocating the abolition of the slave trade, were addressed at the Congress of Vienna. The most significant achievement was the understanding that all of this would create stability in Europe, with negotiations replacing armed conflict.

The Congress of Vienna was also a major social event. Delegates were invited to balls, concerts, and other forms of group entertainment where serious networking took place. Indeed, many agreements were reached on the ballroom floor before being decided at the conference.

The delegates could congratulate themselves on creating a new Europe that would hopefully be more peaceful and amicable. However, in March 1815, those diplomats received the shock of their lives.

Napoleon was back.

from Britannica.com: https://www.britannica.com/biography/Charles-Maurice-de-Talleyrand-prince-de-Benevent.

Chapter 11: The Hundred Days and Waterloo: Napoleon's Last Stand

Exile did not sit well with Napoleon. The former master of Europe was now confined to a small island off the coast of Italy. He had once commanded hundreds of thousands of men; now, he had to settle for a garrison of one thousand soldiers. Napoleon had to sit around and read accounts of what the Congress of Vienna was doing to change everything he had accomplished. He was more than just bored; he was angry. Finally, on February 26th, 1815, Napoleon Bonaparte escaped from Elba. He eluded the British ships that were supposed to guard him and landed in France on March 1st, 1815. He immediately set off for Paris.

His progress to the French capital was less of a journey than an imperial parade. Marshal Ney, who had pressured Napoleon to abdicate, was part of the Bourbon administration. He was sent to arrest Napoleon, but when Ney met his old commander, the marshal changed sides and joined ranks with Bonaparte. That kind of meeting was repeated constantly during the march as old veterans flocked to their emperor's banner.

Although their love of Napoleon was genuine, many French soldiers deserted the Bourbons because of their dissatisfaction with the new government. The army was reduced to peacetime levels, and approximately eleven thousand officers were cashiered with half pay.

Those who stayed in the army were forced to report to superiors who were reinstated to ranks they held before the revolution. This angered those men who had risen through the ranks due to their bravery and merit. Even Marshal Ney, now a Peer of France, was looked down on by the restored aristocrats because he was a commoner by birth. The veterans remembered the past victories and the prestige they enjoyed as part of the Grande Armée. They wanted a return to their former glory.

The Bourbon dynasty could not mount an offensive against this swell of popular sentiment, and Louis XVIII was forced to flee. The Congress of Vienna declared that Napoleon was an outlaw on March 13th, but that did not stop Bonaparte's advance. Napoleon entered Paris on March 20th, 1815.[94]

<u>The Hundred Days</u>

Ten of Napoleon's former marshals declared allegiance to him, and Napoleon created a government that would help him meet his objectives. He presented himself to the French public as a changed man who was uninterested in autocratic rule or any more conquests. One of his critics, Benjamin Constant, was asked to draw up a new constitution. Constant created a shared power government based on the British model. There would be a bicameral parliament that would work with the emperor. Censorship and the slave trade would be abolished. It was all part of a public relations campaign to convince people Napoleon was finished with empires, but very few believed him. There were even French who opposed him: Brittany and the Vendee regions revolted.

Napoleon had more significant problems to worry about than internal uprisings. His former enemies came together, ratifying a treaty of alliance on March 25th. The Seventh Coalition included Great Britain, Russia, Sweden, Austria, Prussia, and several smaller European states. Each great power was committed to providing 150,000 men, and, interestingly, they declared war not on France but on Napoleon himself.

There was a problem of coordination, though. The British and the Prussians were prepared to move immediately, but the Austrians and Russians were not. Therefore, it was decided that the invasion of France would take place on July 1st when the various armies were in the field.

---

[94] Nackaerts, B. (2024, June 13). The Lack of Opposition to the Execution of Marshal Ney. Retrieved from Napoleon-series.org: <u>https://www.napoleon-series.org/research/biographies/c_executeney.html</u>.

Napoleon was not going to wait that long. He planned to take the battle to the enemy before they could be fully organized. However, he had to move quickly to raise a force to confront the coalition. Despite his earlier abdication, Napoleon was still a very popular figure, and he had the support of many French. Napoleon called for volunteers and reinstated the conscription. The wars had been brutal on France, but many young men were still willing to fight and perhaps share in the glory that Napoleon might achieve. The old military infrastructure Napoleon created was still intact, and the officers were ready to join the campaign. An important task was to reconstitute the Imperial Guard. These were the best soldiers of the Grande Armée and would be necessary in any upcoming battles. Like so many veterans, the guardsmen returned to service.

A combination of enthusiasm, loyalty, and recognition of imminent danger helped bring together a significant force. Although Napoleon could not raise an army comparable to what he had for the Austerlitz campaign or the Russian offensive, he gathered nearly 200,000 troops. The new recruits were rigorously trained, and the old timers were reoriented to military activity. Bonaparte was ready to fight within a matter of weeks.

<u>Napoleon versus Wellington</u>

It had all the makings of a major prize fight. Both Napoleon and the Duke of Wellington had achieved significant victories, and neither feared the other. It would be the French champion against the British champion; only one could win.

The Seventh Coalition began to organize its armies and prepare a strategy to defeat Napoleon. The Duke of Wellington, who was in Vienna attending the Congress of Vienna, was assigned the command of a coalition force that was forming in what is now Belgium. He immediately left the congress and headed toward Brussels to assume command. Once there, Wellington coordinated his activity with the other primary coalition commander, Marshal Gebhard Leberecht von Blücher, for the upcoming campaign.

Coordination and logistics planning required skillful diplomatic communications. Wellington maintained a good relationship with all the coalition forces. Just like Dwight D. Eisenhower in the preparation for D-Day, Wellington proved to be as much a diplomat as he was a general. That was critical because internal squabbling and misunderstanding had ruined earlier coalition efforts to defeat Napoleon. It was decided that the British and Prussian armies would defend the Low Countries. Once the

Austrians and Russians were ready, those two armies would approach France from the east.

Napoleon knew that if he conducted a defensive campaign, it would be a repeat of 1814. He did not want that to happen, and the preemptive strike he decided to execute would enable him to defeat one coalition army and then turn and defeat the next. This strategy had worked before, and the French emperor believed he could force the Seventh Coalition into peace talks if he beat them on the field.

Striking at the coalition army in Belgium made perfect sense. The British and Prussians were dispersed and would have to scramble to organize as a unified force. The British did not have the best troops available, as the veterans of the Peninsular War were in North America, fighting the War of 1812 with the Americans.

Napoleon split his forces into three armies. One was stationed in southern France near the Alps to stop any Austrian advance from Italy. Another was placed on the border with Prussia to resist attacks from the east. Napoleon personally led the final group, the Armée du Nord (the Army of the North), into the Low Countries to confront Wellington and Blücher. Napoleon moved the Army of the North, which numbered 128,000 men, in relative secrecy and crossed into the Low Countries at Thuin near Charleroi on June 15th, 1815, and caught the Prussian army off guard.

<u>The Armies Clash</u>

By nightfall on June 15th, the French occupied Charleroi and had moved north, effectively creating a wedge between the Prussians and the British. Napoleon turned his attention toward the Prussians and, on June 16th, engaged them in a battle at Ligny. There, the Prussians were successfully outflanked and forced to retreat.

While Napoleon was dealing with the Prussians, the French left wing, under the command of Marshal Ney, engaged Wellington at Quatre Bras. Wellington was able to take a stronger stand, but Ney was able to keep the British from reinforcing the Prussians. Although the allies were able to maintain communication, Wellington could not move to aid the Prussians. Conversely, Ney was not able to assist Napoleon in attacking the Prussians.[95]

---

[95] Britishbattles.com. (2024, June 13). Battle of Quatre Bras. Retrieved from Britishbattles.com: https://www.britishbattles.com/napoleonic-wars/battle-of-quatre-bras/.

Wellington decided the best strategy was to retreat, so he moved his forces to the north. He finally stopped at a village named Waterloo, where he could set up a solid defensive position.

Napoleon followed the British retreat. Wishing to keep the Prussians and the British separate, Napoleon ordered Marshal Emmanuel de Grouchy to take thirty-three thousand men and pursue Blücher. De Grouchy's orders on the morning of June 17th were to keep close contact with the Prussians. More specific instructions came later that day, and de Grouchy was to move toward the town of Wavre. The French marshal was expected to keep the Prussians occupied and away from the battlefield where Napoleon would engage Wellington.

June 18th: The Day of Destiny

Waterloo would be the most significant battle fought on European soil for one hundred years. Napoleon had separated the Prussians and the British, and if he could prevent them from joining forces, there was a good chance he would win the next battle. Wellington had a strong defense, but that did not bother Bonaparte.

There was a storm the night before the battle, making the ground wet and muddy. Napoleon waited to allow the ground to dry so that his artillery would be more effective and his men could move more quickly. It is also possible that Napoleon was not feeling well. The French emperor needed some rest before commanding that day. Whatever the reasons, the delay allowed Wellington to prepare his defenses better and allowed the Prussians more time to advance toward the battlefield. The fighting commenced at 11:30 a.m.[96]

Two Farmhouses

There was a walled farmhouse named Hougoumont that was between the two armies. It was on the right flank of the British and protected the soldiers from a French attack. The battle began with a French attack on this farmhouse. Hougoumont would withstand seven attacks by Napoleon's infantry during the day. The coalition forces were able to hold onto the farmhouse, and the attacks on it diverted French soldiers who were needed elsewhere on the battlefield.[97]

---

[96] Lentz, T. (2020, June). Bullet Point #35- How Did Napoleon Manage to Lose the Battle of Waterloo? Retrieved from Napoleon.org: https://www.napoleon.org/en/history-of-the-two-empires/articles/bullet-point-35-how-did-napoleon-manage-to-lose-the-battle-of-waterloo/.

[97] Elmer, B. (2024, June 13). The Defense of Hougoumont. Retrieved from Napoleon-series.org:

Another farmhouse, La Haye Sainte, was at a central point directly in front of the main British lines. Napoleon ordered an infantry assault on the farmhouse at 1 p.m., but the coalition forces held it tenaciously. Once again, considerable forces were expended by the French to take La Haye Sainte. It finally fell in the late afternoon, but the French lost men and time in the assaults, and they could not afford to lose either.[98]

Ney's Charge

Late in the afternoon, around 4 p.m., Marshal Ney saw what he thought was a British retreat. The French marshal assembled the cavalry for a massive charge and led five thousand men in an assault. Unfortunately for Ney, those were not retreating British soldiers. They were wounded men being evacuated to the rear. Ney led the cavalry into British squares and artillery. Ney tried several times to break the squares, but he did not have infantry units backing them up, and half of the French cavalry reserve was lost in Ney's efforts.[99]

Enter the Prussians

De Grouchy did his best to keep the Prussians away from the Waterloo battlefield, but because he started moving late in the morning of June 17th, the Prussians had a head start. He was not sure where the Prussians were heading, and instead of following the advice of a staff officer to follow the sound of the guns, de Grouchy followed his original orders to head toward Wavre. He engaged the Prussian rearguard in that town, but the main Prussian troops moved directly to Waterloo.

The Prussians arrived on the eastern side of the battlefield at approximately 4:30 p.m. and began to engage the right flank of the French. By 6 p.m., the lion's share of the Prussian army was on the field at Waterloo and wearing down the French.

The Advance of the Guard

Napoleon repeatedly tried to break through Wellington's lines but was unsuccessful. The Prussian army was now engaged, and the situation became desperate for the French. At around 7:30 p.m., Napoleon

---

https://www.napoleon-series.org/military-info/battles/1815/waterloo/c_hougoumont.html.

[98] Simms, B. (2015, August 5). Holding the Farm at Waterloo. Retrieved from Historynet.com: https://www.historynet.com/holding-the-farm-at-waterloo/.

[99] Haskew, M. (2024, June 13). Marshal Ney and His Biggest Mistake at the Battle of Waterloo. Retrieved from Warfarehistorynetwork.com: https://warfarehistorynetwork.com/marshal-ney-and-his-biggest-mistake-at-the-battle-of-waterloo/.

---

ordered the Imperial Guard to advance, hoping this one last move would break the enemy lines.

The Imperial Guard could not break through despite all their efforts. The British held, and the Imperial Guard was finally forced to retreat. That was the turning point of the battle. The French army, upon seeing the retreat of the Imperial Guard, began to panic, and the French soldiers retreated in a disorganized fashion. Napoleon realized the battle was lost and left the battlefield around 8:30 p.m. His army was in retreat, and he needed to reorganize what was left. He probably knew that it was all over for him.

<u>Napoleon's Fate</u>

Napoleon abdicated for a second time on June 22nd, 1815. He wanted to seek asylum in Great Britain but was turned down immediately in favor of having him exiled. An interesting question is why the former emperor was not executed. That would have solved the question of what to do with him permanently.

The answer is complex and reflects the political realities of the time. There were still many people devoted to Napoleon and turning him into a martyr would upset the political situation in Europe, which was already fragile. Moreover, although the monarchs hated Napoleon, they did not want to set a precedent where a deposed ruler would be executed. Political stability was the order of the day, and sending Napoleon into exile removed him from the European stage and put him in a place where he could be closely watched.

Napoleon's days of influencing European policy were over. He was exiled to the island of Saint Helena, a spit of land in the Atlantic Ocean one thousand miles from Europe. Napoleon lived the rest of his life there. He passed away on May 5th, 1821. There is a legend that the former French emperor was gradually poisoned during his exile, but to this day, there is no corroboration of what the poison was or who was the poisoner.

The Second Treaty of Paris was signed on November 20th, 1815 (the first one was signed in 1814) and had firm stipulations. France had to pay an indemnity of seven hundred million francs, and its borders were reduced to those that existed on January 1st, 1790. All the territory it had gained in the French Revolution was lost. France would be required to cover the expenses of any additional fortifications built by neighboring coalition countries, and to add insult to injury, 150,000 foreign troops would occupy France in designated zones. These would stay there until

1818 when they were removed. The allies wanted stability in Europe, and the terms would prevent France from becoming a problem in the foreseeable future.

An interesting development in the Congress of Vienna was the Holy Alliance. This was an idea that Tsar Alexander promoted. His intention was to promote Christian principles in nations' affairs. It was formed in Paris on September 26th, 1815, while negotiations for the Second Treaty of Paris were finalized. The primary advocates were Alexander of Russia, Francis I of Austria, and Frederick William III of Prussia. The irony is that they were promoting Christian principles, and one nation was Roman Catholic, one was Russian Orthodox, and one was Protestant.

The Holy Alliance was more an enforcer than a moral guide. It was there to uphold the new conservatism regimes, and many liberals suspected that the alliance would be used to suppress liberal tendencies. The Holy Alliance did stifle dissent, but it was also an example of cooperative effort that gradually became the norm for European countries in the 19th century.[100]

<u>The Demise of the Empire</u>

Not one event or reason brought an end to Napoleon's empire. The man was a military genius, but he made mistakes. Some were easy to correct, but others created situations that ultimately produced negative consequences. Let's take a moment to look at some of his more critical missteps.

- The Continental System

  It was a disaster, pure and simple. Napoleon wanted to choke Great Britain economically but did not appreciate that British trade was global. A loss of trade in one country could be compensated for by additional commerce in the Americas or India. Capitalism permitted Great Britain to rebound from the embargo.

  The Continental System created difficulties and encouraged smuggling. The nations forced to be a part of it faced an economic downturn, and that included France.

  France's international image was also hurt. Enforcing the Continental System made Napoleon look more authoritarian

---

[100] Britannica, T. E. (2024, June 13). Holy Alliance. Retrieved from Britannica.com: https://www.britannica.com/topic/Holy-Alliance.

than ever before. He was no longer the great liberator but the oppressive enforcer. The animosity and resentment caused by the Continental System would haunt him a few years later.

- The Russian Campaign

This was the worst military decision Napoleon ever made. The logistics alone were enough to defeat any army, but Napoleon's stubborn ego was a big reason for the defeat. He was smart enough to know that the Russians were deliberately retreating in front of him, drawing the Grande Armée deeper and deeper into Russia. He could have stopped and waited for the Russians to come to him, but Moscow was an obsessive objective for him. France never fully recovered from the losses.

- The Peninsular War

It was an open wound that bled France's treasury. Napoleon was required to station thousands of troops in the Iberian Peninsula, regiments he could have used elsewhere. British persistence and guerrilla attacks created significant problems the French emperor could not solve.

- The Cost of War

The French were at war almost continuously in the first fifteen years of the 19th century. It put an enormous strain on the French economy, but it also affected France's allies and subjugated territories. France was unable to match Great Britain when it came to raising money. Napoleon had to rely on increasing taxes, tribute from the empire and the satellite states, and the indemnities imposed on defeated nations.

- Poor Quality of Leadership

Napoleon was a military genius, but his governing style was more autocratic than egalitarian. He was prone to rule by decrees and not compromise. Placing his family members on various thrones was not a good idea. His siblings were nowhere near as competent as he was. His dream of Bonaparte dynasties all over Europe quickly collapsed when he started to lose.

- Nationalism

Napoleon spread the ideals of nationalism by crippling old empires. The demise of the Holy Roman Empire led to the creation of the Confederation of the Rhine, which meant that large German states took the place of autonomous cities. Italy was more unified than ever before; Bonaparte gets the credit for that.

However, with nationalism came the idea of self-determination. Countries began to turn against French domination, and nationalist movements that resisted French hegemony started to rise.

- Military Reforms

  It required several disastrous military campaigns, but Napoleon's enemies finally understood they could not hope to beat the French emperor unless serious military reforms were enacted. Prussia and Austria, in particular, made significant changes in military management. Several coalitions tried and failed to beat Napoleon, but the Sixth Coalition finally got it right. Members of the alliance put their differences aside temporarily and united in a common purpose to defeat France. The Battle of Leipzig demonstrated what the European powers could do once they were united in achieving their goal.

The era of the Napoleonic Wars was over. Conflicts and wars would still be fought on the European continent, but these actions did not involve all the nations. A conservative frame of mind became the dominant mood and would be so for several decades. The Napoleonic era was finished; the Age of Metternich began.

Conclusion

The Napoleonic Wars were an epoch of change, often accompanied by violence. Yet, as the years unfolded, Europe's resilience shone through, transforming the continent. Europe emerged as a new entity, forever altered from its prewar state, a testament to its ability to adapt and evolve.

The Age of Metternich, spearheaded by the influential Prince Metternich, was a significant attempt to restore Europe to a conservative mindset. While it succeeded initially, the revolutionary ideas that had been implemented in the early 19th century were never entirely abandoned. The significant convulsion that Europe experienced in 1848 marked a profound shift from conservatism to liberalism, a turning point in history.

After the Napoleonic Wars, Europe underwent a societal shift. The societies of Europe, having tasted a degree of freedom that had been absent in the 18th century, were not willing to revert to the Ancien Régime. Europe was now a new world of nations, with Italy and Germany no longer mere geographical expressions. This societal transformation was a direct result of the Napoleonic Wars.

Europe needed to go through that period of turmoil. Some changes were so dramatic that military action was the only way to guarantee these innovations would be part of the social and political order. Millions died, but the changes were made, and some of the reforms, such as the Napoleonic Code, are still significant influences.

The Napoleonic Wars were not just a chaotic period of change but also a defining moment in European history. The break from tradition was not peaceful, but it was permanent. Today, Europe's social, political, and geographical landscape traces its roots back to that epoch, a testament to the profound and lasting impact of this historical era.

Here's another book by Enthralling History that you might like

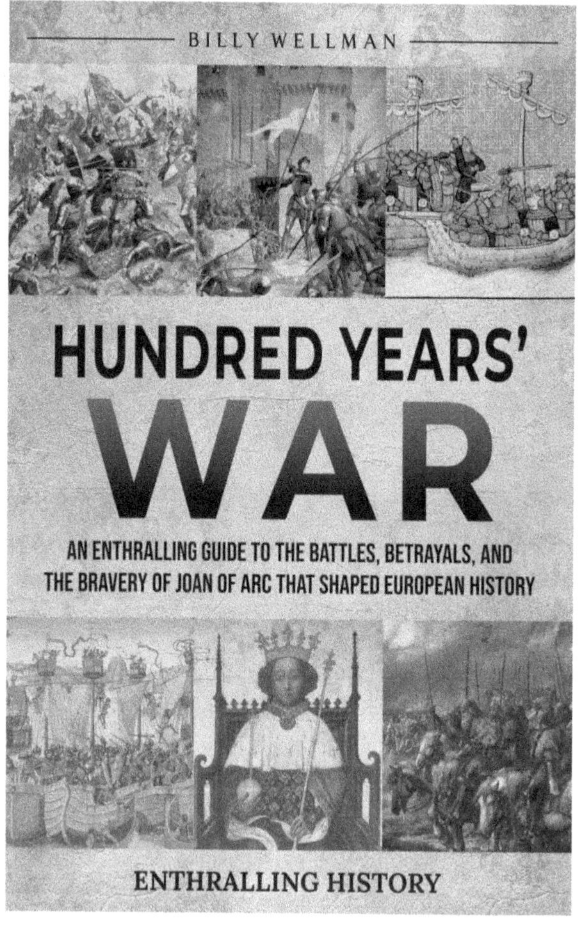

Free limited time bonus

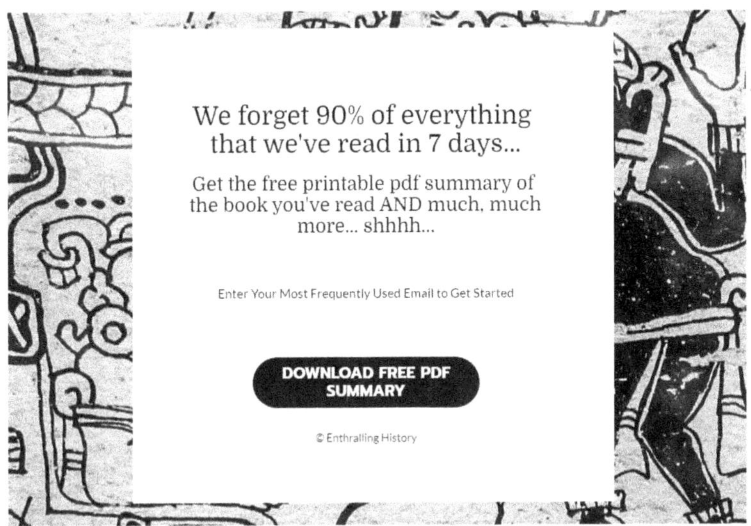

Stop for a moment. We have a free bonus set up for you. The problem is this: we forget 90% of everything that we read after 7 days. Crazy fact, right? Here's the solution: we've created a printable, 1-page pdf summary for this book that you're reading now. All you have to do to get your free pdf summary is to go to the following website:

https://livetolearn.lpages.co/enthrallinghistory/

Or, Scan the QR code!

Once you do, it will be intuitive. Enjoy, and thank you!

Bibliography

Part 1: Napoleon Bonaparte

Abell, Lucia Elizabeth. *Recollections of the Emperor Napoleon during the First Three Years of His Captivity on the Island of Saint Helena.* London: John Murray, 1844.

Bourrienne, Louis Antoine Fauvelet de. *Memoirs of Napoleon Bonaparte.* Edited by R. W. Phipps. London: George Bell and Sons, 1885.

Broers, Michael. *Napoleon: Soldier of Destiny.* London: Faber & Faber, 2014.

Broers, Michael. *Napoleon: The Decline and Fall of an Empire, 1811-1821.* London: Faber & Faber, 2020.

Broers, Michael. *Napoleon: The Spirit of the Age, 1802-1810.* London: Faber & Faber, 2018.

Chandler, David G. *The Campaigns of Napoleon.* New York: Macmillan, 1966.

Elting, John R. *Swords Around a Throne: Napoleon's Grande Armée.* New York: Free Press, 1988.

Las Cases, Emmanuel Auguste Dieudonné. *Memoirs of the Life, Exile, and Conversations of the Emperor Napoleon.* 4 vols. London: Henry Colburn, 1823.

Lieven, Dominic. *Russia Against Napoleon: The Battle for Europe, 1807-1814.* London: Allen Lane, 2009.

Markham, Felix. *Napoleon.* New York: Mentor Books, 1963.

McLynn, Frank. *Napoleon: A Biography.* London: Pimlico, 1998.

Mikaberidze, Alexander. *The Napoleonic Wars: A Global History.* Oxford: Oxford University Press, 2020.

Roberts, Andrew. *Napoleon: A Life.* New York: Viking Press, 2014.

Zamoyski, Adam. *Moscow 1812: Napoleon's Fatal March.* New York: HarperCollins, 2004.

Part 2: The Napoleonic Wars

Anne S. K. Brown Military Collection. (2024, June 4). Napoleonic Satires. Retrieved from library.brown.edu: https://library.brown.edu/cds/napolcon/time2.html.

Anonymous. (2024, June 8). War of the Fourth Coalition. Retrieved from Resources.saylor.org: https://resources.saylor.org/wwwresources/archived/site/wp-content/uploads/2011/05/War-of-the-Fourth-coalition.pdf.

Bainbridge, S. (2016, June 2). Romanticism and War. Retrieved from Oxford Academic: https://academic.oup.com/edited-volume/43514/chapter/364255284?login=false.

Britannica, E. o. (2024, May 14). Battle of Ulm. Retrieved from Britannica.com: https://www.britannica.com/event/Battle-of-Ulm.

Britannica, E. o. (2024, May 18). Napoleonic Code. Retrieved from Britannica.com: https://www.britannica.com/topic/Napoleonic-Code.

Britannica, E. o. (2024, May 14). Siege of Toulon. Retrieved from Britannica.com: https://www.britannica.com/event/Siege-of-Toulon

Britannica, T. E. (2024, May 24). Banque de France. Retrieved from Britannica.com: https://www.britannica.com/money/Banque-de-France.

Britannica, T. E. (2024, May 14). Battle of Dresden. Retrieved from Britannica.com: https://www.britannica.com/event/Battle-of-Dresden.

Britannica, T. E. (2024, June 12). Congress of Vienna Summary. Retrieved from Britannica.com: https://www.britannica.com/summary/Congress-of-Vienna.

Britannica, T. E. (2024, May 23). Haitian Revolution. Retrieved from Britannica.com: https://www.britannica.com/topic/Haitian-Revolution.

Britannica, T. E. (2024, June 13). Holy Alliance. Retrieved from Britannica.com: https://www.britannica.com/topic/Holy-Alliance.

Britannica, T. E. (2024, May 9). Manuel de Godoy. Retrieved from Britannica.com: https://www.britannica.com/biography/Manuel-de-Godoy#ref112973

Britannica, T. E. (2024, April 30). Peninsular War. Retrieved from Britannica.com: https://www.britannica.com/event/Peninsular-War.

Britannica, T. E. (2024, June 11). Treaty of Schonbrunn. Retrieved from Britannica.com: https://www.britannica.com/event/Treaty-of-Schonbrunn.

Britannica.com. (2024, June 12). Decisions of the Congress. Retrieved from Britannica.com: https://www.britannica.com/event/Congress-of-Vienna/Decisions-of-the-congress.

Britannica.com. (2024, June 4). End of the Holy Roman Empire. Retrieved from Britannica.com: https://www.britannica.com/place/Germany/End-of-the-Holy-Roman-Empire

Britannica.com. (2024, May 28). Great Britan, France, and the Neutrals, 1800-1802. Retrieved from Britannica.com: https://www.britannica.com/event/Napoleonic-Wars/Great-Britain-France-and-the-neutrals-1800-02

Britannica.com. (2024, May 14). The Austrian Attempt at Mediation. Retrieved from Britannica.com: https://www.britannica.com/event/Napoleonic-Wars/The-Austrian-attempt-at-mediation

Britishbattles.com. (2024, June 13). Battle of Quatre Bras. Retrieved from Britishbattles.com: https://www.britishbattles.com/napoleonic-wars/battle-of-quatre-bras/.

Burkholder, S. H. (2024, June 10). Treaty of Fontainebleau (1807). Retrieved from Encyclopedia.com: https://www.encyclopedia.com/humanities/encyclopedias-almanacs-transcripts-and-maps/fontainebleau-treaty-1807.

Cheikh, M. (2020, September 24). Were Metternich's Peace Ouvertures in 1813 Genuine? Retrieved from Thenapoleonicwars.net: https://www.thenapoleonicwars.net/forum/napoleon/were-metternich-s-peace-ouvertures-in-1813-genuine.

Colley, L. J. (2024, June 8). The Napoleonic Wars. Retrieved from Britannica.com: https://www.britannica.com/place/United-Kingdom/The-Napoleonic-Wars.

Collinson, A. (2015, May 11). In Literature and Song: The Legacy of the Napoleonic Wars. Retrieved from Ageofrevolution.org: https://ageofrevolution.org/in-literature-and-song-the-legacy-of-the-napoleonic-wars/.

Coppa, F. J. (2018, May 18). Concordat of 1801. Retrieved from Encyclopedia.com: https://www.encyclopedia.com/philosophy-and-religion/christianity/roman-catholic-and-orthodox-churches-councils-and-treaties/concordat-1801.

DailyHistory.org. (2024, May 26). Why Has the French Civil Code Had a Lasting Influence on Contemporary European Law. Retrieved from DailyHistory.org: https://www.dailyhistory.org/Why_has_the_French_Civil_Code_had_a_lasting_influence_on_contemporary_European_law.

DetailedPedia.com. (2024, June 11). Battle of Smolensk (1812). Retrieved from Detailedpedia.com: https://www.detailedpedia.com/wiki-Battle_of_Smolensk_%281812%29.

DetailedPedia.com. (2024, May 26). Napoleonic Code. Retrieved from DetailedPedia.com: https://www.detailedpedia.com/wiki-Napoleonic_Code.

Editors, H. (2023, April 24). Napoleon Bonaparte. Retrieved from History.com: https://www.history.com/topics/european-history/napoleon.

Elmer, B. (2024, June 13). The Defense of Hougoumont. Retrieved from Napoleon-series.org: https://www.napoleon-series.org/military-info/battles/1815/waterloo/c_hougoumont.html.

Emerson Kent.com. (2024, May 25). Taxation in Pre-Revolutionary France. Retrieved from Emersonkent.com: http://www.emersonkent.com/history_dictionary/taxation_in_pre_revolutionary_f rance.htm.

Encyclopedia.com. (2018, May 23). Battle of Trafalgar. Retrieved from Encyclopedia.com: https://www.encyclopedia.com/history/modern-europe/wars-and-battles/battle-trafalgar.

Ernest McNeil Eller, R. L. (2024, June 4). Ships of the Line. Retrieved from Britannica.com: https://www.britannica.com/technology/naval-ship/Ship-of-the-line.

Foscolo, U. (2024, June 11). Ugo Foscolo-Opere Omnia. Retrieved from Foscolo.letteraturaoperaomnia.org: https://foscolo.letteraturaoperaomnia.org/foscolo_dei_sepolcri.html.

Franciscogoya.com. (2024, June 10). The Disaster of War, 1810-1820 by Francisco Goya. Retrieved from Franciscogoya.com: https://www.franciscogoya.com/disasters-of-war.jsp.

Frithowulf, H. (2024, February 29). Battle of Wagram: Napoleon's Masterstroke. Retrieved from Malevus.com: https://malevus.com/battle-of-wagram/.

Globallytaught.com. (2024, May 26). Education Systems Around the World: A Look at 4 Top School Systems. Retrieved from Globallytaught.com: https://globallytaught.com/blog/education-systems-around-the-world/.

Godechot, J. (2024, May 13). Charles-Maurice de Talleyrand, Prince de Benevent. Retrieved from Britannica.com: https://www.britannica.com/biography/Charles-Maurice-de-Talleyrand-prince-de-Benevent.

Green, J. (2002, April). Michel Ney's Retreat. Retrieved from Warfarenetwork.com: https://warfarehistorynetwork.com/article/michel-neys-retreat/.

Green, J. (2004, April). Napoleon Bonaparte's "Roland": Marshal Jean Lannes. Retrieved from Warfarehistorynetwork.com: https://warfarehistorynetwork.com/article/napoleon-bonapartes-roland-marshal-jean-lannes/.

Haskew, M. (2024, June 13). Marshal Ney and His Biggest Mistake at the Battle of Waterloo. Retrieved from Warfarehistorynetwork.com: https://warfarehistorynetwork.com/marshal-ney-and-his-biggest-mistake-at-the-battle-of-waterloo/.

Hickman, K. (2015, March 10). Napoleonic Wars: Battle of Aspern-Essling. Retrieved from Thoughtco.com: https://www.thoughtco.com/napoleonic-battle-of-aspern-essling-2361108.

Hickman, K. (2019, September 4). French Revolutionary Wars: Battle of Valmy. Retrieved from ThoughtCo.: https://www.thoughtco.com/french-revolution-battle-of-valmy-2361106.

Hickman, K. (2020, January 2). Napoleonic Wars: Marshall Jean-Baptiste Bernadotte. Retrieved from ThoughtCo.com: https://www.thoughtco.com/napoleonic-wars-marshal-jean-baptiste-bernadotte-2360137.

Hicks, P. (2024, June 4). The Royal Navy, 1793-1802. Retrieved from Napoleon.org: https://www.napoleon.org/en/history-of-the-two-empires/articles/the-british-navy-1793-1802/.

History Skills. (2024, June 10). What Was Napoleon's Revolutionary Continental System and How Did It Shape Modern Europe. Retrieved from Historyskills.com: https://www.historyskills.com/classroom/modern-history/continental-system/.

Historyskills.com. (2024, June 11). Napoleon's Catastrophic Invasion of Russia: A Military Miscalculation of Epic Proportions. Retrieved from Historyskills.com: https://www.historyskills.com/classroom/modern-history/napoleon-s-russian-invasion/.

Jacques Godechot, E. P. (2024, April 30). Arthur Wellesley, 1st Duke of Wellington. Retrieved from Britannica.com: https://www.britannica.com/biography/Arthur-Wellesley-1st-Duke-of-Wellington.

Jensen, N. D. (2024, May 25). Organization of French Revolutionary Armies 1791-1801. Retrieved from French Empire.net: https://www.frenchempire.net/articles/armies/.

Keene, R. (2024, June 10). Napoleon and Goethe: Touchstone of Genius. Retrieved from Thearticle.com: https://www.thearticle.com/napoleon-and-goethe-touchstone-of-genius.

Lee, A. (2018, March 3). Beethoven and Napoleon. Retrieved from Historytoday.com: https://www.historytoday.com/archive/music-time/beethoven-and-napoleon.

Lentz, T. (2020, June). Bullet Point #35- How Did Napoleon Manage to Lose the Battle of Waterloo? Retrieved from Napoleon.org: https://www.napoleon.org/en/history-of-the-two-empires/articles/bullet-point-35-how-did-napoleon-manage-to-lose-the-battle-of-waterloo/.

Lord Byron. The Works of Lord Byron Vol. 2. https://genius.com/Lord-byron-the-works-of-lord-byron-vol-2-to-inez-annotated.

Marino Berengo, C. M. (2024, June 4). Italy-The Napoleonic Empire 1804-14. Retrieved from Britannica.com: https://www.britannica.com/place/Italy/The-acquisition-of-Venetia-and-Rome.

Mark, H. W. (2022, March 7). The Three Estates of Pre-Revolutionary France. Retrieved from World History Encyclopedia: https://www.worldhistory.org/article/1960/the-three-estates-of-pre-revolutionary-france/.

Mark, H. W. (2023, July 24). Battle of Eylau. Retrieved from World History Encyclopedia: https://www.worldhistory.org/article/2258/battle-of-eylau/.

Mark, H. W. (2023, July 25). Battle of Friedland. Retrieved from World History Encyclopedia: https://www.worldhistory.org/article/2259/battle-of-friedland/.

Mark, H. W. (2023, June 19). Battle of Jena-Auerstedt. Retrieved from World History Encyclopedia: https://www.worldhistory.org/article/2256/battle-of-jena-auerstedt/.

Mark, H. W. (2023, August 16). Battle of Wargram. Retrieved from World History: https://www.worldhistory.org/article/2267/battle-of-wagram/

Mark, H. W. (2023, August 3). Continental System. Retrieved from World History Encyclopedia.com: https://www.worldhistory.org/Continental_System/.

Mark, H. W. (2023, July 6). Coronation of Napoleon I. Retrieved from World History Encyclopedia.com: https://www.worldhistory.org/article/2251/coronation-of-napoleon-i/.

Mark, H. W. (2023, October 3). Hundred Days. Retrieved from World History Encyclopedia: https://www.worldhistory.org/Hundred_Days/

Mark, H. W. (2023, August 7). Peninsular War. Retrieved from World History Encyclopedia: https://www.worldhistory.org/Peninsular_War/.

Mark, H. W. (2023, July 10). Ulm Campaign. Retrieved from World History Encyclopedia: https://www.worldhistory.org/article/2249/ulm-campaign/.

Mark, H. W. (2023, July 28). War of the Fourth Coalition. Retrieved from World History Encyclopedia: https://www.worldhistory.org/War_of_the_Fourth_Coalition/.

Mark, H. W. (2023, September 4). War of the Sixth Coalition. Retrieved from World History Encyclopedia: https://www.worldhistory.org/War_of_the_Sixth_Coalition/.

Mark, H. W. (2023, July 18). War of the Third Coalition. Retrieved from World History Encyclopedia: https://www.worldhistory.org/War_of_the_Third_Coalition/.

Musee Goya Castres. (2024, June 10). Goya-Picasso: A Cross-View. Retrieved from museegoya.fr: https://www.museegoya.fr/en/goya-in-piccaso-s-eye.

Nackaerts, B. (2024, June 13). The Lack of Opposition to the Execution of Marshal Ney. Retrieved from Napoleon-series.org: https://www.napoleon-series.org/research/biographies/c_executeney.html.

Napoleon & Empire. (2024, May 14). Battle of Eylau. Retrieved from Napoleon &Empire.net: https://www.napoleon-empire.net/en/battles/eylau.php.

Napoleonguide.com. (2024, May 25). Lazare Carnot. Retrieved from Napoleonguide.com: https://www.napoleonguide.com/carnot.htm.

Napoleon.org. (2010, March). The Marriage of Napoleon I and Marie-Louise of Austria. Retrieved from Napoleon.org: https://www.napoleon.org/en/history-of-the-two-empires/timelines/the-marriage-of-napoleon-i-and-marie-louise-of-austria/.

Napoleon.org. (2020, December). Napoleon I and His Family. Retrieved from Napoleon.org: https://www.napoleon.org/en/young-historians/napodoc/napoleon-i-and-his-family/.

Napoleon.org. (2024, May 28). Louis-Alexandre Berthier. Retrieved from Napoleon.org: https://www.napoleon.org/en/history-of-the-two-empires/biographies/berthier-louis-alexandre/.

Napoleon.org. (2024, June 11). Napoleon's Russian Campaign: The Retreat. Retrieved from Napoleon.org: https://www.napoleon.org/en/history-of-the-two-empires/timelines/napoleons-russian-campaign-the-retreat/.

Napoleonistyka.atspace.com. (2024, May 28). Russian Army of the Napoleonic Wars. Retrieved from Napoleonistyka.atspace.com: Napoleonistyka.atspace.com.

National Army Museum. (2024, June 10). Peninsular War. Retrieved from Nam.ac.uk: https://www.nam.ac.uk/explore/peninsular-war.

New World Encyclopedia. (2024, June 4). Battle of Austerlitz. Retrieved from New World Encyclopedia.org: https://www.newworldencyclopedia.org/entry/Battle_of_Austerlitz.

New World Encyclopedia. (2024, June 11). French Invasion of Russia. Retrieved from New World Encyclopedia.com: https://www.newworldencyclopedia.org/entry/French_invasion_of_Russia#Retreat_and_losses.

Pisa, J. d. (2011, October 5). Napoleon's Nightmare: Guerilla Warfare in Spain (1808-1814). Retrieved from Smallwarsjournal.com: https://smallwarsjournal.com/jrnl/art/napoleon%c2%b4s-nightmare-guerrilla-warfare-in-spain-1808-1814.

Pock, T. (2024, June 4). Battles of Cape St. Vincent and the Nile. Retrieved from Britannica.com: https://www.britannica.com/biography/Horatio-Nelson/Battles-of-Cape-St-Vincent-and-the-Nile.

Pocock, T. (2024, June 4). Horatio Nelson at Trafalgar. Retrieved from Britannica.com: https://www.britannica.com/biography/Horatio-Nelson/Victory-at-Trafalgar.

Powerplace.org. (2023, July 28). Top 51 Timeless Sun Tzu Quotes: Mastering Strategy and Leadership. Retrieved from Powerplace.org: https://powerplace.org/blogs/quotes/mastering-strategy-and-leadership-unveiling-51-timeless-sun-tzu-quotes.

Royal Navy. (2024, June 4). Trafalgar Day. Retrieved from Royalnavy.mod.uk: https://www.royalnavy.mod.uk/news-and-latest-activity/events/national/171021-trafalgar-day.

Savoie, P. (2024, May 26). Lycée. Retrieved from Faqs.org: http://www.faqs.org/childhood/Ke-Me/Lyc-e.html.

Schneid, F. C. (2024, June 12). Congress of Vienna. Retrieved from Encyclopedia.com: https://www.encyclopedia.com/history/encyclopedias-almanacs-transcripts-and-maps/congress-vienna.

Setterfield, R. (2019, November 18). Horatio Nelson: From Frail Boy to National Hero. Retrieved from Onthisday.com: https://www.onthisday.com/articles/horatio-nelson-from-frail-boy-to-national-hero.

Simms, B. (2015, August 5). Holding the Farm at Waterloo. Retrieved from Historynet.com: https://www.historynet.com/holding-the-farm-at-waterloo/.

Sparknotes.com. (2024, May 25). The French Revolution (1789-1799). Retrieved from Sparknotes.com: https://www.sparknotes.com/history/european/frenchrev/section1/.

The Clark. (2024, June 10). David & Napoleon. Retrieved from Clarkart.edu: https://www.clarkart.edu/microsites/jacques-louis-david/david-napoleon.

The Open University. (2024, June 10). 3 Gros and the Napoleonic Propaganda Machine. Retrieved from Open.edu: https://www.open.edu/openlearn/history-the-arts/history-art/napoleonic-paintings/content-section-3.1.

Thenapoleonicwars.net. (2024, June 11). Napoleon's Invasion of Russia. Retrieved from Thenapoleonicwars.net: https://www.thenapoleonicwars.net/invasion-of-russia.

Wesson, M. J. (2024, May 28). The Development of the Corps d'armée and Its Impact on Napoleonic Warfare. Retrieved from The Napoleon Series: https://www.napoleon-series.org/military-info/organization/c_armycorps.html.

Williamson, M. (2016, August 5). French Napoleonic Artillery in Action. Retrieved from Weapons and Warfare: https://weaponsandwarfare.com/2016/08/06/french-napoleonic-artillery-in-action/.

Wordsworth, W. (2024, June 19). Elegias Stanzas Suggested by a Picture of Peele Castle in a Storm, Painted by Sir George Beaumont. Retrieved from Poetryfoundation.org: https://www.poetryfoundation.org/poems/45516/elegiac-stanzas-suggested-by-a-picture-of-peele-castle-in-a-storm-painted-by-sir-george-beaumont.

Image Sources

1 https://commons.wikimedia.org/wiki/File:Napoleon-Studying.jpg

2 https://commons.wikimedia.org/wiki/File:Henri_F%C3%A9lix_Emmanuel
   Philippoteaux-_Portrait_of_Napoleon_Bonaparte.jpg

3 Histoirefr, CC BY-SA 4.0 <https://creativecommons.org/licenses/by-sa/4.0>, via
   Wikimedia Commons, https://commons.wikimedia.org/wiki/File:
   Portrait_de_Pasquale_Paoli_par_Joseph_Chabord_(1820).jpg

4 https://commons.wikimedia.org/wiki/File:Napoleon_%C3%A0_Toulon_
   par_Edouard_Detaille.jpg

5 https://commons.wikimedia.org/wiki/File:Octobre_1793,_supplice_de_9
   _%C3%A9migr%C3%A9s.jpg

6 https://commons.wikimedia.org/wiki/File:Charles_Monnet_-
   _The_Journ%C3%A9e_of_13_Vend%C3%A9miaire.jpg

7 https://commons.wikimedia.org/wiki/File:Jos%C3%A9phine_de_
   Beauharnais_vers_1809_Gros.jpg

8 https://commons.wikimedia.org/wiki/File:Rampon_Monte_Legino_(cropped).jpg

9 https://commons.wikimedia.org/wiki/File:1801_Antoine-Jean_Gros_-
   _Bonaparte_on_the_Bridge_at_Arcole.jpg

10 https://commons.wikimedia.org/wiki/File:Louis-
   Fran%C3%A7ois_Baron_Lejeune_001.jpg

11 https://commons.wikimedia.org/wiki/File:Jean-
   L%C3%A9on_G%C3%A9r%C3%B4me_002.jpg

12 https://commons.wikimedia.org/wiki/File:Mather_Brown_-_Battle_of_the_Nile.jpg

13 https://commons.wikimedia.org/wiki/File:Antoine-Jean_Gros_-
   _Bataille_d%27Aboukir,_25_juillet_1799_-_Google_Art_Project.jpg

14 https://commons.wikimedia.org/wiki/File:Bouchot_-
_Le_general_Bonaparte_au_Conseil_des_Cinq-Cents.jpg

15 https://commons.wikimedia.org/w/index.php?curid=6107787

16 https://commons.wikimedia.org/w/index.php?curid=150005

17 https://commons.wikimedia.org/w/index.php?curid=254055

18 David Liuzzo via Wikimedia Commons,
https://commons.wikimedia.org/wiki/File:Crown_of_Napoleon_I.png

19 https://commons.wikimedia.org/w/index.php?curid=546742

20 https://commons.wikimedia.org/wiki/File:Ulm_capitulation.jpg

21 https://commons.wikimedia.org/wiki/File:La_bataille_d%27Austerlitz._2_
decembre_1805_(Fran%C3%A7ois_G%C3%A9rard).jpg

22 https://commons.wikimedia.org/wiki/File:Iena.jpg

23 https://commons.wikimedia.org/wiki/File:Tilsitz_1807.JPG

24 https://commons.wikimedia.org/wiki/File:Departure_of_H.R.H._the_Prince_
Regent_of_Portugal_for_the_Brazils_(Campaigns_of_the_British_Army_in_Portugal,
_London,_1812)_-_Henry_L%27Ev%C3%AAque,_F._Bartollozzi.png

25 https://commons.wikimedia.org/wiki/File:El_dos_de_mayo_de_1808_
en_Madrid.jpg

26 https://commons.wikimedia.org/wiki/File:Louis-Fran%C3%A7ois_Lejeune_-
_Battle_of_Somosierra,_November_30,_1808.jpg

27 https://commons.wikimedia.org/wiki/File:Strategic_Situation_of_Europe_1809.jpg

28 https://commons.wikimedia.org/wiki/File:Lannes_mortally_wounded_at_
Essling_(E._Boutigny).jpg

29 https://commons.wikimedia.org/wiki/File:Napol%C3%A9on_%C3%A0_
Wagram.jpg

30 https://commons.wikimedia.org/w/index.php?curid=3125554

31 https://commons.wikimedia.org/wiki/File:Fireofmoscow.jpg

32 https://commons.wikimedia.org/wiki/File:Retreat_of_Napoleon_Army_
from_Moscow_1812.jpg

33 https://commons.wikimedia.org/w/index.php?curid=93465893

34 https://commons.wikimedia.org/wiki/File:MoshkovVI_SrazhLeypcigomGRM.jpg

35 https://commons.wikimedia.org/wiki/File:Bouchot_-
_Napol%C3%A9on_signe_son_abdication_%C3%A0_Fontainebleau_11_avril_1814.j
pg

36 https://commons.wikimedia.org/wiki/File:Beaume_-
_Napol%C3%A9on_Ier_quittant_l%27%C3%AEle_d%27Elbe_-_1836.jpg

37 https://commons.wikimedia.org/wiki/File:Battle_of_Ligny.JPG

38 https://commons.wikimedia.org/wiki/File:Battle_of_Waterloo_1815.PNG

39 https://commons.wikimedia.org/wiki/File:Napoleon_sainthelene.jpg

40 David Stanley from Nanaimo, Canada, CC BY 2.0
   <https://creativecommons.org/licenses/by/2.0>, via Wikimedia Commons,
   https://commons.wikimedia.org/w/index.php?curid=44162709

41 Josh Hallett from Winter Haven, FL, USA, CC BY-SA 2.0
   <https://creativecommons.org/licenses/by-sa/2.0>, via Wikimedia Commons,
   https://commons.wikimedia.org/w/index.php?curid=29076946

42 https://commons.wikimedia.org/wiki/File:Vig%C3%A9e-Lebrun,_Elisabeth-Louise_-
   _Charles-Alexandre_de_Calonne_(1734-1802)_-_Google_Art_Project.jpg

43 https://commons.wikimedia.org/wiki/File:Valmy_Battle_painting.jpg

44 https://commons.wikimedia.org/wiki/File:13Vend%C3%A9miaire.jpg

45 https://commons.wikimedia.org/wiki/File:Pappenheim_Curassiers.PNG

46 https://commons.wikimedia.org/wiki/File:David_-_Napoleon_crossing_the_Alps_-
   _Malmaison2.jpg

47 https://commons.wikimedia.org/wiki/File:Murat2.jpg

48 Clem le Nem, CC0, via Wikimedia Commons; https://commons.wikimedia.org/wiki
   /File:France_September_1812_prussia_occupied2.png

49 https://commons.wikimedia.org/wiki/File:Jacques-Louis_David_-
   _The_Emperor_Napoleon_in_His_Study_at_the_Tuileries_-
   _Google_Art_Project.jpg

50 https://commons.wikimedia.org/wiki/File:Boutigny-Surrender_at_Ulm.jpg

51 https://commons.wikimedia.org/wiki/File:HoratioNelson1.jpg

52 https://commons.wikimedia.org/wiki/File:Treaties_of_Tilsit_miniature_(France,_
   1810s)_side_A.jpg

53 https://commons.wikimedia.org/wiki/File:Manuel_de_Godoy,_por_Francisco_
   Bayeu_(Real_Academia_de_Bellas_Artes_de_San_Fernando).jpg

54 https://commons.wikimedia.org/wiki/File:Joseph-Bonaparte.jpg

55 https://commons.wikimedia.org/wiki/File:Sir_Arthur_Wellesley,_1st_Duke_of_
   Wellington.png

56 https://commons.wikimedia.org/wiki/File:Eroica_Beethoven_title.jpg

57 https://commons.wikimedia.org/wiki/File:Jacques-Louis_David_-
   _The_Coronation_of_Napoleon_(1805-1807).jpg

58 https://commons.wikimedia.org/wiki/File:El_dos_de_mayo_de_1808_en_Madrid.jpg

59 https://commons.wikimedia.org/wiki/File:Prado_-_Los_Desastres_de_la_Guerra_-
   _No._03_-_Lo_mismo.jpg

60 https://commons.wikimedia.org/wiki/File:Marie_Louise_von_%C3%96sterreich_
   Napoleon_Zweite.jpg

61 https://commons.wikimedia.org/wiki/File:Battle_of_Borodino_1812.png

62 https://commons.wikimedia.org/wiki/File:Night_Bivouac_of_Great_Army.jpg

63 https://commons.wikimedia.org/wiki/File:Carl_XIV_John_of_Sweden_%26_Norway_
   c_1840.jpg

64 https://commons.wikimedia.org/wiki/File:MoshkovVI_SrazhLeypcigomGRM.jpg

9 798888 765694